C000253092

DICK TURPIN
FACT & FICTION

To Lucy

DICK TURPIN
FACT & FICTION

JONATHAN OATES

PEN & SWORD
TRUE CRIME

First published in Great Britain in 2023 by
PEN AND SWORD TRUE CRIME
An imprint of
Pen & Sword Books Ltd
Yorkshire – Philadelphia

ISBN 978 1 39907 061 4

Typeset in Times New Roman 12/16 by SJmagic DESIGN SERVICES, India.
Printed and bound in the UK by CPI Group (UK) Ltd, Croydon, CR0 4YY.

Pen & Sword Books Limited incorporates the imprints of Atlas, Archaeology,
Aviation, Discovery, Family History, Fiction, History, Maritime, Military, Military
Classics, Politics, Select, Transport, True Crime, Air World, Frontline Publishing,
Leo Cooper, Remember When, Seaforth Publishing, The Praetorian Press,
Wharncliffe Local History, Wharncliffe Transport, Wharncliffe True Crime and
White Owl.

For a complete list of Pen & Sword titles please contact
PEN & SWORD BOOKS LIMITED
47 Church Street, Barnsley, South Yorkshire, S70 2AS, England
E-mail: enquiries@pen-and-sword.co.uk
Website: www.pen-and-sword.co.uk

Or

PEN AND SWORD BOOKS
1950 Lawrence Rd, Havertown, PA 19083, USA
E-mail: Uspen-and-sword@casematepublishers.com
Website: www.penandswordbooks.com

Contents

Acknowledgements

Anyone writing at length about Dick Turpin must make plain their debt to the monumental research work that has gone on before them, principally that by Derek Barlow in *Dick Turpin and the Gregory Gang*, not least for the enormous quantity of bibliographic references contained therein.

Many people have assisted in the making of this book. I owe them all a great debt of gratitude. Professor Sharpe and Lucy Bernacki, as historians, have read and commented on the text. I am much obliged to both for their comments, which have improved the book, and also for their encouragement. In a different but also important way, John Gauss and Paul Lang have kindly read through the text and pointed out errors in English. Any mistakes, though, are of course the author's own. Lucy and Lindsay Siviter have helped with the loan of relevant supporting texts, as well as the latter accompanying the author on a research trip. Dr Anna-Lena Berg provided useful advice about the infeasibility of the ride to York. Staff at Essex Record Office (especially Ruth Costello), The National Archives, Hackney Archives, the British Library, the London Metropolitan Archives, the Guildhall Library and York City Archives have helped with the supply of information on research visits. Staff at the Post Office Archives and at York Castle Museum have also helped. It was also useful to have a conversation with Dr Alastair Hagger, a cultural historian with an interest in Turpin. Dr Melia of the Borthwick Institute at York University provided information about burials and churchyards in York. Other archivists

Acknowledgements

and librarians have also assisted in answering enquiries from afar: those at Croydon, Lewisham, Richmond, Redbridge and Waltham Forest. My family have accompanied me on some visits, including a marathon expedition from south Buckinghamshire to Hempstead in which the family car broke down, and tolerated my absence on many research trips. York Castle Museum kindly allowed the photography and publication of a number of their exhibits.

Introduction

Ask someone who Dick Turpin was. Most people will have heard of him and will be able to say something. My son told me that he rode to York from London and, being pressed, said with more accuracy that he was a bandit. The York ride has also been mentioned to me by others. I asked a friend and she said he was a highwayman who gave money to the poor. Others knew him as just a highwayman. Only a very few decried these myths. Apart from students of the eighteenth century (a small band indeed), very few have ever heard of anyone else from early eighteenth-century history, not even such luminaries as Sir Robert Walpole, though he headed the government for an unprecedented and unsurpassed twenty-one years. Whereas histories of the period cover Walpole and his policies at length, they might at most have a single reference to Turpin. The gap between public perception and historical writing is immense on this subject.

Of all the English highwaymen of the eighteenth century – and there were many – Dick Turpin has been the best known of all since the nineteenth century. He is almost as well known as the mediaeval Robin Hood, but unlike Hood he was a real character. However, as in the case of Robin Hood, Turpin is mostly known as a handsome and heroic figure, and though on the wrong side of the law he is seen as a fighter for justice, especially for the common man against the rich and powerful. Although he allegedly stole from the rich, he is not generally seen as a criminal at all. His fame has been perpetuated in novels, films, TV programmes and by the heritage industry.

In particular there are a number of pubs which claim to have an association with Turpin and some are even named after him, as are some streets, which cannot be said for most criminals. The image of Turpin as a masked horseman holding up carriages and stage coaches in bloodless crimes is a potent one.

This book is in two halves. The first explores Dick Turpin as a historical figure, born in Essex in 1705 and dying in York thirty-four years later. In particular his criminal career is considered, as recorded by contemporaries and near-contemporaries in the press and in histories published shortly after his death. In these accounts Turpin does not appear as the wholesome figure of nineteenth- and twentieth-century depictions, though in his lifetime he gained a brief notoriety that few criminals of his age did. As a thief and a killer he does not shine and his criminal career was not solely dedicated to being a highwayman: he was also a housebreaker and horse stealer and he rarely worked alone. Yet the contemporary accounts of his life and actions vary and it is unclear how many of the crimes attributed to him, or the gang he was a member of, were correctly attributed.

The second half of the book reveals how Turpin was depicted after his death and in particular in the nineteenth and twentieth century and beyond. Here we have a wholly different character. Gone is the vicious thug and housebreaker and here is the gentleman highwayman who robs, it is true, but often gives to the poor, and never uses unnecessary violence. He has a beloved horse called Black Bess, on which he rides from London to York. He is chivalrous towards women and only became a highwayman because he was forced into it by the cruel laws of the day and despotic administrators among the wealthy.

There are parallels in the Turpin story with the way that pirates have been treated, from being the violent robbers and murderers of the eighteenth century to becoming dashing romantic heroes in films in the twentieth century and beyond. This is in part because pirates and highwaymen ceased to be a real danger – when their exploits ended, they could become the subjects of romantic fiction.

We also need to consider the relationship between fact and fiction and the way that historical fact is presented. Despite the positive image of Turpin in the past two centuries, there is no statue to him like those of Rob Roy MacGregor, Ned Kelly and Robin Hood. It is perhaps worth considering Turpin in the light of the two other real-life criminals, Rob Roy and Kelly, who have, for many, become folk heroes. They are different in many ways but share some similarities.

There are difficulties in researching the life of Dick Turpin, compared to more modern criminals for whom police, prosecution and prison files often exist, such as John George Haigh, the acid bath murderer, or his fellow serial killer, John Christie of Rillington Place. Unsurprisingly, Turpin did not keep a diary nor pen an autobiography, and he was not an avid letter writer. His family and friends did not write about him either during his life or afterwards. He was not of interest to the great and good of the eighteenth century who wrote letters; Horace Walpole (youngest son of the statesman) never mentioned him, nor does Lord Hervey, the celebrated court memoirist of the era. There seems no known reference to Turpin until 1735, save for his baptism record in 1705.

What we do have are references in newspapers, judicial records, brief contemporary biographies and the depositions of witnesses, all of which are of use, but also limited. Some were written years after the events, and very little is known for sure about Turpin's childhood and youth. Sources naturally differ and it is not always possible to establish which are accurate. For example, Turpin is known to have been a gang member, and though we know of some of their crimes, it is unclear how many Turpin was involved in and his role in these, until the gang's final two attacks, for which there is eyewitness testimony. Was Turpin responsible for shooting one man dead or two? It is only towards the end of his criminal career that we can be more certain about what happened and when, but even here there is room for doubt in some of the details. This lack of factual certainty has been an opportunity for the mythmakers.

Introduction

There was far more written about Turpin after his death and in particular in the nineteenth century and afterwards. He appeared in many forms of popular entertainment as well as a few history books. Yet this is the legacy of the criminal and how he is remembered and so this construct must be examined as well as the actual man and his crimes.

The book's first half focusses on the real Turpin, the man known in contemporary records. Chapter 1 is a brief introduction to the history of early eighteenth-century England. The next chapter concerns Turpin's early life and youth, and its context. It is fairly sparse. Chapter 3 is lengthier and concerns the criminal gang that Turpin joined, their numerous robberies, and their final collapse. Chapter 4 covers the period of Turpin's greatest infamy, as a highwayman in 1735–37, which saw him descend into murder and become a much-wanted man. Chapter 5 follows his downfall, arrest, trial and execution.

The next chapters deal with Turpin's legacy. Chapter 6 examines his emergence as a popular hero in the nineteenth and twentieth century. It discusses some of the alleged supernatural manifestations and pubs associated with Turpin. Chapter 7 explores the screen portrayals of his life and crimes. These chapters show Turpin in a different vein than the earlier chapters. Chapter 8 looks at what historians have written about Turpin over the centuries.

I was introduced to Turpin as a child, via the *Dick Turpin* TV series broadcast from 1979–82 (discussed in Chapter 7), but my later research and publishing interests were directed towards the Jacobite campaigns of 1689–1746. Later I took to writing predominantly about twentieth-century true crime, and recently these two interests fused to lead me to write about Turpin and his milieu. In the intervening years I saw a documentary about Turpin and read Professor Sharpe's book, both of which led me away from the myths I learned as a boy. In 2013, in an online critique of the TV show, I wrote that the hero of that fiction was as unlike the real Turpin as it is possible to be. My approach can be seen as conservative, as my sympathies are towards the victims of crime and the agents of the law rather than the perpetrators, however romanticised in retrospect. This being said, there is, hopefully, no attempt in my work to heighten the villainy of the criminals nor swell the hurt of the victims or make heroes of the lawmen. The aim is objectivity where possible rather than direct appeals to the readers' emotions, and not to cast the criminals as the real victims.[1]

Chapter 1

Society, Crime and Justice in Early Eighteenth-century England

Before examining Turpin we need to know a little about the environment in which he lived and died; there are many books on the century's history and so what follows is necessarily a brief summary. Needless to say, Turpin's world was a vastly different one to that of the early twenty-first century, 300 years later. For one thing, it was essentially a rural society, with some large towns and cities. England's population totalled about five million (estimated at 5.263 million in 1731) and so was the most populous as well as the richest and largest part of the British Isles. The biggest city by far was London, with a population of about half a million. London was based on both sides of the Thames with outlying villages and towns such as Hackney and Islington to the north, Charlton and Woolwich to the south-east and Fulham to the west. Much of what is now Greater London was country villages. Other cities were far smaller. Norwich, as second city, had a population of about 31,000 in 1700, Bristol had 30,000 in 1725 and Newcastle had 20,000 in 1730. Most of the other cities numbered under 10,000 residents, and the majority of the population lived in villages and small towns.[1]

Most people worked on the land as either tenant farmers or farm labourers, or in allied professions. The Industrial Revolution was yet to come, though increases in trade and commerce, both overseas and inland, were visible, especially in the growth of Liverpool, Bristol and Newcastle. Life expectancy for most was low at birth and in the early years but if childhood illnesses could be survived then it was quite possible for someone to live until their fifties or sixties and in some cases even longer. Mortality was at its highest in London, where burials outweighed baptisms, but the population grew due to constant arrivals from elsewhere. Population growth was on the whole modest in this era.

Great Britain was ruled by several monarchs in Turpin's lifetime. Firstly, there was Queen Anne (1702–14). She was the last of the Stuarts and died without a surviving heir. Parliament requested that George, Elector of Hanover, become king as George I, ruling from 1714–27. He was succeeded by his son, George II, from 1727–60. The monarch was the most important and powerful political figure in the realm, able to choose the members of the government, to make war and conduct diplomacy, and to have a major say in the appointment of officers in the army and navy as well as civil servants and senior clergy.

However, unlike many Continental monarchs the British king or queen was never absolute, nor made any attempt in that direction. The monarch relied on Parliament to rule and needed ministers who were agreeable to their fellow MPs and peers. The leading minister for much of this period was Sir Robert Walpole (1676–1745), a Norfolk MP, who was pre-eminent from 1721–42. His followers in Parliament were men known as the Whigs, but this was not a coherent modern party, and some Whigs formed part of the Parliamentary Opposition, alongside the Tories. The electorate was composed of male property-owning freeholders, about a fifth of the adult male population, and the two-member constituencies varied widely in the size of their electorates. Most MPs were country gentlemen, city merchants, lawyers and army and naval officers. From 1716 elections occurred every seven years and at the death of a monarch, but not all constituencies were always contested.

Below the level of the central government were the counties and boroughs. The former had a titular head held by a nobleman loyal to the monarch, the Lord Lieutenant, a post usually held for life, and the other county level post, this time an annual one, was that of county sheriff. The Lord Lieutenant raised the militia in times of crisis and the sheriff was responsible for the county gaol and for the assizes. Yet neither post was of huge day-to-day importance in the eighteenth century.

Rather it was the justices of the peace (JPs), country gentlemen, who ruled the shires. They had administrative duties as well as judicial ones and met formally in quarter sessions four times a year. However, one or two JPs could examine suspects, hand out sentences for minor offences or commit more serious offenders to prison. In the boroughs were the corporations, headed by a mayor and aldermen, with the common councillors being elected. They had similar responsibilities to their equivalents at county level, but the majority were merchants or professional men.

The lowest administrative rung was the parishes, which had important duties, and it was these that most people had dealings with. The parish vestry was a collection of householders, chaired by the vicar, who met regularly in order to set a rate and to allocate the money raised in that manner to relieve the local poor, to maintain roads and bridges in the parish and to repair the church fabric. Chosen annually for each parish were the churchwardens and the constable/s; the latter were responsible for apprehending offenders and taking them to the JPs and then possibly to the house of correction or the county gaol.

Equally important in society was the role of Christianity. The established Church from the sixteenth century was the Anglican Church, with the monarch at its head. In practical terms the archbishops of Canterbury and York were the principal ecclesiastical figures in England. Beneath them were the bishops of the other twenty-four dioceses in England and beneath them were the archdeacons and the parish clergy, some of whom were responsible for more than one. The Church had a great deal of political and administrative power in society, as bishops were members of the House of Lords and a multitude of church courts administered all wills.

Not all Englishmen were members of the Church of England. There were the various sects of Protestant Dissenters. Since 1689 they had been permitted to worship in their own chapels, as licensed by the JPs. They were not allowed to enter into the full political life of the nation, as most civil and military posts required the post-holder to prove that they were a member of the Anglican Church. For the even smaller minority of Catholics, as well as these restrictions, even worship was prohibited by law, although it frequently occurred. Such religious restrictions for minorities were commonplace in Europe at this time, as it was believed that these minorities were potentially subversive. In the English case this particularly concerned the Catholics.

There was at this time a threat to the ruling Hanoverian dynasty. This stemmed from the expulsion of the Catholic James II in 1688. He, and later his son, James Francis Stuart (James III, or the Pretender) and his grandson, Charles Edward Stuart (history's Bonnie Prince Charlie, or the Young Pretender), claimed the throne by hereditary right. Their supporters were known as Jacobites and were found at all social levels throughout Britain, especially among some Catholics and Tories, namely the religious and political outsiders. They had plotted to restore the Stuarts and this had included an attempted invasion with French aid in 1708, a major insurrection in Scotland and England in 1715 and a lesser one, supported by Spain, in 1719. All had failed dismally, but the will remained. However, there were no further military efforts to promote the cause between 1719 and 1745. The threat, however, remained, especially when linked to foreign support in wartime.

Britain was a socially divided country. A small number of nobility dominated the senior posts in Church and State as well as wielding immense power through their landed and moneyed estates. Temporal peers numbered 160 families in 1688 and had an average annual income of £3,200, but some had far more (the Duke of Newcastle had an annual income of £30,000). The gentry were far more numerous

(12,000 families in 1688) though less powerful individually, with rents from their land providing them with sufficient income to play a part in society as well as dominating local administration at the quarter sessions. There were also baronets, knights and esquires, another 4,600 families. Many younger sons went into the Church, (10,000 families in 1688) the armed forces (9,000 families) and the professions such as law (10,000 families) and medicine. These two groupings were socially pre-eminent in the counties.[2]

However, in the towns and cities, which were increasing in number and population, the dominant groupings were the merchants and the professions, many of whom had larger incomes than many of the gentry. They also provided the rulers of the urban districts. In the 1720s and 1730s Britain was at peace and so trade and industry were prospering. Of lesser importance were the numerous shopkeepers, craftsmen and small traders. Eminent merchants numbered 2,000, with an average income of £400, and lesser merchants, numbering 8,000, had an average income of £200. Shopkeepers, innkeepers and domestic tradesmen numbered 50,000 with an average income of £45.[3]

The majority of the population fell into none of these groups. They lived in variously sized country villages and most worked on the land as small tenant farmers or landless labourers, or at least in a form of labour connected to agriculture, such as blacksmiths and millers. There were also cottagers, small ale-house keepers and paupers, numbering 400,000 families. Lowest of the low were the transient in society: beggars, prostitutes and criminals.[4]

Education would not be compulsory until the next century and so only a minority had any schooling. There were grammar schools in many towns as well as a few public and private schools. Charity and church schools, mostly quite small, also existed and there were numerous private tutors. A few older boys attended university, then essential for entry into the Church and law.

Transport was basic and the fastest way to travel was by water. Ships took coal from Newcastle and other coastal towns such as

Liverpool, London and Bristol were involved in overseas trade. Navigable rivers were also used for commercial transport. It was not until later in the eighteenth century that canals were created to speed up inland commercial travel.

The majority of non-commercial transport was by road. Roads were the responsibility of parishes, which had to use local manpower to repair those within their jurisdiction. From the seventeenth century private companies were employed to form turnpike trusts, which charged travellers for using the roads. This was unpopular, but the money was used to repair the roads, and as Daniel Defoe (1660–1731) wrote: 'great progress had been made in mending the most difficult of ways, and that with such success'.[5] This was not universal, however. Travel speed was variable. Famously a stagecoach company, which ran coaches from York to London in 1706, leaving from the Black Swan inn, boasted of being able to make the journey of 211 miles in only four days, 'God willing'.

Of the many roads in existence, it was believed that the best parts were those nearest the capital, which were most used. The roads from London through Essex and Suffolk to Harwich and Ipswich were much used and were once dangerous or even impassable. The turnpike system was later implemented there, and roads improved: 'they are now so firm, so safe, so easy for travellers, and carriages as well as cattle'.[6]

Crime is impossible to quantify in the light of the lack of comprehensive statistics. It was certainly widely reported in the press, as were the punishments given to those who were taken and found guilty. The knowledge of theft, murder and violent assaults heightened public concerns about crime.

In the nineteenth and twentieth century poverty has often been cited as the cause of crime, but it was not seen in this way in the eighteenth century. Rather it was the reverse. Henry Fielding (1707–54), a London magistrate *inter alia*, believed that increasing wealth was a cause of crime. William Hawkins, looking back over the period

1715–86, agreed and wrote that 'the increase of commerce, opulence and luxury' had 'introduced a variety of temptations to fraud and rapine'. Since there were more people in possession of more money and/or luxury goods, there was more to steal. There was also debate over whether mankind was rational or followed its base, animalistic (i.e. criminal) instincts.[7]

By twenty-first century standards, the maintenance of law and order may appear amateur and haphazard, but it could also be very effective, as we shall see. It was certainly far from uniform and scientific. Each parish appointed one or two constables to serve for a year, and they were paid expenses for taking suspects to a house of correction or county gaol. Towns and cities supplemented them by appointing paid watchmen at night time. For serious emergencies the militia (led by the Lord Lieutenant) or posse comitatus (led by the sheriff) might be summoned, but this was usually only in times of rebellion or feared invasion and not always then. Thief-takers were another means of dealing with crime: these were men who sought rewards for the apprehending wanted criminals. Some were criminals themselves, such as the infamous Jonathan Wild (*c*.1682–1725). The army was often employed to deal with severe rioting and smuggling, but numbers were low in peacetime and much of the army was employed in garrisoning colonies abroad. There was little political appetite for a paid police force because it was thought that it could pose a threat to political liberty, was expensive in terms of higher taxes, and was a potential source of political corruption. The detection of crime and the bringing of suspects to court was not the role of the state but of the citizens, who then claimed the rewards, often quite generous, offered by the state for successful convictions.

Constables could call on the public to aid them:

'By vesting not only the Officers of Justice, but every Private Man, with the Authority, for securing these Miscreants, of which Authority it may be of service, to the Officers, as well the Public in general to be more particularly informed'.[8]

Severe punishments were seen as another way to combat crime. Hanging was a very common punishment and the number of offences for which it was applicable increased in the early eighteenth century. The Waltham Black Act of 1723 was primarily aimed at poachers but added a further fifty capital offences to the statute book. Indeed, grand larceny was a hanging offence and that was for any article valued at or more than one shilling. However, although the number of capital offences increased in this period, the actual number of hangings fell and this was because there were alternative punishments.

Courts dealing with criminals were the quarter sessions and the assize courts. The former dealt with lesser offences, as a rule, though they could send more serious offenders to the assizes. Minor offences, which made up the great bulk of all crime, could be dealt with summarily by one or two JPs in what was known as petty sessions. There was no required legal knowledge or training or qualification to be a JP; it sufficed to own property and to be an Anglican. Otherwise offenders would be brought before the full quarter sessions, though that only met four times a year. Sentences could include fines and whipping, as custodial sentences were rare except in the case of debtors and forgers. Prison was primarily for those awaiting trial, and offenders could not be bailed out prior to the carrying out of the sentence.

The assize courts met twice a year in each county and were presided over by a small number of itinerant professional touring judges sent out from Westminster. They would usually gather at the county town and hear the capital offences in which potentially the death penalty might be awarded. Overseeing the assizes was the county sheriff, chiefly responsible for the security of the prisoners there. The assizes could and often did, impose the death sentence on offenders, and this was by hanging in public. However, by the time Turpin was active, more of those found guilty were transported, following the Transportation Act of 1718, and at this time this meant being sent as indentured servants to work in the American colonies or the West Indies for a period of years, often seven or fourteen. This was effectively temporary slavery. It has been estimated that in the 1730s those convicted of a capital offence had only a one in eight or one in ten chance of being hanged. Those who were young, were first-time offenders, had character witnesses in court, had previous good character, were female and whose crimes were not seen as particularly heinous, were likely to escape death. Even so, between 1703 and 1772, 1,242 people were hanged at Tyburn in London, mostly men, with just over half being tradesmen and apprentices.[9]

The *Gentleman's Magazine*, established in 1731, had a 'historical chronicle' in each monthly issue and this invariably included reports on the trials at the Old Bailey, which was the main criminal court in London. There were eight sessions per year, unlike most county sessions, which were usually held only twice a year, but such was the volume of crime – and population – in and around London, that more numerous sessions were needed.

An examination of this publication's pages for 1733 shows that the death penalty was given for eighteen robberies, eight burglaries, four murders, eleven highway robberies, three shoplifters, two street robberies, a rape, a horse stealing, and five coiners. In total there were fifty-one executions, these being carried out in public at Tyburn (roughly where Marble Arch is now), but the majority of criminals – 192 of them – who were found guilty were transported; four were whipped and eight had their hands burnt. One was pilloried, given six months in prison and fined a mark. A female coiner was strangled and then burnt. One woman tried to escape the death penalty by claiming to be pregnant. There were fewer criminals and executions in the counties: at Taunton in that year there were four executions, two for horse stealing, one for rape and one for infanticide. In Essex a highwayman was hanged. Yet in Newcastle the first execution since

1703 occurred in 1733.[10] Public hangings were immensely popular sights; thousands would assemble to view them.

Retribution was not sufficient in itself. The other major plank in the fight against crime came from an Act of 1693 which enabled rewards and pardons to be given to the accomplices of criminals. This gave rise to the 'thief-takers': men who received cash for apprehending criminals. Often the thief-takers were criminals themselves. The most notable example was Jonathan Wild, eventually hanged for his own crimes in 1725, who had apprehended many other criminals. As we shall see, this method of sowing division and tempting criminals to turn informant led to gangs being broken up. The system had its failings, but was also seen to work. However, one instance where it was almost fatal came in 1755 when two men were persuaded to take part in a robbery by a gang who planned to betray them and benefit from the rewards paid for apprehending them. The two were tried and, on the perjured evidence of the gang, were found guilty and would have been hanged had it not been for the astute observations of the constable for Blackheath.[11]

Another facet of early eighteenth-century society was the growth of the press and especially the county press. Founded in 1665, *The London Gazette* (initially *The Oxford Gazette*) had become the first regular newspaper, but despite other short-lived titles in that century, it was not until *The Daily Courant* and a few other newspapers emerged in the 1700s, all published in London, but many distributed throughout the country, that newspapers were established as regular fixtures. During George I's reign the provincial press grew: Derby, Ipswich, Leeds, Newcastle, Stamford and York all acquired newspapers in this period. These newspapers were weekly and were usually four pages long. Apart from adverts and foreign news, they also covered domestic events, and this included news about crimes, especially those in and around London, and the results of the county assizes. County newspapers covered national news as well as London news and there was much duplication. Turpin, once he was detached from the gang in 1735, often appeared in these and this helped to build his notoriety.

It should be noted that London news predominated in both the national and provincial press; the latter would copy stories from the former, but less so vice versa. Had Turpin committed his crimes in the provinces it is likely he would have gained far less coverage. By committing them in or near London he was guaranteed more column inches. Apart from the newspapers, there were books and pamphlets published about the crimes of well-known criminals, as well as crime dramas such as *The Beggars' Opera*.

In the 1730s (as in the 1720s), the decade in which the early chapters in this book are set, Britain was at peace. Despite the War of Polish Succession of 1733–35, which was engulfing much of Europe and in which George II wished to bring British force to bear, his chief minister, Sir Robert Walpole, persuaded him against it. His government also presided over a low-tax economy and ruled throughout the decade, but not without visible opposition, as satirical pieces appeared both in print and on the stage. The controversial Excise Bill had to be withdrawn in face of fierce opposition in 1733. As for the bulk of the population, these were generally good years, with a low cost of living. There were no epidemic diseases between 1730 and 1741. From 1730–33 there were four good harvests in a row, thus keeping food prices low, and it was only in 1739 that there was a deficient harvest. For landowners, Land Tax was at 2s in the £1 and even in 1731–32 it was as low as a shilling.[12]

England in Turpin's day was a rural society presided over by the gentry. Times for many were good, but crime was ever-present and was increasingly known about. For some, reading about criminals and attending public executions was the nearest they got to crime. For others, though, the effect of crime was only too well known, either as participants or as victims.

Public responses to crime varied. Despite fears about a great criminal underworld or criminal class, the number of professional criminals was small. However, many people did drop in and out of crime in order to meet short-term needs, caused by poverty and unemployment. Much employment was seasonal in nature and so, especially for the unskilled and semi-skilled workers, periods of under-employment were common.[13] It is possible therefore that some of these were sympathetic towards professional criminals such as Turpin.

Finally, a word about money. In the early eighteenth century a private infantry soldier was paid eight pence per day, a labourer six shillings a week, if in work, and a skilled craftsman could earn up to twenty-two shillings per week. Until 1971 twelve old pence (abbreviated to d) made up one shilling (abbreviated to s), twenty shillings made up a pound and twenty-one shillings made a guinea. All money was in the form of metallic coinage.

Chapter 2

The Young Turpin, 1705–34

Unless an individual is of extreme importance, for example a royal prince, so that others write about him or her in their childhood and youth, or unless they are a precocious creature who writes letters and diaries, or unless there is an extraordinary news value in their youthful self, the material for an individual's early years, certainly in the eighteenth century, is minimal. Even the biographer of the rich and powerful Duke of Newcastle, who appears occasionally in this book, admitted that 'little can be confidently said' about his formative years, devoting a mere page to discussion of the Duke's early life.[1] Twentieth-century criminals who were apprehended were often quizzed by psychiatrists, trying to ascertain the roots of their subsequent criminal behaviour, and if sufficiently notorious the criminals themselves often penned autobiographical essays for the press, such as those that appeared in the *Sunday Pictorial* for John Christie in 1953 and Donald Hume in 1958. Quite how reliable these are is another question. Unfortunately for the low-born Turpin, there is relatively little material about his younger years and much of that is speculative.

Richard Bayes was the innkeeper of the Green Man in Epping Forest in 1737 and was Turpin's only contemporary biographer, writing in 1739 to satisfy a perceived demand from the public for information about the recently executed notorious felon. He would seem to be a key source of details about Turpin, but we must question how accurate his information was and what access he had to reliable data. Who did he speak to and to what extent was he inventive? No definite answers can be given, but he did live in Essex and so may have known people who knew Turpin. Where corroborative evidence can be given it will be used.

So we must begin at the beginning: yet this is impossible because we do not even know the date of Turpin's birth (birth certificates were not introduced until 1837). However, there is the parish register. The register with baptisms for St Andrew's church, Hempstead, Essex, records on 21 September 1705, among the seven people baptised there in that year, one Ricardus, son of Johannes and Maria Turpin, or in English, Richard, son of John and Mary Turpin. Apparently there were many Turpins in this part of Essex in the sixteenth and seventeenth century. Edward Saward, in 1739, recalled 'He was born and brought up at the Bell, his Father kept a publick house'.[2] Richard was baptised by the Revd William Sworder (*c.*1670–1726), vicar of Great Sampford and Hempstead from 1701 until his death. It was not unknown for the clergyman completing the entry in the register to include the date of birth of the child baptised, though there was no obligation to do so. Sworder did not, and so we can only speculate about Turpin's birthday. It is probable that it was only a few weeks prior to the baptism. This is the first and last mention of Turpin in any known surviving contemporary record for another three decades. The church is just south of the main road through the village and is on the top of an incline, opposite the Bell Inn.

John Turpin and Mary Parminter (probably born in Little Yeldham, north Essex) were married in Hempstead on 25 March 1695. Turpin was at least the fifth child of at least six born of John and Mary. He had three elder brothers: Thomas (baptised on 29 March 1696), John (baptised on 20 March 1698) and Christopher (baptised on 23 February 1700). There was an elder sister, Mary, (born on 28 April 1702) and a younger one, Dorothy (baptised on 10 February 1708). The parish registers marked a 'p' before the entry, denoting that the parents were parishioners.[3] The family had lived in the parish for at least a decade when Turpin was born and some of its members were to live there for decades afterwards.

Hempstead is a small village in the north of Essex on the border with Cambridgeshire, seven miles to the east of Saffron Walden, a market town, and six miles to the west of Haverhill. It was 44 miles north-east of London. Apparently 'The village consists of a small number of straggling houses and the inhabitants are generally employed in the labours of husbandry'. The parish comprised 3,565 acres. The soil was loam and the subsoil was clay. Wheat and barley were the major crops. There are scanty details about the place in the early eighteenth century, but the 1848 county directory listed sixteen small outlying farms, four boot and shoemakers, four shopkeepers, three carpenters, a cow keeper, a miller, a wright, a corn miller, a blacksmith and a tailor, with a population in 1801 of 574. The church, which is on a hill in the centre of the village, was mediaeval in origin and was chapel of ease to Great Sampford; the pub was to the north of the church. In 1657 the distinguished surgeon and royal physician, Dr William Hervey, born in 1578, and known for his work on human anatomy and blood circulation, was buried there and is commemorated in the church by a monument.[4] In Turpin's time the population was probably less than it was in 1801 and there may have been fewer farmers, craftsmen and shopkeepers, but it was probably fairly similar in other aspects of rural life.

The Hempstead parish book and the poll books for the county give a little additional information about the parish in the early eighteenth century. Each year, up to 1709, the parish appointed two churchwardens, two constables, two overseers and two surveyors; afterwards only one churchwarden was thought necessary. A number of poor parishioners, mostly widows, received weekly sums from the overseers under the provisions of the (Old) Poor Law; in the 1720s this number was usually about nine and they were given between 9d and 2s 6d each, amounting to a total expenditure of £3–4 monthly. The Smith family seem to have held various parish posts in these years. In 1715 there was an electorate of fourteen men in Hempstead; they were property owners, eight of whom lived in the parish, and these included the Smiths.[5]

Descriptions of Turpin in later life refer to him as being 'pock marked' and this suggests that his face, and possibly his body, had been disfigured by the symptoms of smallpox. This was a common ailment at the time and one that was often fatal. The young Turpin was clearly physically robust enough to survive it and grow to manhood, albeit with obvious facial blemishes (so much for the handsome hero of later myth).

The contemporary histories of Dick Turpin have little to say about his childhood and youth, except to record the place and year of his baptism. His first biographer, whose reliability has been questioned by a recent historian, then adds that his father: 'put him to school to one Smith, a writing master'.[6]

This is corroborated by James Smith, who later became an exciseman (in about 1717), and who crucially knew Turpin as a young man. Smith was clearly an educated man and was probably related to the Edward and Samuel Smith of Hempstead who were both eligible to vote and often filled posts as various parish officials, denoting that he was of the middling sort.[7] In 1739 he recalled before the court at York that Turpin, 'was only learning to make Letters, and I believe he was three quarters of a year with me'. He added 'I think he might be about eleven or twelve years old'. He also stated that 'he was at school with me', suggesting that perhaps Smith was an elder boy, a pupil-teacher rather than a teacher himself, as is often stated.[8] It seems that the school was in fact a room in the church, the east wing, which had been an extension built by Sir Eliab Hervey and is now the church vestry.[9]

Edward Saward was another long-standing resident of Hempstead and knew Turpin from about 1717. He had been a close friend of Turpin since the two were boys and he recalled 'I was very great with him' but regrettably said nothing else to detail Turpin's younger days, except to say 'I drank with him' as a young man.[10] Saward may have been related to the Saward of Hempstead who was in receipt of 1s per week poor relief between 1705 and 1707, and if so was clearly not well off. It is perhaps significant that neither John Turpin nor Saward appear on the list of men eligible to vote and so the former probably only rented his home/business premises. Putting these two together suggests that the Turpins were not particularly affluent, but nor were they exactly poor.[11] However, John Turpin is noted as paying 6s per annum to rent the blacksmith's yard from 1730–33; this may have been Turpin's father or perhaps his elder brother.[12] The Turpin family was neither towards the top of the parish hierarchy nor near its bottom.

Education was not compulsory until the late nineteenth century and so relatively few children went to school. Most who did were from the male urban middling sort and many villages, especially small ones, did not have a school. It was not uncommon for the clergyman to give a few local boys a basic schooling. Clearly John Turpin believed that his son was worth having some education and had some spare money for this. A level of literacy would certainly be necessary for the young man to take up his livelihood in business. As we shall later see, Turpin was able to write and presumably read and the origins of this lay in his father's decision to pay for his education.

After the young Turpin had been given a basic grounding in reading and writing, his father allegedly sent him away to complete his training in London. There is no supporting evidence that he did so and London was over 40 miles away. Even so, Bayes went on to write:

'from whence he was placed apprentice to a butcher in Whitechapel, where he served his time, he was frequently guilty of Misdemeanours, and behaved in a loose and disorderly manner'.[13]

Apparently, Turpin later told the hangman:

'That he was bred a butcher and serv'd five years of his time very faithfully in Whitechapel, but falling

into idle company, began to take unlawful measures
to support his extravagance, and went some times on
the highways on foot, and met with severall small
Booties, his not being detected therein encouragement
to steal horses and pursue his new trade in Epping
Forest on Horseback, which he had continued about
six years.'[14]

This sounds remarkably similar to the account of how Jack Sheppard
(1702–24) fell into crime while an apprentice in London: 'he had
given himself up to the Sensual Pleasures of Low Life, Drinking all
day and getting to some impudent Strumpet at night'.

In particular it was women who led Sheppard astray; one named
Elizabeth Lion, 'was the first who engaged him in taking base
Methods to obtain money wherewith to purchase baser pleasures'.
A later woman friend, Mrs Maggot, used him likewise, 'and only
made use of him to go and steal money or what might yield money,
for her to spend in company that she liked better'.[15]

Apprenticeship was a common practice in the seventeenth and
eighteenth century for young men and women. They could either
be pauper children who were apprenticed by the parish, who paid
a master or mistress to take and train the youth, or they could be
apprenticed privately, at cost to the child's parents. Turpin certainly
lived in Whitechapel in early 1735 and was involved in a skirmish
there in 1737, though this does not corroborate his residence there in
earlier decades.

However, there is a strong piece of evidence which suggests that
Turpin's acquaintance with Whitechapel did not begin until later in life
and that he was not formally apprenticed anywhere. Again, according
to his contemporary, James Smith, 'I think he might be about eleven
or twelve years old when I went to the Excise [i.e. 1716–17] and he
worked with his Father, who was a Butcher'.[16] This seems more likely;
Whitechapel was about 40 miles from Hempstead and there is no

evidence that Turpin was apprenticed by the parish as poor children often were, and none that his father had enough money to apprentice him privately. The cost of this was often about £40 (perhaps about his family's average annual income). Smith's comment that he was taught butchery skills by his father seems logical and reasonable and children often worked alongside older family members in the eighteenth century.

Another mystery is Turpin's marriage. Apparently, according to Bayes, 'he married the daughter of one Palmer', but there is no proof that this was his wife's maiden name (this surname was assumed by Turpin when on the run in 1737–38).[17] Virtually nothing is known of this marriage, not even when and where it took place, assuming it ever did. It may have been a common law marriage without recourse to the Church. It was only near the end of his life that Turpin's wife and child were even mentioned. It does not seem likely that in the latter years of Turpin's life he had any association with them. However, other information suggests that the woman in question was Elizabeth Millington. According to Smith, 'He married one of my father's maids'.[18] This suggests that Turpin and his family had little money, for him to marry a servant girl. Very little is known about Elizabeth and she does not seem to have been a native of Hempstead.

Then, with Turpin's schooling and work training over, according to Bayes, he 'set up for himself at Suson [Waltham Abbey] in Essex' perhaps in about 1727 or 1728, after apparently completing his alleged apprenticeship: 'as soon as he came out of his time'.[19]

Again, more reliably, Smith recalled that Turpin was 'set up in the Butcher Trade' (perhaps on marriage and with help from his family), working independently as his own boss, away from his family, and remained so for some time, but for how long replied 'I cannot tell'. Saward recalled, 'Yes, I knew him perfectly well then, and I have bought a good many Joints of Meat from him, upon my soul'. Newspaper references to Turpin in 1735–36 usually refer to him as 'Turpin the Butcher' and this is clearly a reference to his earlier career and not that he was a slaughterer of people, or at least not yet. He abandoned butchery after about six years, 'then kept a publick house'. This was clearly in the locality of Hempstead for Smith then said, when asked if he ever saw him again, 'Yes, I saw him afterwards, six miles from thence'.[20] He added, 'I have been many times in his company, and frequently with him'.[21] Turpin had clearly left the village of his birth but was not living far away. As Saward was later asked, 'Did you know him since he left Hempstead?' and he replied, 'I was with him at his house in Hempstead… I saw him frequently, I can't tell you how often… He came backwards and forwards'. Saward was also asked 'Had he any settled dwelling?' and replied, 'Not that I know of'. Therefore it would appear that in the later 1720s and up to about 1734, Turpin was living in Essex for a time, perhaps relatively near Hempstead, and that he often visited his family there, but had ceased to do so in about 1734. However, there was also a reference in the trial that he lived at a place which was not explicitly identified but could have been Buckhurst Hill, which is rather nearer to London (10 miles distant) than Hempstead, being just south of Epping Forest. Buckhurst Hill was then a cluster of houses on the coaching road from London to Cambridge, being part of the parish of Chigwell and between Woodford and Loughton.[22]

It would certainly have made sense for Turpin to have earned his living as butcher and then publican somewhere other than his birthplace. Hempstead was (and is) very small and probably too small for two butchers or two publicans to have made an adequate living, competing as they would have to have done for the same custom in a limited market. Joseph Symson, an early eighteenth-century mercer of Kendal, encouraged his sons to set up in the same business but outside their home town for this reason.[23]

The Hempstead parish registers suggest that several members of the Turpin family died in the 1730s: his brother Thomas in 1733 and either his sister Mary or his mother Mary in the following year (the other Mary Turpin died in 1728). Meanwhile Christopher had married in Helion Bumpstead and so was probably living there. Dorothy may have also been married at this time but lived elsewhere, possibly outside the county. Only his father was left by 1734 (four years later it was Dorothy and her husband who ran the family pub when their father could not do so). One wonders if smallpox might have carried them off, for at this time if people survived infancy, their lifespan would usually be expected to extend beyond their thirties.

It is also possible that Turpin resided for a time in Thaxted, which is only about four miles to the south of Hempstead. There is a house in Stoney Lane, Thaxted, called Turpin's Cottage. Proclamations concerning him in 1737 refer to him being of the place and though he was not born there, nor grew up there, he may have been in business there as butcher or publican. This certainly ties in with Saward and Smith having dealings with him in the early 1730s.

Bayes gave an account of Turpin's early life and crimes, but this cannot be verified and one major historian has cast great doubt on its accuracy. Accord to Bayes, business was poor because Turpin had no credit and no one would trust him. This led him to crime: 'he was reduced to a necessity of maintaining himself by indirect practices'. He would steal oxen, sheep and lambs from the gentry in the locality. One of these crimes was to steal two oxen from a Mr Giles of Plaistow. He took the beasts home and cut them up. Unfortunately for Turpin, two of Mr Giles's servants saw him, having followed him based on information they had received, which led them to suspect Turpin of theft.[24]

Seeing Turpin slaughter the oxen certainly did nothing to dampen their suspicions, but further proof was sought. They asked where Turpin usually sold his goods and were told that this was at Waltham Abbey market. They went there and saw the hides. They were then convinced that Turpin was indeed guilty. Returning to Suson, they found that Turpin had departed before they could reach him, having been informed beforehand. But only just: he left them in his fore room while he escaped out of a back window. Meanwhile, his wife sold the meat.[25]

Although Turpin had escaped justice, his character was now indelibly blackened and he could no longer seek an honest living in Essex let alone in Suson. Smuggling seemed a possibility. Supplied with what money his wife could spare, he went to the hundreds of Essex and soon found a gang of smugglers to join and 'he followed his new profession for some time with tolerable success'. His luck did not last and he lost all his gains. He wanted another way of making money. He did not have long to look, and as a contemporary biographer noted 'When People are inclinable to Vice, they seldom wait long for opportunities, which was the case with him'.[26] Whether any of this is true is impossible to know and there is certainly no contemporary reference to Turpin as a smuggler.

What is known, from contemporaries who knew Turpin, namely James Smith and Edward Saward who spoke at his trial, is that Turpin kept up his links with Hempstead until about 1733–34. The former was asked in 1739 'How long is it since you saw him last?' and he replied 'I think about five years'.[27] He added 'I do not know more, only the last time I saw him, I sold him a Grey Mare, about five years ago, before my Brother died'.[28]

Meanwhile, there was another opportunity for Turpin. In the early 1730s gangs of criminals stalked the woods of Epping, Waltham and Enfield to the north and north-east of London, hunting for deer. These were not men in the popular romantic mind that only stole to keep themselves and their families from starvation, nor the social bandits of Marxist lore, but were stealing deer on an industrial scale to sell to butchers as an illicit commercial enterprise. These were violent men, too. Warfare between forest keepers and criminals was open. As was noted in 1733, there were 'several persons who had destroyed a great number of deer' in Waltham Forest.[29] Furthermore, there was 'great destruction of His majesty's deer in Waltham Forest by deer stealers who… continue to come daily in such numbers and so well armed'.[30]

Epping Forest once stretched from Waltham to Colchester and perhaps further eastwards. However, since the Middle Ages, deforestation had taken place. As the population increased, land became more valuable for cultivation. The villages which lay within the forests began to encroach on them. In 1793 the district was composed of 60,000 acres and of these a quarter were wooded. It had been a royal forest, but by the eighteenth century this was restricted to the right to keep an unlimited number of deer there and these were mostly red and fallow deer. There were foresters and a forester's court to punish transgressors.[31] Among the forest's environs were several villages including Loughton, Woodford and Chigwell.

The keepers reported 'On Tuesday the 12th of this instant June 1733 seven deer stealers entered the said Chase with firearms, and killed several brace of male deer, but being pursued by the Keepers and others who came to their assistance they fled'. On 25 June the keepers took the war to their enemy, arming themselves with guns, pistols and swords and proceeding to the house of one Colonel Robinson, 'they were come to blow his brains out and set fire to the house'. Robinson and his family escaped, as did the son of their servant, Turpin Mason, who went for help. Meanwhile a labourer on the premises was beaten and the dogs were shot. Had the household been caught they would have been murdered.[32]

The deer-stealers were regularly appearing in strength in the forests, as the keepers stated:

'a great number of deerstealers, supposed to be at least 12 or 14 do almost daily assemble together, and enter His Majesty's said Chase of Enfield with firearms and other dangerous weapons and have killed and carried off great numbers of fallow deer in defiance of the keepers… and that they threaten to murder the said keepers and others and to destroy all the deer'.

The keepers asked that the King set rewards for the capture of deer-stealers and a reward of £10 per stealer was instituted:

> 'For the better discovering the persons guilty of so Heinous an offence, and bringing them to condign punishment, His majesty is pleased to promise his most gracious pardon to any one or two of them who shall discover his or their accomplices, so as they or any one of them maybe apprehended and committed thereof.
>
> And as a further Encouragement for such Discovery, His majesty is graciously pleased to promise to any person or persons making the same, over and above any reward to which he or they may already be entitled the sum of ten pounds for every such offender who by this means shall be apprehended'.[33]

This seems to have been effective because on 14 December 1736, Colonel Martin Bladen (1680–1746) JP and an MP for Maldon, was looking back over this time and considering why the deer-stealing had tailed off, and put it down to the rewards and pardons being issued:

> 'And though no formal information did ensue upon that notice, and consequently the Treasury was put to no expense by it, yet it certainly had a good effect, for there is reason to believe, that it created such a distrust amongst those miscreants, as broke the combination, for they were never known to rob in such numbers together afterwards'.[34]

Deer-stealers naturally needed to deal with butchers in order to make the profits they desired and Turpin, as an Essex butcher in need of meat, was their man.

Chapter 3

Turpin and the Gregory Gang, 1734–35

It is not known exactly how, when and why Turpin took his final step into whole-hearted criminality, but take it he did by 1734 when he ceased any legitimate employment and was no longer seen by residents of Hempstead such as Smith and Saward. As a butcher he had needed a supply of meat to sell to his customers, and based in Buckhurst Hill he was within Epping Forest where the gangs operated. The deer-stealers could provide meat at less than the price offered by legitimate farmers. It is not a major leap of imagination to realise that at some point, perhaps trade being less good than he desired or perhaps motivated by greed, Turpin, who was already a trusted and loyal customer for stolen meat, joined the deer-stealers. How much, if any, deer-stealing he did is another matter because by 1734, the latest year that Turpin could have joined them, the gang had moved onto other targets. Possibly the keepers were proving too dangerous for them and softer targets presented themselves. When Turpin's supply of meat ran out his livelihood was gone and so he needed another.

This gang was known by the newspapers in 1735–38 as 'the Gregory Gang' once the principals were known; sometimes they were known as 'the Essex Gang'. We need to examine the gang members themselves, the men that Turpin consorted with. According to Turpin's account to officials while in York gaol in 1739, 'there were a gang of 21 at the house of James Parkinson of Suson Ferry near Waltham, the landlord of which was one and they would have had him gone out with them but he always refused to go'.[1] The number Turpin cited were never all together in any one raid and there was probably a hard core of professional criminals and others with legitimate employment who flitted in and out of the gang when needed and perhaps were involved in only one or two robberies or possibly none at all, but helped provide weapons or/and horses, acted as fences or perhaps provided intelligence or other assistance. Certainly not all of them were known to John Wheeler, who supplied the following names, addresses and descriptions in February 1735.

The dozen members of the Gregory gang who are known were as follows. *Primus inter pares* was Samuel Gregory, 'a black smith [alternatively a farrier or a carman], about 23 years of age, five feet seven inches high, a long cut on his right cheek'. This had been caused when he was employed by a gentleman in Buckinghamshire; while Sir John Osborne's horse was being shoed there, it had kicked Gregory.[2] He had lived six months in Edgware with Richard Taylor, where he shod horses. He lived with his brother, called Jeremiah, resident in Hackney in 1731 but later in Old Gravel Lane, Ratcliffe, in east London, in early 1735. Jeremiah was a lighterman, who had worked on the Thames barges. He had a record of crime, being apprehended by forest keepers in mid-1730, when they 'ventured their lives in taking him as is well known he being a very desperate fellow and had a pistol in his hand when we took him'. He was committed to Chelmsford prison for deer-stealing and convicted.[3] It has been suggested that Samuel Gregory was the leader on the basis that as a blacksmith he would be a strong man and strength was probably the prize attribute of this gang of criminals, though there was probably more to it than this because another gang member was also a smith.

Jasper Gregory was the third brother and he had been working for one Jeremiah Woodley in 1733, when he complained to a Hackney JP, Henry Norris, that Woodley had been beating him without cause with an iron and a broomstick, as well as refusing to pay his wages.[4] Possibly this led him to leave his job and join his criminal brothers.

Joseph Rose was 'a fresh coloured man', about five feet eight inches high, about forty years of age and a blacksmith. He was probably living with Mary Brasier (see below) as man and wife as she is often referred to as Mrs Rose. As with Jeremiah Gregory he had a criminal record as a deer-stealer, having been taken on 18 July 1733 for this offence.[5] On 31 July 1734 he and Jeremiah Gregory had been found not guilty of unspecified felonies (perhaps deer-stealing) at the Essex Assizes. Humphrey Walker was 'a very pale man, about 50 years of age, fresh coloured, a little marked with the small pox, wears a light wig' and was probably the gang's eldest member. Herbert Haines was 'a very pale man, about 25 years of age, wears a brown wig, about five feet seven inches high, barber by trade'. He kept his barber's shop in Hog Lane, Shoreditch, just south of Hackney. On 1 December 1733, described as being a labourer of Norton Folgate, he allegedly broke into John Sharrat's house and stole a silver tankard worth £9.[6]

Thomas Rowden was 'a little thin man, about 31 or 32 years of age, a pewterer, wears a light natural wig'. On 5 July 1731 a man of his name was a defendant at the Old Bailey, accused of a violent highway robbery against one John Stokes, robbing him of two pairs of stockings and other goods on 24 January 1729. However, he was acquitted through lack of evidence. More certainly, in 1732 he was tried for coining at Kingston upon Thames on the evidence of a fellow criminal, William Faulkner, but the man's evidence was thought to be insufficient so he was acquitted (Faulkner was hanged for theft in 1735).[7] In early 1735, Rowden lived in a property on the Ratcliffe Highway, near the lower end by Shadwell Church, and near to where Samuel and Joseph Gregory lodged.

John Wheeler was the youngest of the gang, aged about fifteen in 1735, the son of John and Thomasin Wheeler of Hackney. His father was a labourer whose wife was continually complaining to Norris that her husband beat her for no reason throughout 1731–35.[8] As a Hackney lad he may have known fellow Hackney residents

Jasper Gregory and John Jones and, wanting to leave a hostile home environment, joined them, though for negative reasons.

William Bush, who also went by the surnames Saunders and Schooling, had been accused at the Old Bailey on 30 August 1731 of assaulting, on 20 July 1731, one Elizabeth Smith on the highway. He took 30s 9d and 'put her in fear'. He was acquitted through lack of evidence. John Jones was born in Hackney and resided there; little is known of him but he may have known Jasper Gregory and Wheeler. He may have been the John Jones who stole four iron bars from Hesther Booth in June 1731, but his name was a common one and it would seem that this Jones was transported.[9]

There was also a woman, Mary Brasier, also known as Mrs Rose, Johnson, Cox and Head. She had stolen, on 1 October 1733, in the parish of Southchurch in Essex, a holland smock (5s) from Ann Turford, a widow, a cambric handkerchief (2s) and a damask coat (10d) from the rector, the Revd Charles Graham (1709–34) and a napkin (12d) and a lace handkerchief (5s) from Peter Morebreck. On 6 March 1734, she and two other miscreants were 'convicted of several petty larcenies must be openly whipt on their back till their bodies are bloody and then be discharged'.[10] She appears later to have been a fence. John Field/Fielder, 'the tall Man in Blew', had, along with Jeremiah Gregory and Joseph Rose, a criminal record for deer-stealing, having been arrested with two others on 4 July 1733.[11] Then there was Thomas Barnfield, a receiver of stolen goods for the gang, of whom little is known.[12]

Finally there was Turpin and here we have, for the first time, a physical description of him as he was in 1735. He was 'very much marked with small pox, about five feet nine inches high, a butcher about 26 years of age' (an underestimate, as he was born in 1705). He 'lived some time ago at Whitechapel [near to the Gregorys and Rowden] and did lately lodge somewhere about Millbank, Westminster, wears a blew grey coat, and a light natural wig'.[13] This and other written descriptions of Turpin (discussed later in this chapter and in the next) are the only evidence for his appearance; unlike fellow contemporary 'celebrity' criminal Jack Sheppard, no one ever produced a picture of Turpin and this is much to be regretted.

Possibly Turpin chose Whitechapel because it was just outside the city walls as represented by Aldgate; close enough to London, but close enough to the country that he knew better. Psychologically being outside the city walls may have appealed to him, and the City was better lit and policed than elsewhere. Most of the gang, therefore, had their haunts at the edge of east London; near enough to both a ready market for their goods and to the country where they would locate their isolated victims. Despite Turpin's later infamy, he was not the gang leader, but one of the last to join. For all that he seems to have fully engaged in their activities. His criminal career was still in its infancy.

There may well have been others in the gang; those named above are those who were apprehended, but others may have been involved, though probably to a lesser extent, and they certainly eluded the law. Not all were present at each of the gang's raids. These occurred in 1734–35 and took place in and near London, the gang moving to attack different locations. Their *modus operandi* was much the same throughout; to identify a lonely house or farm where the inhabitants had money and moveable goods that they could steal. This was easy: most villages consisted of many scattered farms and homes. The gang would approach a property in the evening or at night, and immobilise any servants found outside or in outbuildings. They would then knock on the door and gain entry. The occupants would be bound and blindfolded and threatened at pistol point or worse, if they refused to reveal where the valuables were. They might be physically attacked as well as being verbally threatened. On leaving the thieves would claim that if anyone tried to raise the alarm they would be back. During these attacks, the robbers would be well armed and would often take steps to disguise their identities. Their victims were neither the titled rich nor the poor, but from the ranks of the middling people, who had ready cash and some of the luxuries of life, so were worth robbing but were insufficiently guarded.

The gang was motivated by money. However, most of them had professions which should have enabled them to earn enough money to live, especially given the low cost of living in the 1730s. It can be surmised that they believed that crime would pay more than honest toil, and that it was greed which led them to crime. Once they had started down that path with deer-stealing, it was hard to turn honest again. Moralists might believe that everyone had free choice and could choose between good and evil, but once a downward step had been taken it became easier to carry on than to reform.[14]

Bladen believed that these robberies began when the deer-stealing ended. One reason for these earlier crimes was that the criminals believed they were invulnerable, 'these kind of people originally set out with a full persuasion, that the King has no property; by an easy gradation they soon come to believe that nobody else has any, and when they are disappointed in the forest, raise contributions from the neighbourhood. They are certainly the most dangerous kind of thieves because they generally travel in very large gangs'.[15] Certainly those gang members who had been previously caught were let off lightly (deer theft was a felony not a crime and so was not punished punitively) and this may have led them to thinking they were invulnerable.

It cannot be ascertained when these attacks began or how many took place, though an early biographer, in 1739, put it as occurring five or six years ago, thus in 1733 or 1734, though the latter seems more likely as it was when they were first recorded. Newspapers reported crimes, but in most of these the perpetrators were unknown and eventually most of the gang members were only indicted for the last two, where the victims came forward to testify against them. The first alleged crime took place in Watford. The elderly Mr Strype was a chandler of this Hertfordshire town and 'they took what little money he had scrap'd together, but did him no further Mischief so that he was in some measure content, but they did not behave in the same manner towards everyone' as we shall see.[16] This crime does not seem to have gone reported in the press and so we cannot know when it took place or even if it did. A proclamation made in 1735 lists most of the crimes of which the gang was accused but this one is not listed, and given that it was unreported in the press, it is quite possible it did not occur. Watford is in the western part of Hertfordshire and so some distance from the known sites of the gang's crimes, thus making this raid seem even more unlikely. The 1734 poll book does not list Strype either, though of course this could only be evidence of his not being a property owner.[17]

A contemporary magazine listed the first known crimes. There was one by five masked men on the house of Mr Savage of Brockley Farm, in northern Kent, where they not only stole cash and plate, but also each man took a shirt 'which they said they were in great need of' and then ate and drank and left 'with as much concern as common visitors'.[18] Other victims were Mrs St John of Chelmsford, Mr Peter Split, near Woodford (possibly this crime was conflated with that mentioned in the paragraph above due to the similarity of names of victim and location), Mr Eldridge [Wooldridge?] of Walthamstow (just to the west of Woodford) and the Revd Mr William Dyde of Great Parndon (died 1754) in Essex.[19]

Whether all of these crimes were committed by the Gregory gang cannot be ascertained. All occurred near London, which was their territory, and all involved similar types of crime. The attack on the parsonage at Parndon (detailed later) seems more violent than any other early crime, but other than that has all the hallmarks of the gang. Yet it is possible that other gangs were at work at this time, so it cannot be said categorically that these were all their work. It is not uncommon for crimes which match those of a well-known gang or individual criminal to be seen in retrospect as their work because of similar characteristics, but rarely does one group or one man have a monopoly on that type of crime in that district at that time.

The next crime took place at Ripple Side, near Barking in Essex. This time an unnamed farmer was attacked in his home. No one came to the door once there was a knock, so the gang broke it down and entered anyway. The elderly couple and their maidservant were tied up and when their son-in-law entered, he was also restrained. The house was then ransacked and the gang took about £700. Turpin later said 'Ay this will do, if it is always so'. The share for each man was £80.[20] Again this was not reported by any other source, so as with the alleged Watford crime its veracity is questionable, though Barking is closer to the other crime locations than Watford and the gang targeted a property in Barking later that year.

More reliably, on the evening of 29 October, three of the gang entered a chandler's shop in Loggerheads, Woodford, and called for half a pint of brandy. Two men joined them, then another three. One of them pulled out a knife and threatened the master of the house, his wife and their daughter, with sudden death if any of them cried out. The robbers plundered the place, giving back a suit of clothes worth £6 to the daughter because they had more loot than they could carry, and emptying a sack of meal in the shop in order to take the other spoils away. Woodford was about 10 miles to the north-east of London and was a wooded part of Essex.[21]

Two nights later, eleven of the gang went to the house of Richard Wooldridge of Woodford, who was a gentleman employed in the Ordnance Office at the Tower of London. He and his family were in London and only a servant was in residence. The place was robbed of all brass, pewter, clocks, curtains, beds and bedding, two fine guns and other items to the total value of £2,000. The gang stayed there several hours, drinking rum, brandy, ale and liquors, and loading several horses to remove the goods.[22]

The forces of law and order were not entirely ineffectual in the face of this series of crimes. On 20 November 1734 Norris ordered that Morgan Bynon, the churchwarden, pay out money to convey Jeremiah Gregory and William Saunders (who had recently assaulted and wounded one Robert Iles) to Newgate. However, apparently through the negligence of Mary Best, who lived at the entrance to the gaol, they successfully escaped from prison in January 1735.[23] When a visitor entered the prison in late January, the turnkey was knocked down and some prisoners escaped, among them Gregory and Saunders, though some were retaken.[24]

John Gladwin, a higler (pedlar) of Chingford, who lived between Chingford and Waltham Abbey, had his house broken into on 14 December by Rowden, Jones, Haines, Samuel and Jasper Gregory. Over 40s was stolen on this occasion.[25] The items stolen in detail were one pair of holland sheets (20s), a hat (5s), a wig (15s), a pair of worsted stockings (3s), a pair of yarn stockings (2s), one holland sheet (10s), five pewter dishes (20s 12d), plates (12s), 12 napkins (10s), and a guinea and a half. Fellow inhabitant John Shockley was robbed of a drugget coat (15s), a cloth waistcoat (8s), and a divinity waistcoat (7s). This small haul (£7 9s) the robbers divided between themselves.[26] This was rather small beer compared to the gang's other thefts.

On Thursday 19 December, a gang of ten men, with blackened faces, including Turpin, Rowden, Haines and Wheeler, entered farmer Ambrose Skinner's house in Barking, Essex. Skinner lived at Bush Grove Farm, which had 32 acres of land attached to it, so he was far from being the wealthiest of farmers. The seventy-three-year-old farmer recalled that at 7pm on 19 December:

> 'as I was going to shut the door of the hall in my house which was then unlatched six armed men unknown to me with their faces muffled and disguised rushed in upon me with violence and presenting their carbines to my breast swore they, if I made any noise or resistance, would immediately put me to death or words to that effect'.

Since he was alone with only a maidservant Skinner thought 'it the safest way to submit to their pleasure'.[27]

Both inmates were bound and the attackers spent four hours in the house. During that time Skinner's daughter-in-law and her husband, also called Ambrose, arrived at the house on horseback, and were immobilised at gun point. Some of the thieves stood over the captives. Others got to work. At first, they broke all the locks they could find, before carrying away sacks of plate and clothes to the value of £400. They also took two horses, including a black mare and a sorrel bay gelding. They filled two sacks with the booty.[28] The junior Skinner was also robbed of 95 guineas and five shillings, among other things.[29]

The remainder of the haul was as follows: a silver tankard (£5), a silver cup (40s), four linen table cloths (10s), a silver porringer (20s), four silver spoons (40s), ten linen napkins (10s), four linen shorts (10s), a wig (20s), a hat (5s), a pair of shoes (2s), a cloth riding coat (10s), a hat (2s 6d), a muslin neck cloth (1s), a silver snuff box (10s), a silver buckle (5s), two silver spoons (15s), two gold rings (20s), a coral (10s), a calico night gown (5s), a burdet gown (10s), a silk gown (20s), a yellow gown and petticoat (20s), a brocade gown and petticoat (40s), two silk quilted petticoats (40s), a velvet hood (£1 10s), two almond hoods (10s), two cloth coats (20s), two cloth waistcoats (10s), two pairs of cloth breeches (10s), a pair of buckskin breeches (10s), six linen shorts (15s), six shifts (15s), two suits of laced head cloths (£4), six linen aprons (6s), six pairs of ruffles (6s) and two trinity pockets (2s).[30]

Skinner senior lastly observed:

'I have been credibly informed, [they] were seen to pass with others in their company on foot and part on horseback through the town of Barking, and also through some of the turnpikes in the High Road from Epping to London. And I apprehend that unless some stop be put to these outrageous violences in such great bands and combinations, it will be impossible for any of his Majesty's good subjects in this neighbourhood to be secure either in their lives or fortunes'.[31]

It was not only booty that the gang sought. As their raids were successful, some thought of other schemes. Apparently, Turpin 'flush'd with this success, encouraged his companions to proceed in their villainies. To be revenged on several who had endeavoured to detect them'. One of these men was William Mason, a keeper of Epping Forest. Turpin declared, 'there's Will. Mason who has us'd two or three of us ill, and we'll be revenged upon him'.[32]

Therefore, the gang arranged a time – on the evening of Saturday 21 December – to attack Mason in his home. In the meanwhile, according to Bayes, Turpin went to London for pleasure and there got drunk and forgot the rendezvous with his companions. They waited for a long time, but since he did not arrive, they went ahead without him. Field and Rose commanded the expedition and resolved to leave nothing of value in Mason's house. Jonathan Richards, a twenty-eight-year-old servant there, later stated:

> 'On Saturday last the twenty first of December about six in the evening some person knocking at the master's door, the master's daughter went to ask who it was and a person from without enquired whether Mr Mason was at home. The child answering yes, I immediately run to the door to see whom it was they wanted the master, and having a candle in my hand opened the same'.[33]

Forty-year-old Mason then took up the story:

> 'Several armed persons with their faces disguised, some with black and some with white colouring, violently entered into my house, and one of them immediately shot at me. They afterwards beat and abused me and my wife, and upon my endeavouring as I did to make my escape they discharged three more shots at me, one in the passage of my house and two more after I had got out of it. It was

with great difficulty that I, my wife, and my daughter aged thirteen escaped with our lives, especially myself, they or some of them having threatened to murder me'.[34]

William Roades, aged sixty-eight, Mason's uncle and an unnamed servant girl were then forced to reveal the valuables in the house. The house was ransacked and breaking a punch bowl, glasses, china, windows, cupboards and chests, the gang found 120 guineas, which they took before leaving. Mason estimated the losses at £140 in cash, nine silver spoons, twelve guns and all his wife's clothing.[35]

Not all the gang's planned attacks actually took place. Having been given information by Mary Brasier, they decided to rob the house of George Asher, JP. This was near to the coastal town of Leigh, Essex. The gang met at an inn near Leigh in order to plan their raid. However, on leaving the inn they realised that they did not know the way to the house, so hid behind bushes near a lane in order to waylay a passerby and thus gain the directions they needed. The first to pass by were a group of farmers, on horseback and by their conversation the gang heard that the men had just been to Asher's house, but there were others still there. Thus they called off the attack. Had they not done so they might well have been apprehended, for they had been seen and, in the belief that they were a gang of smugglers, a party of dragoons was scouring the countryside for them. The soldiers found them, stopped and searched them but could find nothing so let them pass. Had the gang been returning from raiding the house they would have had stolen goods with them and so have been arrested for robbery. It was a lucky escape.[36]

One newspaper lay the blame for the gang's robberies on the undefended state of the country, arguing that the crimes were 'chiefly owing to that secure and defenceless state in which the people of England have allowed themselves to live for many years'. The paper stated that the game laws prevented anyone in country districts but a gentleman from legitimately owning firearms as it was suspected they might use them to hunt game illicitly.[37]

Martin Bladen had collected witness statements from the Mason and Skinner attacks and after reading them he drew some tentative conclusions about the robbers. He wrote:

> 'It is certain that the Robbery at Skinner's, and that at Mason's, were both committed by the same gang, in all probability, the same persons were concerned in the two Robberys at Woodford also, and perhaps the same that took the dear stealers, not long since.
>
> I am convinced the persons concerned in these Robberys are Deer Hunters or smugglers or both, and therefore to make the temptation of Discovery still stronger I should apprehend might extend to all offences committed before Discovery, except murder only'.

He concluded, 'the Terror these Robberys have struck into the Country People, especially the wealthy farmers, is incredible, and your lordship cannot do an act of such charity than to endeavour to deliver them out of it'.[38]

Three more attacks took place in January 1735. The first was at Charlton in Kent, just outside London, to the south-east. Mr Saunders was a wealthy farmer there. On Saturday night, 4 January, the gang met at the George at the Thameside town of Woolwich.[39] Then, between seven and eight o'clock, four men knocked on Saunders's door and asked the maid if her master was at home. She said that he was and then the men rushed into the parlour where the family was, and found that they had their neighbours there, playing at cards. The intruders told the company that they should not be afraid and that they would be quite safe if they cooperated.[40] Ironically the expanse of trees between Woolwich and Charlton was called Hanging Wood.

The thieves then took a silver snuff box that they could see on the table, then made Saunders open his scrutoire and took £100 in cash as well as all the plate in the house. The maid ran up the stairs and locked herself in an upper room, but the gang followed her and broke the door down with a poker, took her and bound her, as they did the others below. One person was left unbound and they were forced to show the gang around the house in order that other items could be taken. Linen was also taken. After all this, the thieves sat down to eat and drink, eating a mince pie they found and drinking a bottle of wine. Mrs Saunders meanwhile fainted with fright, but she was given a wafer of water which had drops in it, and they were careful about her. This shows great concern for one of their victims and this was exceptional. The gang then made to leave, telling the inhabitants that if they moved in the next two hours that they would murder them; likewise if they advertised the marks on the plate that they had stolen. The robbers went to an empty house on the Ratcliffe Highway and divided their spoils.[41]

The second robbery that year occurred at Shirley, near Croydon, 10 miles to the south of London, in northern Surrey. After drinking at the Half Moon tavern in Croydon on Saturday 11 January, the gang went to Mr Sheldon's house at about seven o'clock. There were five of them, each armed with a pair of pistols. They were let in by the servants who were soon bound and then Sheldon and his wife were robbed of their money, jewels, lace, plate and other moveables, which filled a total of five sacks. Curiously enough, after all this, the gang returned two guineas to Sheldon and begged his pardon, before riding away.[42] One of the 'Croydon gang' was taken and sent to the New Gaol at Southwark, but his identity is unknown and he does not seem to have been put up for trial.[43]

One result of these crimes was that gentlemen who lived in lonely houses began to arm themselves and to put strong chains and bars to their doors.[44]

The final robbery in the month was on Friday 31 January 1735 when two men arrived at the house of the Revd Mr Dyde, minister of Great Parndon, north-west Essex. Dyde was a wealthy man with lands in Enfield, Middlesex and Waltham Abbey. The gang knocked at the door, which was answered by the manservant (possibly John Wood or William Allen). They asked him if his master was at home and he said no. They cursed him, rushed in and cut him about the face 'in a barbarous manner', before binding the maidservant (possibly Mary Quarne). Contrary to what the manservant had said, the vicar was at home, and came downstairs, pistol in hand. However, he felt unable to shoot for fear of hitting his maidservant, so he rushed out to summon help. The robbers soon left, taking just a silver spoon, and leaving behind a pistol and four bullets and a whip. This crime was the first in which violence is known to have been used and it set a precedent.[45]

Better documented was a later crime, which Turpin's biographer reports (wrongly) as having occurred in the previous year after the alleged attack in Watford. This is usually highlighted as one of the most despicable robberies, and it occurred on Saturday 1 February 1735 in Loughton, Essex, on the edge of Epping Forest. Mrs Ann Shelley was a fairly well-off widow, 'a Widow Gentlewoman', living with her son and her servants in a house there. Apparently, 'this was a scheme of Turpin's, for he acquainted the Gang that he knew an old woman of Loughton [he may well have done, given he once lived in Buckhurst Hill, near Loughton], that he was sure had seven or eight hundred pounds with her, and Damn her, says he, it is as good as in our pockets, as hers and we shall have it'.[46]

The gang planned a time 'for the enterprise' and on Saturday night at seven o'clock arrived at the property. Wheeler stood watch and he knocked at the door. When it was opened:

> 'Turpin and his companions all rush'd in and the first thing they did was to bind the Old Lady, her Son, her Man and Maid and then Turpin began to examine her where her money and Effects were hid, telling her at the same time that he knew she had money and twas vain to deny it for had it they would: the old Gentlewoman being very

loth to part with it, persisted in it that she had none and would declare anything more of the matter'.

Some of the gang thought that this had the ring of truth about it and were annoyed that they had not found what they sought. But not all of them thought so:

> 'Turpin strenuously insisting that she had money as she that she had none, at last cried, "Damn your blood, you old bitch, if you won't tell us, I'll set your bare arse on the grate". She continued Obstinate for all that, and imaging he only meant to threaten her, and so very fond she was of her darling gold, that she even suffered herself to be served as he declared and endured it for some time, till the anguish at last forced her to discover, which when she had done, they took her off the grate indeed, and robbed her of all they could find... upwards of four hundred pounds'.[47]

However, part of this later account is contradicted by a contemporary report in the press, in which prior to her being laid over the fire, Mrs Shelley's anguished son (Thomas), unable to see his mother tortured, told he would reveal the location of her money, and so they went upstairs, leaving her physically unharmed, and took nearly £100, together with silverware (including a silver tankard with 37 guineas, a pair of silver spurs and three silver spoons), plate, household goods and then went to the cellar, to drink some of the ale and wine stored there, and to eat broiled meat and the remains of fillets of veal they found.[48]

Apparently they 'only':

> 'threatened to murder the old lady if she did not tell them where her money lay, which she obstinately refusing for

some time, they threatened to lay her across the fire if she still did not tell them instantly, which she would not do, but her son being in the room, and threaten'd to be murdered, cry'd out he would tell them, if they would not murder his mother, and did'.[49]

There are two important differences here; firstly Turpin is not highlighted as the prime motivator behind the threats against Mrs Shelley and second, in this version Mrs Shelley is not actually tortured. Whichever is correct is a moot point, but neither shows Turpin in a sympathetic light. If he did not actually torture Mrs Shelley he certainly seems not to have been averse to doing it if necessary.

Apparently Mr Turkle, a farmer who rented the far end of Mrs Shelley's house, was also robbed that night as two of the gang went there and took £20, and two of his horses to help carry away the goods belonging to the old lady. These were later found at Old Street, London.[50]

The gang's last two crimes are best documented, as the evidence for the trials of several of the members were brought before the Old Bailey. Only three days after the attack on Mrs Shelley, on Tuesday 4 February at 2pm Samuel Gregory, Field, Rose, Turpin and Wheeler were at the Black Horse pub in the Broadway, Westminster, not far from where the latter four were lodging. John Bowler, the publican, knew Field, Rose and Wheeler as he had seen them there before, suggesting that Turpin had just moved to the locality and was not a regular in this pub. Samuel Gregory told his friends that as a blacksmith he had previously shod the horses of Joseph Lawrence, a farmer of Edgware, 'an ancient man of over 70 years of age', 'and that he was worth a good deal of money'. This determined them to rob the man. Edgware was then a village a few miles outside north-west London. The gang then rode off; Gregory, Rose and Wheeler first, then Field and Turpin, the latter two overtaking the others on the road. They may have ridden along Oxford Street and turned right into Edgware Road, ominously passing Tyburn, and then continued through Kilburn and Cricklewood. They went to the Nine Pin and Bowl at Edgware, drinking there, about two or three pots of beer each, from 4.15 to 5pm. They left together. They then went to the Queen's Head at Stanmore, arriving at about 6.15pm, where they remained for about an hour or an hour and a half. Here they drank more beer and ate bacon and eggs for supper. They then turned back towards London.[51]

Drinking before a crime is a common trait. The gang had done so before the Croydon attack, before one of the Woodford attacks, and they would do so again before their last foray. In part it is to reduce what moral scruples they might have in order to make it easier to commit crime, especially if violence is a possibility. They are also social occasions and help bind the gang together in what they are about to do. And finally they probably enjoy it.

The gang's destination was Joseph Lawrence the elder's house in Earlsbury, which was about a mile from the Nine Pin and Bowl and other houses, so very isolated. He was a married yeoman with a daughter, Ann, who owned land in Harrow and Pinner in Middlesex and Hertfordshire. They arrived there between 8 and 9pm, tying their horses up about a quarter of a mile away. Given that they were all identified, none can have worn a disguise as had occurred on some previous occasions. Fielder entered the sheep yard and took hold of the sheep boy, bound his hands together and then brought him to the house door. James Emerton was the sheep boy and he later said in court that Fielder:

'holding out a Pistol, said he would shoot me if I offer'd to cry out. There were four more with him. He took off my Garter and tyed my hands. They asked me what servants my master kept and I told them. They said they would not hurt me but they would knock at the door, and I should answer and they would give me money. So one of them knocked and my fellow servant answered the door, and they all rushed in with pistols'.[52]

John Pate was the servant who answered the door and in court he recalled:

'I unbolted the door, the two prisoners, Wheeler and three more came in with pistols in their hands, and said Damn your blood, how long have you lived here? We had two candles in their rooms and I saw their faces plainly. They put a cloth over people's eyes, but in five or six minutes they took them off, ty'd my hands and carried me into the room where the boy was'.[53]

Wheeler later testified that Lawrence and his maid were also tied up. He claimed: 'Turpin pulled the old man's breeches down and dragged him into another room and beat him to discover where his money was. Gregory took the maid up to the garret and lay with her there, as afterwards he told us'.

Lawrence's recollection about his own fate was that:

'They swore at me and demanded my money. They took off my neckcloth and tied it over my eyes. They took down my breeches and took out of my pocket a guinea a six and thirty shilling Portuguese piece and between ten and twenty shillings in silver. They said they must have more and they would make me shew where the rest of my money was. They drove me upstairs with my breeches down, and coming to a closet they broke it open though they had got the key of it, and took out two guineas, ten shillings, a silver cup, thirteen silver spoons, two gold rings and what else they could find... They carried me down again and whipt me with their bare hands as hard as they could strike, so that I was black the next day. They broke my head with their pistols. They carried me into the kitchen and took a kettle of water off the fire and threw upon me… Then they haul'd me back again and swore they would rip me up and burn me alive if I did not tell them where the rest of my Money was. One put a bill to my leg and swore he'd chop them off. One of them held a knife under my chin and threatened to cut my throat. Some pulled me by the nose and some dragged me about by the hair of my head. My breeches were down and I was blindfolded'.[54]

There was another description of what happened to the old man, and while it agrees with what he later said in court, it adds additional details:

'not finding the money they expected, upon their coming downstairs most inhumanely and barbarously abused the said Joseph Lawrence, by beating him with a stick till they broke it to pieces, letting down his breeches and whipping him in a violent manner, that they likewise laid a faggot on the fire and laid him down upon it and threatened to burn him [shades of what may have occurred to Mrs Shelley], then took a knife and drew it under his throat, and declared they would cut his throat and afterwards, dragged him by the hair of his head about the kitchen, then took a kettle of water from the fire and threw the water over him'.[55]

More violence was to come. Dorothy Street was the young maidservant and was in the back house, making butter, when she heard a great noise. She recalled:

'They rushed in upon me and tyed my hands... They put me into the Room where my master was.... one of them made me go up and swore I should shew him where my Master's Money was. I said I did not know; but he [Samuel Gregory] carried me to the garret, where he bolted the door, and threw me on the bed. He had two pistols. He laid one upon the chest, and one upon the bed, and swearing he would shoot me if I would cry out, he lay with me by Violence'.[56]

After the rape, she was released and went downstairs in tears and Wheeler later claimed 'I asked her if any body had beat her; she answer'd No, but one of your Men has lain with me', but he did not recall her stating that it was non-consensual.[57]

Emerton had had a cloth put over his face and when it was removed, he was asked what guns Lawrence had, so he told them and they found the old gun and broke it. Meanwhile Rose threatened Lawrence with a knife. Elsewhere, the thieves opened a closet and found a bottle of elder[berry?] wine, which they gave to Emerton and Pate. They also took linen and plate.[58]

Before leaving they asked Emerton if his master's son would be returning that night. He said that he would be. They said that they were going to a house nearby next and would return to Lawrence's in half an hour. If they found that any of the inmates were loose, they would kill them. They would have attacked the farm house nearby but feared that the farmer might return and they could not effectually split their forces.

The thieves' spoil consisted of the following: a silver cup (40s), four silver spoons (20s), four gold rings (40s), a pair of linen sheets (4s), twelve linen napkins (9s), a linen table cloth (5s), six towels (2s), six linen pillowbiers (3s), six handkerchiefs (3s), a waistcoat (2s), fifteen guineas (£15 15s), three moidores – gold coins of Portuguese origin that were usable as currency – (£4 2s) and 30s in cash. This gave a total of £27 15s. They left Lawrence and his three servants locked in the parlour, locked the door and threw the key into the garden. They arrived home at 11pm and divided their spoils, putting them all on a table at Rose's lodgings near the Black Horse, Dawes Street.[59]

Rose bought the linen for 15s (valued at 21s) and also the silver cup and spoons and the gold rings, giving these to Mary Brasier. Gregory boasted over and over that he had raped Dorothy. Wheeler was unhappy, though not about that; only his share of the booty: 'they cheated me in every respect, so out of sixty pounds I had four'. The figure of £60 does not square with the valuation above so perhaps he was adding the booty of more than one robbery. Mary sold most of the items within the next two days, some to Charles Westridge, a gunner at the Tower of London.[60]

Thomas Lawrence, the old farmer's son, returned home at six next morning. He found that his chest had been broken into and linen and £20 were missing. At least the attackers and their horses could be described. The men and their mounts were described thus: 'a tall black man with his own black hair', 'a middle sized man with a large scar on his right cheek' (Samuel Gregory), 'a middle sized man disfigured with small pox' (Turpin), 'a middle sized man', and 'a fresh coloured man aged between 40 and 50' (Rose?). Their horses were a large bay nag, a little bay nag of 13 to 14 hands high, a bay nag of 14 hands, a large black nag and a brown nag 15 hands high.[61]

Three days later another robbery was carried out by the same gang: Humphrey Walker, William Saunders, as well as the five previous participants, Wheeler, Rose, Field, Samuel Gregory and Turpin. This time they met at the White Hart Inn at the upper end of Drury Lane at about 5pm on 7 February. They remained there until about 6.30pm. Possibly the publican, who fled sometime afterwards, was involved in the crime, or at least had guilty knowledge. They then went to the hosue of William Francis (died 1743 or 1751) in Marylebone Park, arriving there between 7 and 8pm. Marylebone was then on the edge of north-west London, described a decade earlier as 'a large village about one mile from London. It contains several handsome houses', and so rather nearer to them than their last target had been.[62]

They first went to the cow house and found there Stephen Manning, a dairyman, and he later recalled, 'I was in the Cow House with a candle and lanthorn, two fellows came in and bound me. Saunders was one of them but I don't know the other, for his face was smutted. They carried me over to the stable and stood sentry over me'.[63]

Edward Jones was in the stables and he recalled, 'I was in the stable feeding the horses, two fellows laid hold of me. One of them had his face all dirty, and he untyed my Garter and bound me. The other was Saunders. They brought Manning to me and they both stood over us, with pistols an hour and a half more'.[64]

Shortly after the two servants had been incapacitated, Francis returned home. As he was opening the gate he was seized, and later recalled 'Three of them came up and clammed me over the head. I thought they were upon some game and said "Methinks you are mighty funny gentleman". Upon that they presented their pistols and carried me to the stables, where they bound me with my men. My eyes are bad and I can't swear to their persons'.[65]

Saunders and Turpin stood guard over the three bound men in the stables while the other four effected entry to the house (unlike in the Lawrence robbery, Turpin was playing a secondary role). They knocked on the door, it now being about seven o'clock. Inside the house were Mrs Francis, her daughter Sarah and Eleanor Williams, their housemaid. They were sitting by the fire and hearing the knock on the door, Sarah went to answer it. Wheeler was first to enter. Eleanor recalled, 'They cock'd their pistols at us, pushed manfully to enter, and so got in'. Sarah asked them 'What have ye done?' and then one or two of them hit her and told her to be quiet or they would shoot her. Mrs Francis said 'Lord, what is the matter?' to which one of the intruders, Rose, replied, 'Damn you for an old bitch. I'll shut your mouth presently'. He hit her on the head, and tied her to a chair, blood streaming from the cut.[66]

The other two women were tied up and put in the kitchen and the thieves raced upstairs to loot the house. Their haul amounted to a silver tankard (£6), a gold watch (£10) and a gold chain (£5), a gold seal (25s), a silver thimble (12d), a silver strainer (10s), a pair of silver spurs (40s), a coral set in silver for a child (10s), a mourning gold ring with a cipher (10s), a gold ring enamelled blue with a stone and diamonds on each side (40s), a gold ring with four diamonds (30s), another gold ring with diamonds (20s), two gold rings with posies (20s), a wig (40s), six handkerchiefs (10s), a silver punch ladle (15s), a silver picture of Charles I (10s), four linen shirts (20s), a velvet hat (12s), two pistols (10s), 37 guineas, £10 in silver and a gold piece with a hole in it (8s). It was a larger haul than that gained at the Lawrences at £86 8s, though to be shared out between more people.[67]

Wheeler then related 'When we had got all ready to go off, we threatened the family, that if they made any noise we could come back, so we left them all bound and went away'.

The gang had got away again, but this time they had made a mistake, by committing another violent crime near London itself and not putting much distance between themselves and their last robbery. This had not happened previously and risked their being seen by one of their victims. Which is what happened. The serious nature of these two recent crimes, the heightened violence and the fact that the gang had gone on largely unchecked, meant that things had clearly gone too far. It led to a governmental proclamation being made by Thomas Holles-Pelham (1693–1768), the Duke of Newcastle, who was Secretary of State for the South and a key political lieutenant of Sir Robert Walpole, the King's First Minister, who on 8 February ordered:

'Whereas the dwelling house of the several persons following, vizt., of Peter Split at Woodford, chandler and grocer, of (blank space) Eldridge at Walthamstow, of Mrs Shelley at Lawton, of the Rev. Mr Dyde at Parndon all in the county of Essex were lately forced into at night time and robbed of money and other things to a considerable value, His Majesty for the better discovering and bringing to justice the several persons concerned in the above mentioned robberys, or other of them, is pleased to prove his most gracious pardon to any of the said persons who shall discover his accomplices or accomplices, in the said facts or either of them, so as he or they be apprehended and convicted thereof, and as a further encouragement His Majesty is also pleased to promise a reward of fifty pounds for every one of the criminals who shall be discovered and apprehended aforesaid to the end of the conviction of the offender or offenders'.[68]

The rapist of Dorothy Street was naturally excluded from this pardon. It was thought that the reward would tempt one of the gang to turn informer. The gang had also stirred up a hornet's nest of family members and servants who were eager to repay the villains and claim the rewards. It is also worth stating that the mental harm caused to the victims of these attacks is hard to measure; being attacked, threatened, tied up and robbed, and sometimes worse, in one's home, a place usually thought of as being a safe haven, is particularly disturbing and harrowing. The Revd James Woodforde (1740–1803) wrote thus in his diary on 2 November 1784, about a robbery at the house of Mr Gurdon at Letton in 1781, 'The above Robbery was supposed to have hastened the death of poor Mr Gurdon'.[69]

Luck for the gang was about to run out and much sooner than they probably imagined. On Tuesday 11 February, just a week after the attack on Joseph Lawrence, Richard Wood, publican of the Nine Pin and Bowl alehouse which the gang had patronised on the evening of the attack, saw a horse belonging to one of the gang outside premises in King Street, Bloomsbury, or as was also reported, at Mr Morgan's Punch Bowl, just to the north of Westminster Abbey. He found a constable and the latter gathered together a few men. Entering the ale house they found a woman and three men drinking punch. Wood knew the men as three of the robbers – Fielder, Saunders and Wheeler – and they were arrested 'after some Resistance' for the men had five pistols among them.[70]

The men were taken before Robert Hind, a JP of Ormonde Street, the next day. There, 'Wheeler, as may be supposed, then began to foresee, that they would be discovered, and sufficient proofs found against them, before they could get out of Jail, whereupon he would confess and inform against the whole gang and so he did', telling of the robberies against Mason, Lawrence and Francis 'together with a great many others'. Wheeler was sent to the Compter prison on Wood Street in the City and the other two to Newgate Prison, just outside the City of London.[71]

This was common, as a Swiss observer noted in the previous decade: if accomplices would 'denounce their accomplices and give evidence against them, will be pardoned. Sometimes they are even rewarded... By this means many criminals who would otherwise escape the gibbets are caught'.[72]

Wheeler provided names, addresses and descriptions for all his fellow gang members who had not yet been taken. He clearly wished to save his own life and could only do so by betraying his former colleagues. He may also have lacked a sense of loyalty to the others because he only joined to escape an abusive domestic situation. Possibly Hind may have suggested he turned King's evidence to save his life and claim some of the reward money. This crucial information was put to good effect immediately. Names of all the wanted men were posted, together with their descriptions, on all the turnpikes leading out of London.[73]

There is a reference to Fielder, Rose and Walker as having robbed (again) the younger Ambrose Skinner, in Westminster, of linen and other clothing, on 15 February. Yet Fielder was already in custody and the trial was not proceeded with because the three men had already been found guilty of other thefts, so no more details of this are known.[74] Their total haul was two silk gowns (£6), two silk petticoats (50s), a silk quilted petticoat (10s), two suits of cambric headcloths (£8), eight muslin handkerchiefs (8s), six cambric handkerchiefs (10s), a linen shift (4s), a pair of leather breeches (10s), a velvet hood (10s), a silk hood (3s) and two linen pockets (2s). Total pickings: £19 7s.[75]

Things now only got worse for the gang. On the night of Monday 17 February, Archelaus Pulleyn, constable of St Margaret's parish, Westminster, who, as a widower, remarried in 1736, learnt that some of the gang were to be found at Mr Lloyd's chandler's shop on, appropriately enough, Thieving Lane, alias Bow Street, Westminster. This was just to the north-west of Westminster Abbey and not far from the Punch Bowl. As constable, he swore eight people to assist him in what he was about to do and for two people, Thomas and Joseph Lawrence, the sons of old farmer Lawrence, this was personal; possibly Emerton and Pate may have been with them. They found Rose and Walker, and Mary Brasier, in a chandler's back room, drinking punch. Lawrence's sons identified the men 'and knock'd 'em down'.[76]

Rose resisted when they tried to arrest him and pointed a pistol at Richard Bartram 'and pulled the trigger, but I clapt my finger between the hammer and the lock and so prevented his firing'. Walker resisted too, and would have shot a chairman, but Harrowfield, a coachman, recalled, 'Walker had hold of his pistol and was pulling it out of his pocket but it hung by something and he could not get it out and so I came upon him and knocked him down'. Turpin was, according to Bayes, also apparently in the room, but he left via a window and rode off on his horse. There is no contemporary corroboration for Turpin's presence here, so Bayes may be trying to improve on the story by placing Turpin at the scene of this action.[77] However, he was described as being in Westminster at the time so may have been in the locality.

Some of the stolen goods were found in property on Duck Lane, very near Thieving Lane, where some of the men had been lodging since Friday 14 February.[78] Some of the linen was found in their possession. There was also a small armoury: fifteen pistols, bullets, a bullet mould and several powder horns. It seems that the arrests were greeted with enthusiasm, 'People are greatly pleased with the Discoverys that was made'.[79]

It is possible that on the same night as this arrest, the remainder of the gang were robbing Mr Berry, a farmer near Gravesend. Certainly on that Monday night between 8 and 9pm five men armed with pistols confronted a servant in the stables and forced him to take them inside the house. There Mr and Mrs Berry were bound and blindfolded. The robbers initially found little, and so threatened Mrs Berry, striking her on the face with a pistol 'which cut her in a violent manner'. They later found money and goods to the value of £160 and took two horses, releasing them in Greenwich or Deptford the next day. On leaving, Mrs Berry asked to be released and one of the men said 'Damn you madam, somebody will release you in the morning and that is time enough'.[80] The crime certainly has all the hallmarks of brutality that the gang were known for.

After the arrests, Saunders, Rose, Walker and Fielder were put in Newgate; Mary Brasier in the Gatehouse, Westminster. Other gang members were also being sought elsewhere. A proclamation was issued, describing Jones and Jasper Gregory's robbery at Chingford in the previous year and it continued:

> 'His Majesty, for the better discovering and bringing the said John Jones to Justice, is pleased to promise a Reward of fifty Pounds to any person or persons who shall discover the said criminal, so as he may be apprehended and convicted thereof, to be paid upon such conviction'.

This was signed by Newcastle's colleague, William Stanhope, Baron Harrington (1683–1756), Secretary of State for the Northern department.[81]

There was also a letter written on 21 February noting that Turpin, Samuel Gregory, Rowden and Haines (like Jones and Jeremiah Gregory) were still at large and it may be significant that Turpin topped the list rather than the supposed gang leader, Samuel Gregory. It did state that Walker, Wheeler, Rose, Fielder and three others (Saunders, Mrs Brasier and another unidentified person) had been arrested, 'for several robberies in Essex, Middlesex, Surrey and Kent' and that a reward of £50 per man was being offered.[82] Rowden, Haines, Jones and Jeremiah Gregory had not taken part in either of the last two robberies and may have been out of London and so were not caught up in the net. Clearly Turpin and Samuel Gregory had also been able to escape.

On 24 February some of the remaining gang members were nearly apprehended, having left London and gone to Essex; these may have included Turpin, Rowden and Jones as well as Samuel Gregory and Herbert Haines, who were drinking in a pub, almost certainly the White Hart, a seventeenth-century timber-framed structure, in Debden near Saffron Walden, not far from Turpin's home village of Hempstead. Then 'In the meantime, one Palmer, an innkeeper from Thaxted' entered and he recognised the two as being criminals. He fetched the constable and some other men and they tried to arrest them. Gregory drew a pistol and pulled the trigger, but the gun misfired. He then drew a dagger and in the ensuing fight wounded two of his would be captors before he and Haines escaped, leaving behind shirts, stockings, powder and ball, and a loaded pistol.[83]

There was press speculation about their whereabouts, which turned out to be way off the mark. They were correct in believing, at least initially, that Turpin and Samuel Gregory were still together, but not where. A newspaper report alleged that in March 1735 'it's supposed that Gregory and Turpin and Hains are concealed somewhere in Town'.[84]

Meanwhile, in London, Walker and Rose were questioned by Nathaniel Blackerby, JP, on 18 February. Some of the goods found on them were identified by Miss Ann Lawrence. They admitted their names to Justice Hinde of Ormonde Street, but denied any wrongdoing. The daughter of Francis identified the goods stolen from her. Meanwhile sixteen warrants were issued for the remainder of the gang.[85]

On 26 February at the Old Bailey, Fielder and Rose (and Gregory and Turpin in absentia) were charged on two indictments: theft and assault. Wheeler had turned King's evidence as, he claimed, he thought that he had been given an unequal share of the loot. The victims of the attack as well as Wheeler gave evidence in court and some of the stolen linen was produced there. Fielder said 'I know nothing of what you are talking of' and Rose said similarly, 'Nor I neither'. The jury, composed of twelve men of the same class as the defendants, found them guilty and so both were sentenced to death.[86]

On the same day in the same court, Fielder, Rose, Walker and Saunders were also indicted for breaking and entering, theft, assault and putting Lawrence in fear.

As previously Wheeler provided much of the evidence taken with that of the three servants, Francis and his daughter giving witness statements, but they could only identify Rose and Wheeler between them. However, the goods produced in court which were found with the defendants, were proved to belong to the victims, including rings and the punch bowl. The armoury found in possession of the defendants was also shown in court.

A number of other witnesses told of the arrest of the defendants and the recovery of some of the loot. The defendants then spoke. Fielder said 'I know nothing of the matter' and the other three said 'Nor I'. The jury found them guilty and they were sentenced to death. There was another indictment against Fielder (who was already under lock and key), Walker and Rose, for having robbed Ambrose Skinner in Westminster of linen and other clothes on 15 February, but as they had already been convicted it was not thought necessary to proceed with this.[87]

Apparently one of the witnesses from Essex had been accused of smuggling and had to find £3,000 in bail money. It was suspected that this might have been a connivance of the gang to prevent their evidence being given.[88]

Mr Baron Thomson (Sir William Thompson, 1678–1739), Recorder of London from 1729–39, made a report to the Cabinet on 3 March, with a list of convicted criminals to be executed (who could now be sentenced to transportation instead) and the King confirmed the names of fifteen of the men who were to hang. These included Fielder, Rose, Saunders and Walker. Instances of violence with robbery were rare; just 9 percent of all Old Bailey indictments of 1714–99 included such cases and so these were seen as being particularly heinous.[89] There was concern expressed by the sheriff of Middlesex that a rescue attempt might be made and so Sir Charles Wills (1666–1741), colonel of the First Foot Guards, was told to 'order a detachment from the three regiments of Foot Guards equal to one entire company and be commanded by a discreet sergeant whom you can confide in to be at Holbourne Barrs at the time appointed [6.30am] and receive his directions from the said sheriffs'.[90]

In the meantime another gang member had been caught. Barnfield was committed to Newgate by Justice Dennet, 'on suspicion of his being one of the Essex Gang; several goods belonging to Mr Woolridge… being found upon him, and of which he could give no satisfactory account before the Justice'. Barnfield died in prison before he could stand trial.[91]

On Monday morning, 10 March, there were fifteen executions at Tyburn (the location of this is now Marble Arch); Fielder, Saunders and Rose were among those hanged. Walker had died in Newgate, but was later hung in chains along with them. The condemned men were guarded by fifty soldiers and as they died the condemned 'appeared bold and undaunted'.[92] Another report elaborated: 'The fellows at the Gallows appear'd very Bold and undaunted; shewing outwardly no great signs of Repentance'.[93]

According to a contemporary author, the condemned men were placed in carts with a parson in attendance, to exhort them to repentance. The hangman then asked for a pardon. A halter was then put around the neck of each condemned man and they were cast off the cart until they were strangled.[94]

The bodies of Fielder, Rose and Saunders were the first of the fifteen executed men to be cut down from the gallows, put back into a cart and carried off for the next part of the proceedings.[95] It had been expected that all four men would be hanged. Suits of chains were bought for them, costing £25 in total, with an additional £7 7s spent in providing guards for them and finally £16 10s was spent in making and erecting gibbets for the four so they could be put in them on the Edgware Road after execution. The remains of all four were suspended there for some time.[96] They now adorned the very road that Fielder and Rose had probably ridden with Wheeler, Turpin and Samuel Gregory to attack the Lawrence farm just over a month previously. For the first of these, retribution had been swift.

Meanwhile, at Chelmsford, Jasper Gregory and one John Rootham had been captured in February by John Gladwin and others and were sentenced to death on 8 March as housebreakers and presumably hanged later in the month.[97]

Rewards were shared out: that for Fielder was shared by twenty people with unequal shares; Joseph Lawrence received the most, with £7 10s; his brother and Pate got £3 15s each, Wheeler and Dorothy Street £1 5s each and Emerton 12s 6d.[98] For Rose, Pullen received £10.[99]

Although the reactions of the remaining gang members to the hangings are unknown, it seems reasonable to suppose that they unnerved them sufficiently for them to move lodgings and change their way of making a living. The gang had been broken up and four of its members hanged; one had died in custody and one had turned King's Evidence. Turpin, however, along with two of the Gregorys, Rowden, Jones and Haines, had escaped, presumably by the good fortune of not being with the others when they were seen and subsequently arrested. Turpin may seem to have been a fairly peripheral figure in these trials, though he seems to have played a leading role in beating up Lawrence, but in the last attack he merely acted as a guard over the servants in the stables. However, though he was indicted in these three trials, he was not actually physically on trial and so the witnesses did not need to focus their attention on him. Furthermore, most had been blindfolded and so could not identify him or most of the others. As with his fellow gang members Turpin appears to have condoned Gregory raping Dorothy, and the numerous boasts he made meant that none of the others could have been unaware of what he had done, an act that was as unnecessary as it was terrible.

It is to be regretted that Turpin escaped, but it enabled him to carve out his own infamy in the years to come. He was about to become known in his own right, rather than as a member of a gang. Had Turpin been captured, convicted and hanged like Fielder, Saunders, Rose, Walker and Jasper Gregory, it is doubtful that anyone would remember him now. He had the fortune to escape and so was to gain notoriety for his subsequent crimes, and those are the ones that fiction loosely focuses on. No one wrote a booklet about any of the other criminals mentioned above, but they would eventually do so about Turpin. It was not only his life that Turpin escaped with in 1735, but the potential for winning eternal fame, though the road was far from straightforward, as we shall see.

The government was aware that not all the gang members had been taken and wanted the job finished. Newcastle wrote to Sir John Willes (1685–1761), then Attorney General (1734–37) in July 1735, when George II was taking one of his trips to the electorate of Hanover, of which he was the Elector, and his wife, Queen Caroline, was Regent:

'Her Majesty being concerned at the frequent Robberies and other Outrages that have been committed of late in and about the Cities of London and Westminster and the neighbouring parts to the great Damage and Terror of Her Majesty's subjects, and the Queen being determined to have the laws out in Execution for the preventing in the most effectual manner such practices for the future, I am commanded to signify to you Her Majesty's pleasure that you should prepare a draft of a proclamation to be laid before Her Majesty in council on Wednesday next, July 8th for Her majesty's approbation and signature, inforcing the several laws now in being for preventing the same; and Renewing the offers of the Rewards for such persons, as shall be concerned in and apprehending and legally convicting any highwayman or Street Robbers in or near the Cities of London and Westminster, and strictly requiring all magistrates and other Her Majesty's subjects to be diligent in inforcing the execution of the laws, with such… as have been usual upon the occasion as you shall think most proper for the purpose'.[100]

Thomas Taylor and James Emerton claimed the reward for apprehending Field, Saunders and Wheeler on 31 March and 26 September. Jonathan Waltham and others claimed they had taken Rose for the Lawrence robbery on 25 September and four weeks later were awarded £50.[101]

Other gang members got their just desserts in the following months. Mary Brasier was tried at the Old Bailey on 16 April 1735 for selling goods that she knew were stolen. She was found guilty and sentenced to transportation to Maryland, which occurred on 9 December 1735.[102] The authorities were certainly on the alert for the others. One John Lyndon was misidentified in Hampshire as being Samuel Gregory, but protested that he was a locksmith from Wolverhampton who had subsequently joined the army and was with a recruiting party at Basingstoke. When brought before Wheeler, the lad was unable to recognise him as his former gang member.[103] The remaining six were still on the loose and we shall now turn to them and their various modes of existence.

Chapter 4

Turpin the Highwayman, 1735–37

The popular image of Turpin as highwayman is indelible, created by both the contemporary press and the man himself, and latterly theatre, novels, circuses, comics and films, but in reality this was only a part of his versatile criminal career. It was a by-product of the failure of the gang of housebreakers of which he had formed a part, and covered the years 1735–37. The gang had been mostly rounded up by April 1735 and Turpin was forced to go into business with another of the survivors, Thomas Rowden. Housebreaking needed a number of accomplices because of the potential size of a household which needed incapacitating before a robbery could safely take place, so was risky with few men. Highway robbery seemed easier, as single travellers or coaches could be successfully targeted by fewer men. Some believed it more lucrative, too, as one contemporary criminal noted, 'more could be made on the highway in one night than by sneaking about the country for twelve months'.[1]

However, as we have seen, we cannot be absolutely sure that all the robberies attributed to a particular gang or individual/s were actually their responsibility. Certainly there were a number of reported robberies by Turpin in and around London in the second half of 1737, when it is known from another source (not known then to contemporaries) that he was no longer in the environs of London and that a few other individuals called themselves Turpin. This chapter relates the crimes ascribed to Turpin by the contemporary media, but the reader should be aware that even those prior to June 1737 might not have been all his work, and there might have been other offences carried out by him which went unreported. No attempt was later made, once he was in custody, to discover which were and which were not his actual crimes.

Highway robbery was nothing new in the eighteenth century. Court records refer to prosecutions of men who attacked and robbed travellers on the road from at least the sixteenth century. It was not just stage coaches, but lone or pairs of riders and foot travellers as well, that were seen as prey. Lacking much of a banking system, travellers were often obliged to carry large sums of money, whether travelling on business or pleasure. More people were travelling, especially the better off, to and from London. Given that there was no system of patrols on the roads – the Bow Street Runners' mounted patrols (which anachronistically feature in some of the Turpin films) did not commence until the second half of the eighteenth century – travellers, especially lone travellers, were vulnerable. Slow-moving transport also presented an easy target to thieves on horseback.

Despite the later romantic image of 'knights of the road' performing acts of gallantry, the reality was, of course, rather different, and a whole lot nastier. Many robbers were men on foot, footpads, not the riders who now command the public imagination. Such robbers, on foot and on horse, were very prevalent around London, as it grew in population and opulence. It was here, on the outskirts of the urban area, that the robbers chose to strike. Few criminals were gentlemen; most were of a low social status.

Concerns about highway robbery were mentioned by contemporaries. In a letter from Thomas Grey to Horace Walpole on 4 February 1735, the former wrote 'I suppose you will come down Essex way, and you do, first you must cross Epping Forest, and there you must be robbed'.[2] Years later, in 1753, the Revd George Woodward wrote 'my wife was in a peck of troubles about the gentlemen collectors [highwaymen], for we had heard both from the public papers and several people, that they were very busy upon

Marlborough Forest, and part of the road I was to go: but we had the good luck not to meet with them'.[3] James Boswell, travelling between London and Oxford in 1763, wrote 'I was a little afraid of highwaymen, but we met none'.[4] In 1775, after the Revd James Woodforde had made a long coach journey to Norwich after passing through Epping Forest, he wrote 'where we got, I thank God, safe and well'. In 1780 he wrote about highwaymen on the Norfolk roads and that his niece was 'much alarmed on hearing the above. It was lucky that I did not go to Norwich last week'. The next year, when the men were arrested and tried, the diarist does not seem sympathetic to the 'Highwaymen that infested these roads last Winter... found guilty and all condemned'.[5] Highwaymen were thus a great terror to travellers in the eighteenth century.

An encounter with a highway robber was recounted in 1728 by John Byrom, who was in a coach travelling from London to Cambridge:

> 'about half a mile or less of Epping, a highwayman in a red rug upon a black horse came out of the bushes up to the coach, and presenting a pistol, first at the coachman and then at the corporation within, with a volley of oaths demanded our money – with a brace of balls amongst us if we didn't make haste. We had two women in the coach, who were so frightened that though they had got their money, they had not strength to offer it; one of the gentlemen who rode backwards flung a guinea into his hat; Mr Collier who sat backwards over against me, threw another; I thought we should be well off if he insisted on no more, but as that seemed to be more than he deserved, I consulted my silver pocket and presented him with five or six shillings of white metal which forsooth affronted him, and he cursed me, and swore he would have gold from me, but not being hasty enough in producing it, he turned to the fourth man, an honest bricklayer of

Lynn – "What, must I wait for you?" He came over to my opinion, and tendered him 5s. and some ha'pences; and then I expected a visit from him on my side of the coach. It happened that Mr Collier's guinea fell upon the road, upon which he made the coachman light and take it him up, and then came round to the other side, from whence he rid into the woods without calling for any second payments, and so we drove on to Epping'.[6]

Byrom continued:

'all these robbers ill-treat only those who try to defend themselves. I have been told that some highwaymen are quite polite and generous, begging to be excused for being forced to rob, and leaving the passengers the wherewithal to continue their journey'.

He rated footpads as being far more vicious as they would usually threaten to kill their victims.[7]

Possibly Turpin's first known highway robbery was on Easter Sunday, 6 April 1735. Three highwaymen, Samuel Gregory (allegedly) and perhaps Turpin and Rowden and either Jones or Haines, attacked a servant of Henry Howard, the 10th Earl of Suffolk, whose seat was at Audley End near Saffron Walden, in Epping Forest. They took a valuable horse worth £80. However, there were other people nearby and they chased the three robbers, and shot at them. One robber's horse was hit and injured so he leapt on the back of that of one of his accomplices. This may have slowed them down, as the country people caught up with them. The three robbers then turned to face their pursuers, presumably armed to the hilt and 'finding them resolute' the pursuers backed away.[8]

Turpin and Rowden's association with Gregory did not last long; Samuel joined his remaining brother, Jeremiah, and together they sought to flee the country. They went to ports on the south coast such as Shoreham, Brighton and Southampton, hoping to take ship to Guernsey or Boulogne. However, they found they lacked the money to pay the full fare, so resorted to robbery to restore their depleted funds.[9]

There is a good reason why Gregory was not involved in the robbery on 6 April in Essex. On 4 April, Sir John Osbourne (died 1743), an Irish baronet and MP, was attacked by the Gregorys on Milford Heath between Godalming and Liphook and robbed of his watch and other belongings. One of them had chatted to him amicably and then the other arrived and pointed a pistol at the baronet's breast while he was disarmed of his own weaponry. Osbourne offered money for the watch but was rebuffed. He made the description of his attackers known. Later that night Mr Spooner, master of the Red Lion at Guildford, was travelling with a companion when they were confronted by the Gregorys. Spooner escaped but his companion had his money taken from him.[10] On 6 April the two attended a cock fight near Petersfield, placing bets on the outcome. Samuel Gregory's greatcoat blew open and onlookers saw his pistol. Next day, having heard of the recent robbery and the description of the robbers, some wondered if these were the men.[11]

On 8 April, two men on horseback arrived at the Flying Bull near Liphook and Petersfield in Hampshire and took a room for the night. The landlord thought they matched the description of the two highwaymen who robbed Sir John and he told his neighbours. A crowd of people gathered, including three members of the Cooper family, William Richards and perhaps four others, although another account claimed they numbered four; two young men armed with both swords and pistols and two older men, one similarly armed and the other with a scythe. There are two accounts of what happened. One claims that when the two guests rose early next morning, they were confronted by the crowd. The two men fired their pistols and wounded one man. The attack did not falter and the two men barricaded themselves into their room. The crowd broke through. The other account states that the four men entered the alehouse, broke down the Gregorys' door and the men inside said they were innocent and would come quietly.

They then drew their pistols. Samuel Gregory shot one of the men and then closed with him, nearly killing him, but another man cut the tip of Gregory's nose off with his sword. The other Gregory was shot through the thigh. Eventually the two men were overpowered and disarmed. Among their possessions were Sir John's watch and other items which were his. The two prisoners were sent to a magistrate and he sent them to prison. The two identified themselves as William Johnson and Lisle, but the former was thought to be Samuel Gregory, identified by the two scars on his face; one an old one and one recently caused by one of his victims.[12] The other man was Jeremiah Gregory and he soon died of the wounds incurred during the struggle.[13] Now only Turpin, Rowden, Haines and Jones were at liberty, as the former gang members diminished in number yet further.

After spending some time in Winchester Prison, Samuel Gregory admitted that he had robbed Sir John and taken his valuable horse, which he had used to commit another robbery, and that he had been involved in the robbery on the Lawrence farm. He denied assaulting the maidservant.[14] He told his story but declared he wished to 'be used civilly' while he lived and said he did not want to be hung in chains on a gibbet after his death nor did he want his body to be given to the doctors who would use it for dissection.[15] The younger Lawrence also visited the gaol and he identified Gregory. The latter told him that, after the trial of Rose, Fielder and Walker, there had been a plan to ambush him, his father and Wood in order to hang them in revenge, for providing evidence against their three colleagues, but the gang missed the three.[16]

Samuel Gregory was brought to the New Prison on 13 May. Wheeler was shown him, 'who, tho' his face was very much disfigured, swore directly that he was the man'.[17] Gregory had at least two visitors while he was in prison. Pulleyn was one, visiting him the day after he arrived there, and he later recalled, 'He told me he lay with the Girl, but that she was as willing as he, or else she was afraid, for he said he had two Pistols and laid them down by her. He confest likewise that he was concern'd in the Robbery'. Thomas Lawrence also visited the man who broke into his father's home and attacked and robbed the occupants. He recalled 'he own'd to me that he shew'd the others the way to our house, for he thought we had a great deal of money. Why did you think so, says I. Because you paid every body very well says he and therefore I thought you must be very rich. He told me too that he lay with the Maid and that he had twenty five shillings of the money that was taken'. Dorothy Street also visited him but 'when he was brought to her, she fell into such an Agony that she declar'd she could not tell whether he was the person or not'.[18]

On 22 May Samuel Gregory stood trial at the Old Bailey on several counts: breaking and entering Lawrence's house, stealing from him and assaulting him, raping Dorothy Street, stealing from Thomas Humphries, breaking and entering William Francis's house and assaulting him. The elder Lawrence was the first witness and he gave very similar evidence to that given at the trial of Rose and Fielder. Wheeler gave evidence as before as to Lawrence being robbed, stripped and assaulted, but elaborated on what he had given on the previous occasion. He stated that Gregory claimed to have raped Dorothy.

'Did he say by force?'
'He said he bolted the garret door and laid with a pistol on the bed while he lay with her'.

Gregory replied to this:

'I don't deny I was with them at the prosecutor's house but I had nothing which came from thence, for they were taken that day se[ven]night.

'He was with us when we divided the money, and had his part, perhaps more than I, for they cheated me in every respect'.

'But when you went away did you see no sacks carried out?'

'Not to my knowledge'.

Dorothy gave her evidence about being raped by Gregory, as she had at the previous trial.

> 'How did he force you? Were you dresst or undresst?
>
> 'I was dresst. He pulled up my coats and took out what he had – and into me – And he pushed as hard as ever he could for the life and soul of him'.
>
> 'Did you perceive?'
>
> 'Yes, and when he asked me if ever I was lain with before? And I said no and then he let me on down; and I cry'd and one of them said What's the matter, and I said one of your Men has lain with me.'

The publicans then gave evidence of the gang being at their premises together prior to the crime. Thomas Lawrence and Richard Taylor said that they had previously employed Gregory as a blacksmith. Archelaus Pulleyn stated that Gregory had confessed to being involved in the robbery but had naturally claimed that intercourse with Dorothy was by consent. Gregory stated: 'I have no witnesses, nor one friend in the world, and so I must leave it to the court'.

Gregory clearly had no witnesses to testify on his behalf to prove an alibi or plead good character. It was looking hopeless and he clearly realised this. Witnesses from the previous trial then came in to provide evidence against him. He admitted:

> 'I'll give the Court and Jury no further trouble. I own that I was at that house and took the money and goods, and had two guineas for my share'.
>
> 'What do you say as to stealing the horse?'
>
> 'I am guilty of that too – My lord, there are two gold watches in the custody of Sir Simeon Stewart, a Justice of the Peace in Hampshire – ought they not to be brought into court?'

'Are they a part of the goods for which you are indicted?'

'No, one was Sir John Obston's watch; it had a gold case. The other was a little watch with a shagreen case'.

'Then they are not before this court and we can make no order about them'.

'Besides they took my silver buckles (which cost me 18s) out of my shoes and took away all of my linen, in Winchester Gaol'.

The jury found Gregory guilty of all six indictments and he was sentenced to hang.[19] Gregory and four others were ordered to be hanged at Tyburn.[20] Unsurprisingly, 'Gregory declared a particular Enmity and Malice against Wheeler, the Evidence' and it was believed he had a concealed pistol which he would use to shoot Wheeler. He was searched but none could be found.[21] Apparently 'Gregory feigned a laugh, even at the last moment'.[22] He was hanged in chains on 4 June along with four others. It was noted that Gregory's behaviour 'shewed he had no Regard for Religion, and as little sense of the crimes he had been guilty of… his obstinacy did not proceed from a mad Despair or from being always intoxicated with strong liquor… he was carried to the gallows, he appeared quite sober and more tranquil than is usually observed in persons just going to submit to Fate'.[23] Despite his earlier stated wish, Gregory's corpse was put in chains, gibbetted and set on the Edgware Road, alongside his four fellow gang members.[24] Given his crimes, he deserved no better.

Richard Cooper petitioned for the £50 reward for taking Samuel Gregory for the Lawrence robbery on 19 June and was awarded this on 23 October 1735. William Richards claimed £60 on 18 August 1735 'For persons who apprehended Jeremy Gregory a notorious highwayman'.[25]

What the four remaining gang members thought about the hanging of Samuel Gregory, which they could have known about from the newspapers, is unknown, but their actions are clear. They did not stay together long. Haines and Jones went their own way, as we shall see later. Turpin and Rowden remained together for some time; presumably they felt they could trust one another and felt secure in each other's company. It is noteworthy, perhaps, that Rowden had remained with Turpin and not with the erstwhile gang leader, Samuel Gregory, whom Rowden (and presumably Haines and Jones) may have felt was unreliable, given the recent round-up of the rest of the gang. They were not inactive for long. Having left their known London haunts in the aftermath of the arrests of their companions in west London, on the night of Sunday 20 April 1735, 'Sir Caesar Child, baronet [of Woodford, Essex], was attack'd upon Epping Forest by two highwaymen, supposed to be Gregory and Turpin, who fir'd at the coachman without bidding him stand, and shot off the tip of his nose; they robbed Sir Caesar, and were with difficulty prevail'd upon not to murder him'.[26] However, as noted, Gregory had been arrested, so the supposition about Gregory must be incorrect and it was probably Rowden who was with Turpin. This may also be the first known explicit reference to Turpin in the press as a highwayman.

Epping Forest was certainly a suitable place for robbers to ply their trade as a verse from a poem, 'An Horrid and Barbarous Robbery' by John Byrom stated:

> 'Thro' the wide brakes of Epping Forest lay:
> With Travellers and Trunks, a hugeous Load,
> We hagg'd along the solitary Road:
> Where nought but Thickets within Thickets grew,
> No House nor Barn to cheer the wand'ring View;
> Nor lab'ring Hind, nor Shepherd did appear,
> Nor sportsman with his Dog or Gun was there;
> A dreary Landscape, bushy and forlorn,
> Where Rogues start up like Mushrooms in a Morn'.[27]

As early as 10 May Turpin was nearly captured. On that evening, a Saturday, he was seen drinking in a pub in Whitechapel, perhaps one of his old haunts. A man recognised him, so left to find a constable. On arriving to arrest him they found that Turpin had fled, leaving behind half a guinea for his refreshment, not having waited for the change. A few days previously he had been seen a quarter of a mile from Woodford by people who knew him well. [28]

Yet the thieves did not restrict their activities by geography. Another early crime was as follows:

'On Wednesday last [28 May] at 6 o'clock in the evening, Turpin, the Butcher, one of the companions of Gregory in the Essex Gang, was seen with two of his new companions, well mounted, within a pistol shot of Fulham, and had the impudence to speak to a young woman, who knew him, and desired her to go with them to a public house, but she refused. Mr Bareau, an old French gentleman, who passed by, was bid to deliver his money, and robb'd of four shillings, his silver watch and a sword. The young woman ran to the next house and alarmed the neighbourhood, but could not find Men enough to pursue them, so they got away with their Booty'.[29]

Some of the hold-ups took place to the south of London. On the evening of Thursday 3 July, at eight o'clock, Richard Vane of Richmond and James Bradford of Southwark were travelling from the latter to the former. Between Wandsworth and Barnes Common they were robbed by Turpin and Rowden of all their money. They were then forced to pull off their horses' bridles and let their horses wander off, so they could not quickly ride off to summon help. Shortly afterwards Turpin and Rowden rode further to the west to Roehampton and there robbed a man of £3 4s and a watch.[30]

On 21 July, a Monday, one Mr Omar of Southwark, who was riding from there to Barnes, encountered 'Turpin the Butcher, one of

Gregory's gang' and another horseman, again between Wandsworth and Barnes Common. Mr Omar 'not caring for their company, clapp'd his spurs to his horse' to try and flee, but they pursued him and 'obliged him to dismount'. Turpin suspected that Omar knew who he was, so he pulled his gun on him and was about to shoot him, but his companion managed to persuade him not to. It seems that Turpin had no compunction about shooting those who might identify him, but his companion was less bloodthirsty.[31]

Turpin remained to the south-west of the capital for his next exploit. On the afternoon of Sunday 10 August, a number of gentlemen were riding and some were in coaches between Putney and Kingston Hill to the south-west. They were confronted by Turpin 'the Butcher' and Rowden 'the Pewterer'. Mr Wise, a saddler, and two of the gentlemen were unhorsed on Putney Common, tied up and left in a ditch, where they lay until released. Several others were robbed near Barnes Common that day.[32]

Meanwhile, Turpin and Rowden's former gang members were caught. Herbert Haines, despite his description being circulated widely, eluded capture at first, having parted from Turpin, Rowden and Jones. He planned to flee to Holland on a Dutch trading sloop, the *Baudois*, under the name of Joseph Butler, but either his mistress (the wife of a tradesman called John Carroll, whom Haines had once worked under as a journeyman) wrote to him and pleaded with him to return, or he wanted to take leave of her or to see her one more time.[33]

He may have read her letter to him, which asked him to meet her so they could then live together abroad. He replied in the affirmative and sent a letter to a pub in Gravesend for her to call for.[34] His mistress went to see him when his boat stopped at Gravesend but she was recognised there by Henry Palmer, a man who knew both her and her husband, who knew that Haines was a wanted man by having read the *London Gazette*. Palmer told Carroll, who already suspected his wife, and they went together to the ship, and after some initial reluctance on the part of the crew, found the two together and hauled them onshore on 12 April.[35]

Haines was committed to Newgate on 11 May 1735 by Sir Richard Brocas and then sent to Chelmsford prison. This was because the evidence for his crimes came from those which took place in Essex, not Middlesex, and Wheeler provided evidence against him for robbing William Mason. In August he was sentenced to death and to be hanged in chains at Chelmsford, with Wheeler providing evidence that Haines had taken part in the Skinner robbery.[36]

Haines was hanged along with four other convicted criminals on 8 August. Apparently while in prison he behaved very well, in a sedate manner, and was never known to swear. His mistress, who was much older than him, visited him there and claimed to be pregnant and said they would eventually be reunited. On his way to the gallows, he was given a glass of wine by a man in a laced hat at the Black Boy pub and the two men chatted for a while. His body was hung in chains after death.[37]

Henry Palmer petitioned the Treasury on 2 September 1735. Mary Mason petitioned likewise, but on 5 July 1738 it was Palmer who received £50 for the arrest of Haines, one of the 'Essex Robbers'.[38]

John Jones was not at liberty much longer, being arrested at his home in Hackney on 14 December when Nicholas Graves, the constable, with Francis Francis and Dison Green, entered his house with a warrant and began searching for him. Green found him in the yard and Jones struck him and the others came to his aid, so after 'some struggle' took him to Norris and Samuel Tyler, who as JPs had him sent to Newgate by the end of 1735 and examined by Nicholas Blackerby, JP, three days later and confessed to a robbery undertaken by himself, Samuel and Jasper Gregory.[39] Jones was subsequently moved to Chelmsford gaol where he was sentenced to death for burglary and felony at the assizes in March 1736, though he was pardoned and was transported, on the *Dorsetshire*, to Virginia on 25 December 1736.[40] Dison Green, Francis Francis and Nicholas

Graves petitioned for the reward on 30 November and were given £50 between them a week later.[41]

It was reported that one Arnold was allegedly another gang member and he was arrested in Chelmsford, but his companion, thought to be yet another gang member, escaped. Arnold was sent to Newgate.[42] He does not seem to have been put on trial at the Old Bailey so may have been released or died in prison.

The Gregory gang, once so strong, was now reduced to a rump of two. At the end of 1735 it was thought that Turpin had been caught. One newspaper proclaimed 'Turpin the Butcher, who for his Robberies on the highway, has been the bugbear of the Neighbouring counties for a considerable time, was apprehended yesterday and confined to Newgate'. Alas this was not true, and the newspaper had to retract the earlier story. 'Turpin the Butcher is not yet taken, but a Person very like him having been apprehended, gave rise to that Report, and to the mistake in our last'.[43] Clearly there was hope among respectable law-abiding folk that Turpin would be apprehended.

Turpin and a companion were seen on 24 December at Worthey, within a mile of Winchester, having stopped at a blacksmith's to have their horses shoed. They pretended they were in a hurry to get to Winchester, but left in the direction of London. Turpin had several pistols and hangers under his greatcoat.[44]

Turpin and Rowden eventually parted. In late February 1736 Rowden left London's environs and returned to his old game of coining, making half crowns and shillings as he had in 1732. However, he passed off a coin at a baker's in Stroud, Gloucestershire, and a few days later the baker's wife realised the money was counterfeit and told her husband. Thomas Davis and Giles Bishop located Rowden and he was arrested on 2 July in the town and said his name was Donald Crisp. He was found guilty and at trial sentenced to two years in prison and fined 20 marks.[45]

However, in the summer of 1737, when Rowden's sentence was nearing its end, one Richard Arundell came to the prison as a visitor to see a fellow prisoner. By chance this man was one whom Rowden was playing a game with at the time. Rowden asked Arundell if he knew a man called Donald Crisp and he said he did, so Rowden asked him to remember him to him. At market day a few days later Arundell spoke to a friend who said he did not know Crisp but did know Rowden as a coiner and Arundell returned to the prison and identified Rowden. He then rode to London to tell a magistrate of Crisp's true identity. The magistrate told him that he must tell a Gloucestershire JP. He did so and an affidavit was made out to convey Rowden to Newgate.[46] William Robinson, sheriff of Gloucester, spent £14 moving him.[47]

However, once Rowden was at Newgate, it was decided to send him to Chelmsford Prison to stand trial at the forthcoming assizes there, for he was not being accused of any crimes that had occurred in Middlesex. His legs were chained together under the horse which he rode upon. On 20 July he was found guilty of felony and burglary against Ambrose Skinner at the Essex assizes and sentenced to death, though the judge believed he and others should be reprieved 'as fit objects of mercy on condition of transportation for the term of fourteen years'. He was transported to Virginia on 15 June 1738 on the ship *Forward*.[48]

On 8 August 1737, Arundell and Thomas Bayliss claimed the reward for apprehending Rowden. On 1 November 1738, they, and Benjamin Henning and Thomas Cavanagh, gaoler at Newgate, were awarded £50.[49]

John Wheeler, on the other hand, who had been instrumental in helping break up the gang, had spent over a year in the New Prison, Clerkenwell, in order that he be used to give evidence in the various trials of his fellows in London and Chelmsford. Poor as Wheeler claimed to be (though he had been awarded £5 as part of the reward for Haines and £1 5s for Rose), the gaoler, Thomas Cavanagh, had to spend a shilling a day to feed and clothe him and by 30 September 1736 had paid £31 10s. Wheeler had been committed on 8 February with his fellow gang members, but had to be taken out of the prison at various times to provide testimony at both the Old Bailey and against Haines, Rowden and Jones at Chelmsford.[50] He was pardoned, left gaol in October 1736 and apparently worked honestly until he died in Hackney on 12 February 1738, when it was noted that all the Gregory gang except Turpin had been hanged (this was wrong, as three had been transported and three died in prison).[51]

In 1736 Turpin was seen by various witnesses. One claimed that 'Turpin the Butcher, one of the Gregory Gang' was seen on the morning of Friday 13 September, drinking at a pub in Clapham. A man told the landlord who he was, but before they could decide how to take him, he and his companion left, taking horses and throwing down 1s for the beer they had drunk. They were last seen riding eastwards towards Wandsworth. The man thought to be Turpin was on a fine gelding, the other on a dark bay horse. Turpin was 'dressed in a red waistcoat and a brown coat'.[52] Shortly after this it was alleged that Turpin had left the country 'We hear that Turpin has been in Rotterdam, Holland, from where he returned about six weeks ago in the Ostend packet Boat'. He allegedly tried to persuade one Daniel Malden, later in Canterbury prison, to leave the country forever and enter into foreign employ, though one account claimed that Rowden was there at the time and they were drinking with Malden at the Sign of the Three Dutch Skaters in Flushing, though this seems unlikely.[53]

Turpin's new companion may have been Matthew King. According to Bayes, Turpin allegedly decided to make the main road from London to Cambridge his hunting ground, because he was unknown there as well as it being a source of rich pickings. A contemporary historian puts Turpin's extravagance as a key factor in this decision.[54]

Turpin may well have wished to have a reliable ally in his thefts and at some stage he had an encounter that was to change all that. As his first biographer wrote:

'King, the highwayman, who had been towards Cambridge, on the same account, was coming back to

London. Turpin, seeing him well mounted and appear like a gentleman, thought that was the time to recruit his pockets, and accordingly bids King stand, who keeping him in discourse some time, and dallying with him, Turpin swore, if he did not deliver immediately, he would shoot him through the head, upon which King fell a laughing, and said, What! Dog eat Dog! Come now brother Turpin, if you don't know me, I know you, and should be glad of your company. After mutual assurances of fidelity to each other and that nothing should part them but death, they agreed to go together upon some exploit and met with a small booty, that very day after which they continued together committing divers robberies'.[55]

How accurate this account of their meeting is, or whether the meeting even took place, is unknown. Possibly the two were already acquainted (a servant called Elizabeth King was present at one of the robberies committed by the Gregory gang in 1734). When it happened is another question; perhaps some time in 1736 after Rowden and Turpin had gone their separate ways. Bayes, who first related it, may have heard it from the dying King in 1737, for he had no opportunity to speak to Turpin himself. Or he may have invented it, or have embroidered what he was told. Virtually nothing is known about King save that he was married and was a few years younger than Turpin, as we shall see, and that the two did work together. If the story of the meeting is true then it certainly indicated a radical change in Turpin's territory, but this could have been a wise decision to avoid being taken, and he certainly knew the district through his time in the Gregory gang. All that is certain is that Turpin and King worked together in the first half of 1737; perhaps King was attracted to Turpin because of his reputation in the press and perhaps by word of mouth.

Bayes writes a few pages about the Turpin–King partnership, but how much of it is true is another question. Because King and Turpin were well known, no innkeeper would accommodate them. So they decided to make their own home. This was in Epping Forest, 'pitched upon a place enclosed with a large thicket, situate between Loughton Road and King's Oak Road'. It was large enough to conceal both of them and their horses and contained numerous spy holes so they could see passers-by on the roads and steal from them. This made the stretch of road very hazardous for travellers. The hideaway was known as their 'cave'. Turpin's wife supplied them with food and would sometimes stay the night there.[56]

The cave was also used as a base for lengthier forays. On one occasion King and Turpin travelled to Bungay in Suffolk. There they saw two young market women receive £13 or £14 for corn and so Turpin planned to rob them. King tried to dissuade him: 'they were pretty girls and he would not be concerned in it'. Turpin refused to heed the urgings of his friend and robbed them and this 'occasioned a dispute between them'.[57]

At Fair Maid Bottom, one Mr Bradele of London was taking the air with his two children. King was the first of the two highwaymen to confront him. Thinking there was but one assailant and being 'a man of spirit', Bradele made out to resist. On this King called out 'Jack' and Turpin came to his friend's aid. Bradele's resistance collapsed and first they demanded his money, which he gave without any dissent. Then they demanded his watch, but he refused to part with it. One of his children, frightened by the proceedings, implored him to hand it over. He did so. The children also told him to part with an old mourning ring. Bradele insisted it was only worth eighteen pence, but he prized it much. King demanded the ring and so received it, then he returned it explaining that he was a gentleman and would not deprive another gentleman of something he valued so much. Bradele then asked if he could buy his watch back. King said to Turpin: 'Jack, he seems a good honest fellow, shall we let him have the watch?' 'Ay, do just as you will' came the reply.

Bradele enquired about the price and King told him 'Six guineas, we never sell one for more, if it be worth six and thirty'. Bradele promised he would leave the money on the dial in Birchin Lane and would not inform against them. Turpin said 'Ay but King, insist on no questions ask'd'.[58]

Barnes Common was once again a scene of operations. One Tuesday at nine o'clock, a gentleman, a lady and their son were travelling in a coach with six horses. Turpin and an unknown companion, presumably King, held them up. They robbed them of watches and money to the value of £40, before riding away over the fields.[59] However, there may have been others working with Turpin. A reference to King in 1739 states that he was 'one of Turpin's gang'.[60]

Turpin was seen to the north of the capital later that year. On 9 October he was seen riding through Edgworth towards Harrow on the Hill, riding 'a strong big horse'. He called on one Moreland, a drover, near Edgworth, but not to rob him.[61] However, other reports put him to the south of London, as on 5 October he allegedly, along with a companion, 'had the insolence to ride through the City at noon day and in Watling Street they were known by two or three porters who plyed there, but had not the courage to attack them, they were but indifferently mounted and went towards the Bridge, so that tis thought they are gone upon the Tunbridge Road'.[62]

There were rumours of Turpin being caught soon afterwards, as there had been in the previous year. 'The notorious highwayman Turpin' was to be sent to Newgate with a strong guard and he had been 'concerned with that hardened and wicked fellow Gregory in the robbery of farmer Maurice [presumably Lawrence]'.[63] Yet another newspaper had to report that the man sent to Newgate was not Turpin but a rioter sent from Bristol.[64]

There was a report that Turpin and his two fellows quarrelled over the spoils of one of their robberies in early 1737. They had taken £50 but Turpin took £30 of it. This enraged the other two and they threatened to kill him. He escaped to Holland and then wrote a letter to them from Rotterdam, addressing it to a pub in Southwark. It was taken to the JPs in March, but nothing more came of this.[65]

There were, apparently, other robberies. Allegedly, at the gallows, Turpin told the hangman, or at least it was reported that he had done so, that:

'Some Time after he returned to the Forest again, and attempted to rob Captain Thompson and his Lady in an open Chaise, but the Captain firing a carbine at him, which miss'd, Turpin fir'd a pistol after the Captain, which went through the chaise between him and the Lady, without any further damage, than tearing the left sleeve of his coat, the Captain driving hard, and being just in sight of a town, Turpin thought it best not to pursue any further.

Next he stopp'd a Country Gentleman, who clapping spurs to his horse, Turpin followed him, and firing a pistol after him, which lodged two balls in his horses' buttocks, the Gentleman was obliged to surrender: He robbed him of fifty shillings, and asking him if that was all, the Gentleman saying he had no more, Turpin stripp'd him, and found two guineas more in his pocket book, out of which he returned him five shillings, but at the same time told the Gentleman, it was more than he deserved, because of his Intention to have cheated him.

After this he stopped a Farmer in Epping Forest, who had been to London to sell Hay, and took from him fifty shillings, and hearing of several coaches coming that way, laid wait for them, but they being informed of the frequent Robberies in these Parts, took another Road.

Another time, meeting a Gentleman and lady on horseback, in a lane near the Forest, he stopp'd them and presented a pistol, at which the lady fell into a swoon, he took from the Gentleman seven guineas and some silver, and from the Lady, a Watch, a Diamond Ring, one Guinea and fifteen shillings in silver'.[66]

Turpin was even referred to by a French traveller in England in 1737–39, who later wrote up his experiences and shows that his fame was not restricted to England. Jean Bernard Le Blanc (1707–81) referred to him as '*Le célèbre Turpin*' and '*Le Cartouche de La Nation*' and '*M. Turpin, touché de ses bonnes manières*'. He added, '*Les voleurs célèbres sont ici des espèces de Heros*'.[67]

Le Blanc then went on to relay an experience that a friend of his had with Turpin on the road to Cambridge:

> 'after having repeated in vain the word of command to stand, in order to punish him for his disobedience, fir'd a pistol at him, but the ball happily missed him M.-, fearing a second summons of the same kind, resolved to obey. The first man took his money, his watch and his snuff box, leaving him only 2s to continue his journey. Before he left, he required his word of honour that he would not cause him to be pursued, nor inform against him before a justice, which been given they parted courteously'.[68]

The year 1737 marks a turning point in Turpin's career for a number of reasons. Firstly he was to shoot and kill at least one man, perhaps two, and secondly, doubtless not unconnected with these shootings, he radically changed both his mode of life and his abode.

Sometimes his would-be victims were ready for him, as this report illustrates:

> 'On Saturday last a Gentleman of West Ham, and others in a coach were going to Epping to dinner, on the Forest, the famous Turpin and a new companion of his, came up and attacked the coach, in order to rob it, the Gentleman had a carbine in the coach, loaded with slugs, and seeing them coming, got it ready, and presented it at Turpin, on stopping the coach, but it flash'd in the pan, upon which

says Turpin, God damn you, you have missed me but I won't miss you, and shot into the coach at him, but the ball missed him, passing between him and a lady in the coach and then they rode off towards Ongar'.

Apparently several coaches between Loughton and Romford were robbed later that night.[69]

On the other hand, the Hon. Mr George Stirling, returning from Newmarket, was robbed of six guineas by Turpin in Epping Forest.[70] However, he did have a narrow escape when at Finchley his horse was taken three minutes after he dismounted and he was forced to flee on foot in the forest.[71]

Turpin seems to have been acquiring celebrity status, as a newspaper report stated:

'The famous Turpin, who rides with an open gold lac'd hat, and his companion (who sometimes passes for his man) were last week at Bedford, and have since been seen at Market Street and Coney, and last Saturday they lay at a house in Whetstone, where Turpin left his Dun horse and took away next morning a Grey mare of the landlord's in his room and 'tis supposed they have changed their road to rob'.[72]

Not all Turpin's recorded life concerned robbery. On Thursday 3 February Turpin met his wife, Elizabeth, with Hannah Elcombe, her alleged maid and Robert Nott, once huntsman to a Mr Harvey of Chigwell, at an inn in Puckeridge, Hertfordshire. This could have been the 600-year-old White Hart on the High Street. He had probably seen her at the end of the previous year, too, for reasons which we shall later note. He had written to her, asking her to meet him, and he greeted her using a fictitious name. He also allegedly met a butcher there, to whom he was in debt to the tune of £5. The butcher took him to one side and said 'Come Dick, I know you have money now, if you'd pay me, it would be of a great service'. Turpin said that his wife was in the next room and he could obtain the money from her. Meanwhile the butcher told other men that he would take his money and then they could take him. However, Turpin left the inn by a window, took horse and rode away to Cambridge.[73]

As usual, the sequel for those left behind by Turpin was grim. Elizabeth, along with Nott and Hannah, was arrested and sent to Hertford Prison, 'committed on the 10th of February 1736 [1737] by Thomas Rolt Esq., on a violent suspicion of being dangerous rogues and robbery upon the highway'. However, they were all released shortly afterwards. Presumably they were questioned about Turpin's whereabouts but could not supply any useful evidence.[74]

Turpin did not only rob the moneyed, but also the poor. On Tuesday morning, 29 March, at two o'clock, he robbed several higlers between Enfield Wash and Waltham Cross – these were poor men travelling to work with their meagre wares. He took a total of £4 and was later seen counting his money at a turnpike gate.[75] But Turpin did not discriminate on grounds of wealth, as the next month he robbed William Hucks Esq. (1672–1740), an MP for Wallingford since 1715, the King's brewer, and a supporter of the government, who was travelling in a four-horse coach in Epping Forest, taking 11 guineas.[76] Turpin and his accomplices were then seen on Sunday 24 April at Finchley Common, on their way to London.[77]

However, matters were about to become far more serious and bloody. On Saturday 30 April, Turpin met King and Stephen Potter, whom they had just taken up with. There is a note that Potter was known for robberies in Leicester and Essex and so probably had prior criminal experience. They decided to seek victims once it was dark. Riding towards London they arrived within 300 yards of the Green Man pub in Epping Forrest when Turpin's horse began to tire. They held up a Joseph Major, owner of the race horse White Stocking. This was taking a risk as the robbery took place near houses. They took his money as well, seven guineas, a knife and a horse whip and then, perhaps curiously, exchanged horses, presumably because Major had a better one (Turpin having stolen a poor bay mare at Hare Street, a suburb of Romford, on the previous night). Turpin had threatened Major with a blunderbuss. They then rode to London.[78]

Major went to the Green Man and spoke to the landlord, Richard Bayes, and told his sad tale. Bayes said 'I dare swear tis Turpin has done it, or one of that crew, and I'll endeavour to get intelligence of your horse, this that they have left you is stole, and I would have you advertise it [i.e. by having pamphlets printed or by placing an advert in a newspaper]'. Apparently the horse's saddle had belonged to one Arrowsmith.[79] One of the robbers was Matthew King and on the next day, he took his new horse to the Red Lion Inn, Whitechapel Road, a district that Turpin had once known well, as he had resided there in early 1735. Most inns had stables nearby where the horses belonging to those travellers staying at the inn could be accommodated. This inn was probably the Old Red Lion pub at 217 Whitechapel Road, which closed in 1991, as it is described as such. King had left the horse in the inn's stables. Bayes found where the horse had been taken. Major went to the inn and saw an ostler watering his horse in the stables. Asking the man who had left the horse there, he was told that the man would return on Monday morning. Major then summoned others, perhaps constables, and they lay in wait.[80]

Their patience was rewarded because at either 11pm or at 4am the new owner returned for his horse. The men stopped him and took him inside. He said he had bought the horse and could prove it. Bayes saw his whip and identified it as belonging to Major. The bottom part of the whip with the owner's name on it had been broken off and that seemed to prove it beyond doubt. A constable was summoned and King, on promise of release, confessed that his brother Robert was in Gloucester Street in Goodman's Fields, which is to the south of the Red Lion, and that Turpin was with him. Or that is one version;

another is that King told them that Turpin was wearing a white duffel coat and was waiting at Red Lion Street, further to the north and in Spitalfields, so Bayes and others went there. Bayes claimed the latter and as he was there in person, weight should be given to his account, though it was written two years later, and this is corroborated by a contemporary newspaper. Red Lion Street no longer exists (replaced by the wider Commercial Street in about 1850), but it was a fairly small street that ran north to south between part of Bishopsgate Street to the west and Brick Lane to the east and was named after an inn adjacent to Red Lion Court, confusingly also known as the Red Lion. Robert was found on foot and Turpin was on horseback. Then: 'King, being taken, Turpin fired, shot King in his left breast, and rode off'. The newspaper put the shooting down to being an accident.[81]

However, there was another newspaper account of the same incident which relocated it to the pub itself:

> 'Last night at about twelve o'clock, the two Kings, Brothers and accomplices with the noted Turpin the Highwayman, were apprehended and taken at an Inn, in Red Lion Street by Mr Bayes, Keeper of the Green Man on Epping Forest, Turpin was first seized by Bayes, but had his heels struck up by Turpin, and receiv'd a shot or two, but without much damage, and 'tis believed Turpin was dangerously wounded in this Engagement by a ball from Bayes, Turpin made his escape without his horse, but the other two were secured by Bayes as they were about to take horse'.[82]

Another account claimed that it was Mr Bayes who shot King, not Turpin: 'Mr King the highwayman was shot by Bayes... on his making resistance when apprehended... He was not shot by Turpin by Accident, for Turpin rode off and left him when he was taken'.[83]

Bayes's own account, published two years later, ran as follows:

'Mr Bayes immediately went out and finding him as directed [in Red Lion Street, dressed in a white duffel coat], perceived that it was King, and coming around upon him, attacked him, King immediately drew a pistol, which he clapp'd to Mr Bayes' breast, but it luckily flash'd in the pan, upon which King, struggling to get out his other, it had twisted around his pocket and he could not. Turpin, who was waiting not far off on horseback, hearing a skirmish, came up, and King cried out, "Dick shoot him or we are taken by God", at which instant Turpin fired his pistol, and it mist Mr Bayes and shot King in two places, who cried out, "Dick, you have killed me", which Turpin hearing, he rode away as hard as he could'.[84]

Naturally, Bayes would not admit to shooting a man dead, for legal trouble apart, he might be the victim of a revenge attack. It was alleged that, on the gallows, Turpin recalled:

'he was a Confederate with one King, who was executed in London some Time since, and that, once being very nearly taken, he fir'd a pistol amongst the Crowd, and by mistake shot the said King into the Thigh, who was coming to rescue him'.[85]

It is not now possible to discern who shot King and thus gave him his fatal wound, the location of which seems so variable. There was no investigation into it. He was shot in a confused mêlée involving himself, Turpin, Bayes and others. There was very little street lighting in London and often travellers had to bring their own or employ a servant to do so. This meant that confusion would be at its maximum. Turpin and Bayes were both armed with pistols. The account claiming that Bayes shot Turpin may well be incorrect in that, but correct in that Bayes fired his gun – and perhaps hit King. It is also possible that both men might have hit him as there is a reference to King later dying of his wounds, suggesting more than one pistol ball (breast and thigh), though this could also refer to other wounds caused by other weapons in the struggle.

The location of the fatal encounter is also in doubt, but it would seem that it took place near to the Red Lion inn in Red Lion Street, Spitalfields, and that by coincidence, earlier, the horse had been found, and then Matthew King taken, at the Red Lion inn in Whitechapel, further to the south.

The two King brothers were taken before Justice Richard Ricketts. Robert was sent then to the New Prison and his brother to Bridewell. Robert was found to have a brace of pistols and a bag of bullets on his person.[86] King said that it was he, Turpin and Stephen Potter, now in Newgate, who had robbed Mr Major recently. He also told what he knew of Turpin's haunts.[87]

In detail, Bayes recorded:

> 'King… gave Turpin the character of a coward, telling Mr Bays, if he had a mind to take him, he knew he might be found at a noted house on Hackney marsh, and that when he rode away he had three brace of pistols about him, and a carbine slung'.[88]

Apparently when Turpin arrived at the house in question, he vented his anger, or so Bayes recorded, to strengthen his previous account of who shot King:

> 'What shall I do? Where shall I go? Damn that Dick Bayes, I'll be the death of him, for I have lost the best fellow-man I ever had in my life; I shot poor King endeavouring to kill that dog'.[89]

That night it was learnt that Turpin would be sleeping at a house near to Well Close Square. This was not far south-east from Goodman's

Fields, just to the south of Cable Street and north of the Ratcliffe Highway; Well Street was to the square's immediate west. At the beginning of 1735 had Turpin lodged there, so he might have been staying with someone he knew. Very early on Monday morning three men arrived at the house to seize him. They were seen by a woman (perhaps Turpin's mistress or a prostitute) and she called out to Turpin. He had been in bed, but made his escape over the roofs of houses. Meanwhile, Matthew King was being attended to by two surgeons and there were hopes he would recover.[90] He did not do so, and died of his wounds in prison on 24 May, aged twenty-five.[91] On 10 May, however, he had written his will, curiously stating himself to be 'in good health in body and sound in mind', and describing himself as 'a labourer' (a common fiction of the time) and leaving all his worldly goods to 'my loving wife, Elizabeth King', although there is no clue about the extent of these goods (probably meagre), or any information about Elizabeth, who was possibly a servant. The will was proved by the Prerogative Court of Canterbury on 1 June 1737.[92] Potter may have been sent to Chelmsford to stand trial at the Essex assizes because it was thought that he had committed robberies there with King and Turpin.[93]

Later in the year there was an unpleasant sequel for Bayes. On Sunday morning, 31 July, at two o'clock, assailants tried to break into his pub. It was supposed that they were members of 'Turpin's gang' bent on revenge. Fortunately Bayes's maid put the light on and this deterred the would be housebreakers. Whether they were related to Turpin or not is another question; they may have been other bandits wanting to break into an isolated inn.[94] Bayes leaves Turpin's story for now.

The second fatal shooting took place shortly afterwards, on Wednesday 4 May, and this time there was no doubt who pulled the trigger. There are a number of accounts of what happened, but the fatal outcome is undisputed. A contemporary newspaper noted:

'a Man belonging to Mr Thompson, one of the Keepers of Epping Forest, having Intelligence that Turpin lay hid in a certain place in the Forest, got a higgler to go with him to assist in taking that arch Rogue, who they at last met with. Mr Thompson's Man seized him by the collar, and told him he was his Prisoner, upon which Turpin pulled a pistol out of his pocket and shot the man dead on the spot'.[95]

There was another newspaper report, which differed in details:

'On Wednesday Night last, a servant of Mr Thompson's, one of the Keepers of Epping forest (who lives at Fair Maid Bottom), saw the famous Turpin in the Forest, and suspecting he was going to steal some particular Horse in the Neighbourhood, went to a House near King's oak and borrow'd a Gun, and charg'd it, and said he would go and take Turpin, who was not far off, and accordingly went with the Gun, after him, but approaching him with his Gun too near, (apprehending, 'tis supposed, he only had pistols), Turpin saw him and immediately discharged a carbine at him, loaded with slugs, and shot him into the belly, dead on the spot, and he now lies at the oak'.[96]

Bayes gave yet another near-contemporary account:

'The Reward for apprehending him and set several on to attempt it, among the rest this fellow, needs go in Company with a Higgler; Turpin was unarmed, standing alone, and, for not knowing the man, took him for one poaching for hares, and told him, he would get no hares near that thicket, No says the Fellow, but I have got a Turpin, and presented his piece at him, commanding him to surrender, Turpin stood talking to him, and creeping up to his cave, laid hold of his Carbine and shot him dead'.[97]

The higler ran off, though he was himself armed, having been much surprised at what had happened. He found help and a number of gentlemen, who were out hunting, returned to the crime scene. They hunted for Turpin and found his lair in a thicket, though their quarry was gone. There was his bed of straw, a half-eaten loaf, part of a bottle of wine and three clean shirts.[98]

There was another near-contemporary account which was the version allegedly given by Turpin himself at the gallows:

> 'Having been out one whole day without meeting any Booty, and being very much tired, he laid himself down in the thicket, and turned his horse loose, having first taken off the Saddle; when he wak'd, he went to search after his horse, and meeting with Mr Thompson's servant, he enquir'd, if he had seen his horse? To which Thompson's man answer'd that he knew nothing of Turpin's horse, but he had found Turpin: and accordingly presented his Blunderbuss at Turpin, who instantly jumping behind a broad oak, avoid'd the shot, and immediately fired a carbine, at Thompson's servant and shot him dead on the spot; one slug went through his breast, another thro' his right thigh, and a third thro' his groin. This done, he withdrew to a yew tree, hard by, where he concealed himself so closely, that though the noise of Mr Thompson's man's blunderbuss and his own carbine had drawn together a great number of People about the Body, yet he continued undiscovered for two whole days, and one night in that tree, when the company was all dispersed he got out of the Forest, and took a Black Horse out of a close near the Road and there being people working in a field at a distance, he threw some loose money amongst them and made off, but afterwards the same evening stole a chestnut mare, and turning his black horse loose, made the best way for London'.[99]

An inquest was subsequently held by the Essex coroner, but no record of it survives, the papers having been subsequently sent to York by the Duke of Newcastle. This was murder, but Turpin had no real alternative. Had he allowed himself to be taken, it is hard to see how he could have avoided the fate of his former gang members and swinging from a rope at Tyburn. His strong sense of survival kicked in and led him to committing the ultimate crime. Regrettably next to nothing is known about the unfortunate victim, whose name was not even given by most newspapers, but who was subsequently stated as being Thomas Morris, evidently a man of very humble social status. Most murder victims are forgotten when their murderers often are not (for example, most can name Peter Sutcliffe as being the Yorkshire Ripper, but few can recall the names of any of his many victims), and nowhere is this more true than with Morris.

Turpin had vanished: his horse was apparently found at Waltham Abbey. The whole district was allegedly searching for him on the day after the shooting. It was surmised that he had gone northwards.[100]

However, another report suggests he remained in the forest for a few days, at least a week after shooting Morris, 'but 'tis imagined he has changed his Road or lies conceal'd'. Apparently 'The Report of his being taken was first raised by some his Relations of his, as 'tis imagined, for him to Escape the more easily'.[101]

Other stories in the press refer to Turpin being at Market Street and Colney in Bedfordshire and at Whetstone, where he took his landlord's grey mare in return for his own dun horse.[102] At the same time there were stories of his being arrested; being taken either to Hertford or Chelmsford prisons.[103] The latter may originate from the fact that Howlett, a pork butcher of Waltham Abbey, was taken to the latter on suspicion of being Turpin.[104]

Turpin certainly appeared to be as active as ever, if newspaper reports are to be believed. On Friday 6 May, at 11am, he robbed a gentleman on horseback and a coach with a family inside in Epping Forest, between the Green Man pub and the Eagle, netting £60. On the next day he robbed a gentleman on Buckworth Hill of his money and his horse.[105] More menacingly, he told the latter gentleman that 'he designed to kill but two persons and then he did not care if he were taken', words that were remarkably prophetic.[106]

Another newspaper reported:

> 'Turpin the famous highwayman still continues to levy war on the good people of England without distinction. After he had left the man dead in Epping Forest, he attacked four Ladies in a coach and six, and then a gentleman on horseback, got good Booty. This week he marched his forces into Middlesex and, passing by an Excise man on his way in Barnet, he said only Good morrow, Brother! The Report of his being taken is false [there was a claim on 19 May of his being taken in Hertford on 10 May]'.[107]

There is more evidence that Turpin's highwayman days were not quite over. On 10 May a gentleman and two servants were travelling on horseback from London to Portsmouth and were crossing Putney Heath when they were robbed of 'considerable Booty'. Apparently the thief 'was very well mounted and dress'd and told the gentlemen his name'; Turpin.[108]

Another report ran as follows:

> 'On Sunday [19 May] night last, the noted Turpin robbed several gentlemen in their coaches and chaises at Holloway and the back lanes at Islington ['a large village or market town... extends over a mile in length'], and took from them several sums of money. One of the gentlemen signified to him, that he had reigned a long time. Turpin replied, 'Tis no matter for that, I am not afraid of being taken by you, therefore don't stand hesitating, but give me the Cole'.[109]

Apparently this was at midnight and he relieved two gentlemen of a purse of guineas; he was also active on the Highgate Road.[110]

Turpin was not always successful, as a report stated:

'On Friday last [13 May] Turpin the highwayman attempted to attack a Gentleman on Hertford Road, but the Gentleman having a better horse than Turpin, out rode him, and sav'd a great quantity of money he had about him'.[111]

There was yet another case of mistaken identity. A higler woman of Bishop's Stortford, Hertfordshire, was given brandy by a man in order to drink Turpin's health when the man told her that he was Turpin. She raised other people and they pursued him for five or six miles, before capturing him and sending him to Hertford Prison.[112] He was not the wanted man.

There was criticism in the press about the state of law which allowed Turpin to carry on his evil work, 'If the laws were more severe in the harbouring of known highwaymen, this desperate fellow could not have escaped long'.[113]

The killing of Mr Thompson's man had a number of important consequences. First, there was a better description of what it was thought Turpin looked like. Since there is no contemporary picture of him, this provides the best clue as to his appearance, being fuller than those given in 1735. It was as follows:

'The said Richard Turpin was born at Thackstead [sic] in the county of Essex, is about 30 years of age, by trade a Butcher, about five feet nine inches high, of a brown complexion, very much marked with the small pox, his cheekbones broad, his face thinner towards the bottom, his visage short, pretty upright, and broad about the shoulders'.[114]

This incident certainly added to Turpin's notoriety, and his hand was seen, rightly or wrongly, in a great deal of crime; after four coaches had been robbed on Hounslow Heath in May the following was observed:

> 'they gave out it was Turpin, but that Fellow having done so much Mischief of late, runs in Everybody's Head – the people about Epping Forest say he will never be taken till a proclamation is published offering a Reward for apprehending him, and give their Reason that he will never be taken alive, but will kill, or be killed, it will be dangerous to attempt it, and if they should take him, he'll be tried for the murder of Thompson's man and if convicted in that, the persons that apprehended him, will then be intitled to no reward, unless by proclamation, which makes them backward in endeavouring to take him'.[115]

The Duke of Newcastle caused the following notice to be drawn up, which indicates that Turpin was viewed as no ordinary footpad but a very dangerous fellow indeed, for although violence in London was common, murder was not and in 1731 there were only a dozen indictments for it in London. The notice read:

> 'Whereas it has been represented to the King that Richard Turpin, did, on Wednesday the 4th of May last, barbarously murder Thomas Morris, servant to Henry Thompson, one of the keepers of the Epping Forest; and that the said Richard Turpin hath, at divers times, committed several notorious Felonies and Robberies in and near the said forest, and other places near the Cities of London and Westminster, His Majesty, for the better discovery and bringing the said Richard Turpin to Justice, is pleased to promise his most gracious pardon to any one of the

accomplices of the said Richard Turpin who shall discover him, so that he may be apprehended and convicted of any of the said offences. And as a further encouragement, His Majesty is pleased to promise a Reward of £200 to any person or persons who shall discover the said criminal, so as he may be apprehended and convicted as aforesaid, to be paid upon such conviction, over and above all other rewards to which the said person or persons may otherwise be entitled'.[116]

This notice would have led anyone who had any idea as to where Turpin was and how to apprehend him a great incentive to do so; £200 was four years' wages for a skilled craftsman. The previous rewards of £50 for the members of the Gregory gang had been effective. But quadrupling the reward for a man who was not only a robber, but also a murderer would seem to make his capture even more likely. Morris had tried to apprehend Turpin for £50; despite the known risks, more would probably do so for £200. Staying in and around London where people knew him was now extremely dangerous for Turpin. It is noteworthy that no such reward was offered when King was killed, perhaps because of the uncertainty over who shot him.

Although literacy was far from universal in eighteenth-century England, knowledge of newspaper content was not uncommon and for all ranks of men. As Cesar de Saussure observed in the previous decade, at least in reference to London, 'all Englishmen are great newsmongers. Workmen habitually begin the day by going to coffee rooms in order to read the daily news' and he marvelled at common people discussing national and foreign politics.[117] It seems safe to suggest that the reward for Turpin was widespread and well known by many people, making his stay in or near London increasingly dangerous.

At some point in May Turpin was allegedly at Cunnington, near St Ives, which seems far from his usual beat. Apparently he was waiting for booty from graziers and butchers on the road to market. He missed them and so rode to London. It was thought that Rowden, the only surviving member of the Gregory gang, still accompanied him, but this cannot be true as Rowden, now known as Crisp, was in Gloucester prison and the man in question is unknown.[118]

It seems worth noting that contrary to the impression given by later dramas, Turpin did not necessarily conceal his face, or certainly not by using a mask over the top part or a scarf over the bottom. The Gregory gang had sometimes blackened their faces, but otherwise they did not bother, presumably relying on inadequate descriptions being given of them and the fact that their victims would not know them. However, Turpin did ride an unnamed horse and carry pistols and a sword.

As we shall see in the next chapter, Turpin had left his usual haunts around London by the beginning of June, yet reports of his alleged activities continued to be reported in the press. It would seem in some cases that other robbers used his name in order to cast fear into the hearts of their victims and thus make their crimes easier, reducing any resistance. Journalists, keen on material about a 'celebrity' criminal, did not question these reports, and to be fair, they did not know that Turpin was elsewhere. Similarly, after 1888, some journalists attributed subsequent prostitute murders in Whitechapel to Jack the Ripper, knowing that this would sell newspapers. Furthermore, other highwaymen, knowing Turpin's name and reputation, may have used his name to further terrify their victims.

Fielding observed:

'How long have we known Highwaymen reign in this Kingdom after they have been publicly known for such? Have not some of these committed Robberies in open Daylight, in the sight of many people and have afterwards rode solemnly and triumphantly throughout the neighbouring Towns without any Danger or molestation?'[119]

On 5 June Mr Loan of Bristol and another Quaker were riding to London for a general meeting of their sect, when a man rode up to them on Hounslow Heath. His pistol was cocked, but he did not demand any money from them, and told them that he was Turpin but they should not be afraid. He rode with them for a while and as they crossed the heath they saw a criminal hanging in chains. Turpin said 'that would be his fate, they said, if he thought so, they wondered why he pursued his trade. He could not help it, for he could trust nobody nor make his escape; besides he would never rest till he was avenged of the man who took his companion; and if he could kill him, he did not care what became of himself afterwards'. Turpin then spied a gentleman and rode towards him. 'You get your money easily, I must speak with you'.[120]

Reports on Turpin's robberies continued into the next month. In mid-June he was reported to have met Sir Charles Turner (1666–1738), an MP for King's Lynn, near Epping Forrest, and saluted him:

> 'Sir Charles Turner, I am Turpin and do not design to offer you any incivility or rob you of anything. In a little time I will come to the Gallows and hope that when I have occasion, you will do me your best service'.[121]

A few days later Turpin held up another coach on Hounslow Heath, near the powder mills, robbing several coaches. In particular, 'a Gentleman and his lady who live in Cork street, Burlington Gardens, and were coming into Town, from whom he took upward of 30 guineas'.[122]

One newspaper gave this report: 'last Tuesday, at ten o'clock in the morning, three gentlemen coming from Highgate in Mr Decosta's coach, were robbed of £17 by a single highwayman, who they supposed to be the famous Turpin'.[123]

Another alleged hold-up took place when the Saffron Walden and the Bishop's Stortford coaches were travelling towards Epping

Forest with over twenty passengers and a total of £10 was taken. Apparently 'the famous Turpin' 'used the passengers with a good deal of civility'. [124]

At the end of July 1737, the following comment was published:

'Turpin, the noted Butcher Highwayman, almost Every Day this Month, committed some Robbery on the roads near this City and gave out that he wanted to kill two men, and then he should not much regard being taken'.[125]

There were reports of Turpin being seen in Coventry, Epping Forest and near Harwich, then riding to London.[126] On Monday 1 August Turpin was seen at Tottenham High Cross, at 9am on a grey horse, with a servant boy riding with him on a brown horse with a black velvet hat and a silver tassel. Although men recognised him, no one molested them.[127] Turpin was subsequently spotted with the same youth at gambling tables and a race course in Manchester.[128] He was also seen on a dun horse at Walworth going to Camberwell.[129]

Not all were complacent on seeing Turpin. Apparently he was pursued in Upton Lane, near Stratford, by four horsemen, well armed, having been told about him by a servant, and they were riding after him at the full gallop.[130]

Reports of Turpin's supposed capture also made the press, as they had in the previous year. The first is instructive as regards the fame that had surrounded him. It was reported in early July that he had been captured and was at the Swan ale house in Butcher's Row, London 'which occasion'd such a concourse of people out of curiosity' who paid the landlord three pence to cast their eyes on the man they believed was the notorious criminal. It turned out that what had been caught was a vociferous owl. Next there was a tale of his capture in Leicester. A highwayman apprehended near Reading was also thought to be Turpin. Neither report was true, though many doubtless wished it to be so.[131]

There were also rumours that Turpin had been active in Scotland, having allegedly been seen in Longton on the Borders, with his servant. There had been a robbery of the Edinburgh mail coach and he was the suspected perpetrator.[132] A highwayman who robbed the Ipswich mail coach near Colchester was referred to by the coachman as Mr Turpin.[133]

Reports of thieving apart, there was also a rather different and rather momentous event, if true, taking place at a house near Chingford on 11 August: 'the wife of the noted Turpin was brought to bed of a Son and Heir'.[134] John Turpin, son of Elizabeth and Richard Turpin, was baptised at Holy Cross and St Leonard's, the parish church of Waltham Abbey, on 31 August 1737.[135] It is not known if both parents were present, because Turpin had left the district over two months earlier and to reappear, when he had a price of £200 on his head would have been very dangerous. What subsequently happened to his son is another question, but a John Turpin died in Little Bardfield, Essex, on 11 February 1827 at the grand old age of ninety, who may have been the child. Another John Turpin was aged twenty-six in 1763 when he married a Jane Biggs in Finchley on 28 June, though this Turpin had lived in Flampstead in Hertfordshire for five years. Given the scarcity of genealogical material it is difficult to be sure.

Turpin's fame was now at its peak. In 1737 Turpin was so well known that he was discussed in Opposition political satire, comparing him to Walpole, as a piece in *The Craftsman*, titled 'The nation excited against a great Robber' showed:

> 'the flagrant, undisturbed success if the infamous Turpin, who hath robbed, in a manner, scarce ever known before, for several years, and is grown so insolent and impudent, as to threaten particular persons, and become openly dangerous to the lives, as well as Fortunes, of the People of England'.[136]

It continued:

> 'That a Fellow, who is known to be a Thief by the whole
> Kingdom, shall for a long time continue to Robberies,
> and not only to, but to make a Jest of us, shall defy our
> Laws, and laugh at Justice, argues a want of Publick Spirit,
> which should make every particular Member sensible
> of the publick calamity, and entitle us of the honour of
> extirpating such a Notorious Robber from society, since
> he owes his success to no other cause than his monstrous
> impudence and the sloth or pussillanimousity of those
> who ought to bring him to Justice'.[137]

Likening the ministers and in particular Walpole, who had been the King's first minister since 1721, to criminals, was long established; John Gay had done likewise with *The Beggars' Opera* in the previous decade. Not all agreed with this and the comment in one magazine, after reproducing this, was 'If this writer really means Turpin the highwayman – it is a matter of wonder he did not think to employ our idle soldiery for the security of the Roads, as is done by the wise emperor of China'.[138] Another criticism came in an essay: 'I could never yet hear a Reason why a Man of State should be compared to Turpin'.[139] In another newspaper, at the year's end, there was a remark, in a similar vein, about why Turpin should not lay claim to be as eminent a man as Julius Caesar 'or any other Roman Robber or Trickster'.[140]

Other references made to Turpin also attest to his fame. When John Goodall was incarcerated in York Castle in May 1737 it was stated that he was 'as terrible in those Parts as Turpin has been in Essex' and as a precursor to what was to happen to Turpin it was noted that many people flocked to visit him.[141] In the next year John Ashwood in Kent cursed George II and was sent to Canterbury gaol. He claimed to be called Turpin.[142]

There is only one surviving contemporary non-newspaper publication about Turpin. It is the first glimmer of the Turpin myth, but because it was contemporary it will be examined here. It is unknown whether Turpin knew of it or even read it. Had he done so it is likely he would have revelled in it. However, clearly the writer and publisher envisaged that it would find a market, albeit limited as it only went through one edition as far as is known. It was published in 1737, clearly after early May, when Turpin was at the height of his infamy and just as he disappeared from the public view. It was titled '*New's News; great and wonderful news from London in an uproar or a Hue and Cry after the great Turpin, with his escape into Ireland*'.

Much of the account was fiction, interspersed with accounts from the press, and so was a mix of the untrue and partly true. For example, the robbery of Major was placed after the shooting of Matthew King. There are tales of Turpin being at the White Lion pub in Westchester and at the Bird in the Hand at Huntingdon, escaping by shooting a wig off a constable and being at the Bell at Stilton, then Yoxley, escaping the law again. There was an account of a fictional encounter between Turpin and a lawyer:

> 'Turpin saluted a gentleman in the following manner; Good-morrow Sir, do not you hear of one Turpin, a robber? O Lord, sir, I heard an account of him in the public newspapers. Turpin replied, Sir, I have a small matter of money at me, and am very much afraid of being robbed, but for security I have put it in my boot tops. Sir, says the Gentleman, that is a very good place.
>
> Place! Well, Sir, my money is all carried in the cape of my coat. Riding about two miles further, Sir, says Turpin, Pray Sir, what might be your business or calling? Sir, says the gentleman, I am a lawyer. Then says Turpin, if you are a lawyer, I am a cutter, and must cut the cape of that coat of yours before we go any further'.[143]

There was also a crude and bawdy ballad therein and its importance lies in it containing the genesis of a major plank of what would become the Turpin legend, represented in countless dramas, namely that he robbed the rich to give to the poor, for which there is no foundation whatsoever. Another less well-known and short-lived myth it introduced was that Turpin fled to Ireland, instead of the Continent. It is also important in that it is an illustration of Turpin's fame at this time.

'Of all the famous robbers
That does in England dwell,
The noted Richard Turpin
Does all the rest excel;
Tho' to Ireland he did go, go, go, &c.

He is a butcher by his trade
And lived in Stanford town
And eight men did at Leicester rob
As it is full well known;
Now to Ireland is gone, gone, gone &c.

He only taketh from the rich
What they well can spare;
And after he hath served himself,
He gives the poor a share,
Tho' to Ireland he is gone, gone, gone &c.

He met with a poor tenant
Upon a certain day;
Whose landlord would seize upon his goods
'cause his rents he could not pay,
Tho' to Ireland he is gone, gone, gone &c.

Then Turpin he does lend him
Directly fifty pounds
That when the landlord called for's rent
He might pay the money down;
Now to Ireland he is gone, gone, gone &c.

The landlord came and got his rent
But was met upon the day
By Turpin who did take it all
And then run quite away
Now to Ireland he is gone, gone, gone &c.

The very next that he did meet
At the highway side
Was a gentleman and lady fine
Who in a coach did ride:
But to Ireland he is gone, gone, gone &c.

He soon made the gentleman
Deliver all his money
But madam she did put her watch
Onto her hairy c—y
Tho' to Ireland he is gone, gone, gone, &c.

But Turpin quickly found it out
Which made the lady cry
Because he handled her twat
And stroked her soft plump thigh
But to Ireland he is gone, gone, gone &c.

Then he killed the Keeper's man
On Epping Forest wide
For which if ever he is caught
He must to Tyburn ride;

Tho' to Ireland he is gone, gone, gone &c.

But if ever he returns again
Unto the English shore
They'll hang him up on Tyburn Tree
Where he can rob no more
Tho' to Ireland he is gone, gone, gone, &c.'[144]

One reason for Turpin's fame was perhaps his longevity. Highwaymen often had a short career. In 1738 two highwaymen were arrested only three weeks after they began to ply their trade; Turpin had been a highwayman for nearly two years and seemed to have got away with it.[145] As the pamphlet noted:

'of all the Rogues that ever grac'd Tyburn, (whether Whitney, Nevison, the Golden Farmer or Hind) none ever came up to the famous Turpin… who had the good fortune to reign so long in their villainies, as to become a Terror to Gentlemen and others that are oblig'd to travel through the whole kingdom'.[146]

In the following year virtually nothing was heard him of Turpin, but ironically, in the light of what was to happen, there was the following report in York in May 1738:

'a person who calls himself John White (but is supposed by some to be the famous Turpin) was committed to prison at Ouse Bridge Gaol for deceitfully, fraudulently and unlawfully taking half a guinea out of the shop of Thomas Watkinson, and refusing to find sureties for his next appearance at the General Quarter Sessions, to be held in the said City. He is a broad set man about five foot eight inches high, pock broken, full faced and a scar on

102

his right cheek, wants three fingers on his right hand, and is about fifty years of age'.[147]

Another pointer to his fame is the paragraph below:

'On Saturday [20 May] night last, a noted deer stealer and a member of Turpin's gang, fell out of a waggon in Epping Forrest and was killed, on the spot by one of the store wheels running over his head'.[148]

Another alleged gang member was William Clifford, taken to Oxford prison in November 1737 and rumoured to be an accomplice of Turpin's.[149]

From being a member of the Gregory or Essex gang in 1735 journalists were now crediting Turpin as being a gang leader himself, but this is to exaggerate, for at most Turpin is only known to have worked with one or two other men after the break-up of the Gregory gang. It is unfortunate that the man's name went unrecorded.

However, interest in Turpin in 1738 was at a lower ebb, with the general consensus being that he was abroad, as various newspapers attested. There was talk in the press that Turpin went abroad for some of this year. In April it was claimed 'by some' that he was in Hamburg, trading as a merchant in gold and other watches.[150] Later that year he was apparently seen in Lisbon.[151] It was thought that the 'infamous Robber and Murderer' was in Holland and Robert Trevor, the King's representative in that country, asked the States General for an order to arrest him in Delft, but he was too quick for the officers.[152] In the previous year traveller John Loveday had noticed there were the remains of two men in gibbets just outside Delft; hardly a welcome sight to Turpin.[153] Another report was that he had been seen in Dunkirk.[154] As with the case of Lord Lucan in the years following his disappearance in 1974, numerous sightings in numerous places were reported of this wanted man. None proved to be accurate.

Yet despite this, there was a report that on 8 October:

> 'Counsellor St John and his Lady, going over Banstead Downs in their chariot, were attacked by a single highwayman, well mounted on a black gelding, who robbed them of two gold watches, eight guineas, and some silver. The person who committed the robbery had a great scar on his face, and answered pretty exactly the description of the famous Turpin'.[155]

However, the description of the man with the scarred face matched that of Samuel Gregory, hanged three years previously, not Turpin, and so the robber's identity must remain unknown, except to state that it was not Turpin; one reason is the scar, but there was another as we shall see. Having examined Turpin's notoriety, we shall now discover where he really was and what he was doing.

Chapter 5

Turpin's Capture and Trial, 1737–39

The disappearance of Turpin from the environs of London in May and June 1737 led to the appearance of a man called John Palmer in the little village of Brough in the east riding of Yorkshire. These two events appeared to be unconnected at first and did not apparently give rise to much comment anywhere else, but in the following year they did.

Robert Appleton of Beverley, Clerk of the Peace to the East Riding quarter sessions, recalled in 1739 that in 1737, 'a Person came out of Lincolnshire to Brough, near Market Cave in Yorkshire, and staid for some time in the Ferry House Brough' and said his name was John Palmer; his surname was later also referred to as Paumer and Pawmer, possibly mispronunciations of the same name. He lived at nearby Welton too, and had lived in these places cumulatively for fifteen or sixteen months. He also spent time in Lincolnshire, allegedly to see his friends there. Palmer claimed to have been a butcher but was now making a living as a horse dealer. It was noted that he 'frequently brought three or four horses back with him, which he used to sell in Yorkshire'. His customers were Yorkshire gentlemen. When he lived in Brough and Welton he often went out shooting and hunting with the county gentry.[1]

To be exact, as shall be noted below, Palmer arrived on 6 June 1737 as stated by William Harris, innkeeper of the Ferry Inn, in Brough; a small village on the north side of the River Humber, and he lived there for several months. Then, from October or November

1737 he lived at an inn in nearby and slightly more inland Welton, perhaps at the Green Dragon. One day Palmer was talking to Harris, his landlord, and the latter later recalled that Palmer said:

> 'if he could go along with him, and have a good heart, he would show him how he might as easily take £20 as take up that 2d which he had laid down upon the Board. Says Harris, What signifies my going along with you, you HAVE NO Arms? Palmer replies Have not I? I'll show you such pistols you never saw in your life before?'[2]

Palmer was virtually telling Harris that he was an armed criminal, but Harris seems not to have taken any further action because of it. Possibly he was sounding out Harris to see whether he might want to team up with him in criminal activity. After having associated with others in crime from 1734–37, Turpin may have been in search of a new companion.

Meanwhile, in July 1738, a horse was stolen from the Revd Charles Townsend of Pinchbeck, Lincolnshire, a recently ordained deacon. It was a brown bay gelding, worth £5, and the thief took it to John Turpin, who later admitted that 'he bought the said gelding from his son Richard Turpin'. Perhaps Turpin was seen by neighbours in the little village and perhaps they wondered where John Turpin had suddenly acquired a new horse from. Someone told the constable and/or a JP and so John Turpin was committed to Chelmsford prison on 12 September 1738 'for stealing'.[3]

Returning to Yorkshire, there is always the likelihood that a man who carries a gun will use it. On Monday 2 October 1738, Palmer, returning from a day's shooting, was walking along the high street of Brough and saw one of the cockerels belonging to Francis Hall. He shot and killed it. A neighbour by the name of John Robinson saw what happened and said 'Mr Palmer, you have done wrong in shooting your landlord's Cock'. Palmer replied, 'If he had only staid whilst he charged his piece, he would shoot him too'.

Robinson left the scene and went to see Hall and told him what had happened. The two men then went to see George Crowle (1696–1754) of Springhead, an MP for Hull from 1724–42 and a Commissioner for the Navy from 1732. As a JP, he signed a warrant for Palmer's arrest and on the next day Palmer was taken.[4] There is no record that Palmer put up any resistance and this seems strange; nor did he try to escape, and as shall be noted, he was allowed to ride his own horse to the court on the next day. Firstly, he was armed with at least one pistol, and secondly, when members of the Gregory gang had been apprehended in 1735, they usually put up a stiff resistance before being taken. He had shot dead Morris in 1737 when he was in danger of being apprehended. Perhaps Palmer did not appreciate the peril he was in, or perhaps he did not care, given how he had boasted to Harris about being an armed robber. This attitude would not bode well for him if he kept it up. His once strong instinct for survival seems to have deserted him.

Furthermore, quite why Palmer shot a cock in broad daylight and in front of a witness is never explained. He may have been angry and wanted to let off steam, but he must have also known that he was committing a crime. Yet thoughtless anger not only led him to the deed, but stopped him from apologising and promising to recompense the owner, which should have settled the matter reasonably amicably and was commonplace at the time as it saved all concerned the time and expense of court proceedings. This would be ultimately fatal and would take him one step nearer the gallows. Possibly, having escaped the law for so long, he was contemptuous of it.

At a General Quarter Sessions, held at Beverley on 3 October, Palmer was brought before the assembled JPs. These were Crowle, Marmaduke Constable and Hugh Bethell, a former sheriff of Yorkshire from 1734–35. They demanded from Palmer sureties for his appearance at the next court sessions, but these he refused to give. Why he chose to do this, unless he was really friendless and moneyless, is again hard to imagine, unless he did not realise how serious matters were. He was committed to the house of correction. The order read as follows:

> 'To the Master or Keeper of the House of Correction at Beverley
>
> Whereas it appears to us, upon the Informations of divers credible persons, That John Palmer of Welton of the County of York, is a very dangerous person, and we requiring sureties for his good behaviour, until the next General Quarter Sessions of the Peace for the East Riding of the County of York, which he said the John Palmer refused to find, These are therefore to command you to receive into your Custody the Body of the said John Palmer, and him safely keep until he shall be discharged by the due Course of Law, and hereof fail not at your peril. Given under our hands and seals the 3rd day of October 1738'.[5]

Evidence of Palmer's culpability had been provided by witnesses. The first testimony was from Abraham Green and John Robinson, labourers of Brough, both of whom were illiterate:

> 'This informant Abraham Green saith that John Palmer of Welton aforesaid did on the second day of October instant at Brough aforesaid with a Gunn did kill a tame fowl which did belong to Francis Hall of Brough aforesaid Neatheard and did throw the said Fowl into the fields of Elloughton in the said riding and Brough aforesaid and this Informant John Robinson saith that he did see the said John Palmer on the second day at Brough aforesaid kill the said Fowl belonging to the said Francis Hall and this informant reprimanding the said John Palmer concerning the same he the said John Palmer did threaten to shoot this Informant'.[6]

Harris, who was literate, gave additional information:

'This Informant Saith that on or abt Trinity Monday [6 June 1737] was Twelve months one John Palmer came to this Informant's house at Brough aforesaid and boarded with this Informant at Brough aforesaid four or five months and during that time went from this Examinant's house over the water into the County of Lincoln at divers times and at the said times returned to this Informant's house att Brough aforesaid with severall horses at a time which he sold and disposed off to diverse persons in the County of York and this Informant inquiring of the said John Palmer the place of his abode he the said John Palmer told his Information that he lived at Long Sutton with his Father and that his Sister kept his Father's house there and the reason of the John Palmer's leaving his Father was for debt and was feared of being arrested by bailiffs and say'd that if they once catched him they would kill him and this Informant answered and say'd it would be very hard to kill a man for debt and that he went unarmed but the said Palmer then told this informant if he would go over the water with him he the sd Palmer wod shew him such a pair of pistolls as he this informant never saw in his Life and that he did not fear the Bailiffs for in plain terms I am every thing or words to that effect and further this Informant saith that at the same time the said Palmer wod go over with him says the said Palmer twenty pounds is as easily gott as two pence he then had laid upon the Table to pay for a pint of ale and then say'd drink about not catch me not have me but before they do catch me a great deal of blood shall be spilt'.[7]

The magistrates continued in their investigation and procured information from people in Welton and Brough. It seemed that Palmer often went to Lincolnshire and returned with horses and plenty of money. The horses were then sold and the suspicion emerged that he was 'either a Highwayman or Horsestealer'. They questioned Palmer again, in particular about where he had lived and what his business was. He replied:

'He had about two years before lived at Long Sutton in Lincolnshire, and was by Trade a Butcher, That his Father then lived at Long Sutton, and his Sister kept his Father's House there, but he having contracted a great many Debts, for sheep that proved rotten, so that he was not able to pay for them, he was therefore obliged to abscond and come to live in Yorkshire'.[8]

This was not a clever story, not only because it was false, but it could also be proved to be false. The truth was soon to come out and would make matters worse. A little of the story was true; he had been a butcher and since September 1738 his sister and her husband had kept his father's house. Perhaps the part about debts and rotten sheep is also autobiographical, referring to the collapse of his former legitimate occupation, though several years previously. When people tell lies or invent new names, it is common for them to retain some of their former identity and biography.

The JPs decided to send a messenger into Lincolnshire to verify this story. Appleton wrote a letter to Long Sutton and this letter was sent by special messenger to Mr Delamare, a Lincolnshire JP. Appleton received the following reply:

'That the said John Palmer had lived there for three quarters of a year, and was accused before him of sheep stealing, whereupon he issued out a warrant against Palmer, who was thereupon apprehended, but made his escape from the Constable, and soon after such an escape, Mr Delamare had several informations lodged before him against the said Palmer, for Suspicion of Horse stealing, And that Palmers' father did not live at Long Sutton, neither did he know where he lived, therefore desired Palmer might be secured and he would make further Inquiry about the horses stolen, and he would bind over some persons to prosecute him at the next Assizes'.[9]

On receiving this letter, Appleton communicated with Crowle and he went to Beverley the next day. Crowle concluded that such was Palmer's villainy that he should be transferred from Beverley to the county prison in York.[10] The situation for Palmer was now becoming far more serious; he was no longer a petty offender but a serious one indeed. Again it is uncertain whether he realised the gravity of his situation. The full extent of his crimes in Yorkshire and Lincolnshire are unknown and he may have committed more than the known animal thefts.

George Smith and Joshua Miller took Palmer to York on 16 October, handcuffed, and were reimbursed £2 2s at the Michaelmas sessions by order of Jonathan Midgeley, the county treasurer.[11] Palmer made no attempt to escape. This was the real ride to York; not from London but from Beverley; not pursued by lawmen but accompanied by them as their prisoner. A month later two men came from Lincolnshire and challenged Palmer for having taken a mare and a foal from them which had been subsequently sold to a Captain George Dawson of Harrison's battalion of infantry, and of Ferriby, Yorkshire (not far from Welton), and also that the horse Palmer had ridden into Beverley had been stolen from Heckington Farm in Lincolnshire.[12]

Palmer was now residing in the purpose-built Baroque York prison, only three decades old, built in 1705. Apparently it was 'a prison the most stately and complete of any in the Kingdom, if not Europe... The felons are allowed straw, and their beds are now raised from the Ground: and there is an infirmary apart from the Common Prison, to which the sick are conveyed, and a Surgeon has an appointed salary to attend'.[13] It was perhaps the first time Palmer had been to York, but he was probably unable to appreciate the beauties and glories of the city as described by Daniel Defoe in the previous decade. Palmer was housed in one of the cells on the ground floor; each held up to three prisoners.[14]

Thomas Griffiths (1696–1751) was governor of York prison. He was also a tanner, entrepreneur and local property-owner and left much of the running of the prison to the under-gaoler. He was later to acquire an unsavoury reputation, having been allegedly involved in the death of a prisoner in 1741, but his responsibility could not be proved. In January 1746 he was alleged to have stopped well-wishers supplying prisoners with food and drink. He was dismissed in the next month and was later imprisoned in the same prison as a debtor. Ironically Marmaduke Constable, who was one of the three JPs who sent Palmer to York Castle, also spent time in prison in 1745–46 under suspicion of Jacobitism.[15]

Meanwhile, Turpin's father claimed that the horse he was accused of having stolen was allegedly left to him by his son in order to pay for his son's diet and lodgings; this is the one Turpin had stolen from Charles Townsend.[16] Turpin became aware of this because he later wrote a letter to his brother-in-law, not his father, and so must also have known that his taking the horse to his father had been the cause of the old man's troubles.

It was early in the new year that Palmer's real identity was revealed. Despite Turpin's description having been circulated since June 1737, no one in Yorkshire realised who Palmer really was. This is despite him arriving as a stranger in a small Yorkshire village, clearly from afar as he did not have a Yorkshire accent and so would clearly stand out (the author, Yorkshire bred, recalls on arriving at university in the south of England that his accent was noticeable and initially indecipherable) as an obvious outsider. Possibly they did not conceive that a man who committed crimes in and near London could be in their northern county. His arrest and incarceration went initially unreported in the press, as it seemed that this was merely a run-of-the-mill offender, of no great importance. A journalist stated, after noting the description circulated, 'Yet people are so regardless of these Publick notices, or throw them by, that he has been undiscover'd'.[17]

This all changed when a letter was sent by Palmer to Pomp Rivinal, his brother-in-law, apparently on 6 February 1739. Palmer had been in York prison for four months; enough time to realise that he was in mortal danger and that he needed to swallow his pride and try to seek help from the only ones who might help him: his family. The following letter is deemed to have been sent by him, and though the actual text is disputed as the original no longer survives, there is no reasonable doubt about a letter being sent by him with some of the following sentiments therein:

> 'Dear Brother [in law],
> I am sorry to acquaint you that I am now in confinement at York Castle, for horse stealing. If I could procure any evidences from London, to give me a character, that would go a great way towards me being acquitted, I have not been long in this county before being apprehended, so it would pass off the readier; for Heaven's sake, dear brother, don't neglect me, you'll know what I mean when I say
>
> I am yours
> John Palmer'[18]

It is not certain who could have been found in London who would have given Turpin a good character. Having witnesses to give character references was certainly a useful device to help a defendant either be acquitted or to receive a lighter sentence, so to ask for this made sense. In 1775, at a trial at Wells, the Revd James Woodforde was asked by the defendant to be a character witness as he was a neighbour of his, yet since he thought him guilty he did not attend.[19]

The letter was addressed to the Bell in Hempstead, which was being minded by Rivinal and Turpin's sister, for the elder Turpin was incarcerated in Chelmsford prison on suspicion of being involved in his son's horse theft. In the eighteenth century, it was the recipient who paid the postage for letters addressed to them; there were no pre-paid postage stamps until the next century. Rivinal saw that the letter was sent from York, but as he claimed to know no one in the city, he refused to pay the postage.[20] Assuming the letter was a single sheet of paper the cost would have been 7d in total, as post had to be routed through London and rates were 4d for over 80 miles and then a further 3d for under 80 miles from London. It might also have to be collected from the nearest town, Saffron Walden.[21] Alternatively Rivinal might have recognised the handwriting and refused to have anything to do with his villainous brother-in-law, whose criminal record he would have known all too well. Whatever his reason, the result was the same. He did not collect the letter. Had he paid the postage, Palmer's true identity might never have been revealed.

In early February James Smith recognised the handwriting on the letter, and reported this to an Essex JP. There were other letters from York, the texts of which do not survive in any form, and they demanded £10 and two witnesses. Another referred to Betty Millington, allegedly Turpin's cousin, but really his wife. Meanwhile, a written description of Palmer was asked for from York and was supplied; Smith thought that Palmer was Turpin. Smith then came to York and identified him. Smith was also examined by George Nelthorpe, John Adams and Thomas Place, three Yorkshire JPs, and a copy of his testimony was sent to the Duke of Newcastle. This read as follows:

> 'That he saw a letter directed to one Pomp Rivernall of Hempstead in Essex with the York post stamp upon it and the said Rivernall refusing to take the letter in [he] acquainted one Thomas Stubbing of Bumpstead Helion in the County of Essex Esquire, who sent to Saffron Walden Post office and payd the postage. And this informant

upon perusing the said letter had a suspision that it was Turpin's handwriting, and four of his majesty's Justices of the Peace in the County of Essex desired this Informant to go to York Castle to see whether it was the said Turpin or not who says and declares before us that the person now shewn to this Informant is Richard Turpin and no other person. And this Informant is the better able to know the said Turpin by being bred and Born in the same Town with him also went to school with this Informant and hath constantly for several years since been in company with him till within these three or four years, and further saith that the said Pomp Rivernall Marryed one Dorothy Turpin, the said Richard Turpin's own sister'.[22]

Meanwhile in York, rumours about Palmer were circulating and wagers were laid on the incarcerated man's real identity, with 10 guineas to one that the man in question was really Turpin.[23] In the eighteenth century gambling was rife among all classes and this seemed a novel approach to one of life's pleasures. Turpin became incredibly popular once his identity was known and so, 'A great concourse flock to see him, and they all give him money'.[24]

William Jessop, a farmer and apothecary in Holmfirth in the west riding of Yorkshire, relayed rumours that came his way on the subject. In one diary entry on 24 March he noted; 'I hear it is not Turpin who is confined at York Castle'. Eight days later he wrote, 'It is confirmed that it is Turpin who was confined in York Castle, and hath took his trial for horse stealing & is condemned'. This is indicative of the interest that Turpin engendered, as well as the rumours that were passing as news.[25]

Those in authority were convinced of Palmer's identity and the next question was what to do with this new information. Knowing that Turpin was a criminal of national importance, Thomas Place, who was also Recorder of the City of York, wrote to Newcastle on 24 February, beginning with the information that Palmer had been at York Castle since 16 October, suspected of stealing sheep and horses. He continued:

'From ye information taken yesterday before me & the other two gentleman, whose names are subscribed to it (of which ye enclosed is a true copy) & from many other circumstances concurring it severally appeared that ye person is Turpin against whom a proclamation issued: he long persisted in denying his knowledge of ye informer & of everything contained in ye information. I went to him again in ye evening he then confessed to me that ye information was true & that he was Turpin & that he had been in the neighbourhood of Hull for about ye last two years so that I think no doubt can remain as to ye identity of this person. I thought it my duty to give your Grace ye most early notice of this. Orders are given for his strict confinement till His Majesty's pleasure concerning him can be known'.[26]

Newcastle evidently passed on the letter to a colleague, Dudley Ryder (1691–1757), the Attorney General since 1737, who in turn gave, on 28 February, his opinion to Newcastle:

'In obedience to your Grace's commands, by [Andrew] Stone's letter, of yesterday, whereby I am desired to give my opinion what orders it may be proper for your Grace to give, with regard to the removing Turpin, the noted highwayman, and murderer, from York, or to the prosecution of him afterwards.

I have taken the papers transmitted to me therewith, and which are herewith enclosed, into consideration, but there being no informations laid before me relating to the crimes mentioned in his Majesty's proclamation, I am not able to advise your Grace what orders may be proper to be given for his prosecution: but as it appears, by His Majesty's proclamation, that he be charged with divers capital crimes, committed in or about London, I am humbly of opinion it may be proper to give directions for his removal hither by Habeas Corpus, from York gaol, in order to be tried here'.[27]

On 1 March Newcastle replied to Place:

'I have received the favour of your letter of the 24th of last month, giving an account of Turpin, the highwayman, being confined in York gaol. I shall immediately take the opinion of His Majesty's Attorney General, in what manner it may be proper to proceed upon this occasion, with which I will acquaint you, as soon as possible. In the meant time you will take the most effectual care, that the prisoner may be kept and the safest custody and that all necessary securities be used to prevent any possibility of his making his escape'.[28]

Clearly Newcastle saw Turpin as a very important prisoner and as a dangerous criminal who had to be kept secure. Newcastle sent another letter, presumably having received Ryder's additional advice on legal matters, providing further information to show Place that Turpin was indeed a dangerous man:

'I send you herewith the coroner's inquest for the county of Essex taken in May 1737 by which you will see that Richard Turpin now a prisoner in the county Gaol of York stands charged with murder.

I also inclose several informations relating to other felonies committed by the said Richard Turpin. And I desire that you would lay them before the judge of the Assizes when Turpin is tried, to the end, that in case he should be acquitted at the present assizes at York of the felony for which he is to be there tried, he may not be discharged upon such acquittal, but be continued under close confinement in the Gaol at York till he shall be removed in which case of the trial of the facts mentioned in the inclosed inquest and informations'.[29]

Another letter claimed:

'He has been examined this morning before two or three more JPs and confronted by his countryman, who they say, knows him very well and affirms that he is Turpin and he has been seen by abundance of gentlemen, as well as by many of the inferior sort, this afternoon, and several persons were present at his examination, who were all of opinion that he is the man'.[30]

Unusually the magistrates garnered praise from the press on this occasion:

'We cannot help observing upon this Occasion, that each of the Magistrates before mentioned have acted with great prudence and Assiduity in Discharge of their Trust, and deserve the Thanks of their Country for bringing so Notorious and dangerous a Rogue to his due Punishment'.[31]

An extract from a letter in York on 24 February claimed, 'You have heard that a man has been committed to our castle for horse stealing, who by means of a letter written by a prisoner here, which fell into honest hands near London, is suspected to be the notorious Robber, Turpin'.[32]

Most criminals, when choosing an alias, use name/s which are already familiar to them. Turpin was no exception. John was his father's Christian name and also that of one of his brothers, as well as being a very common name. Palmer was a corruption of Parmenter, his mother's maiden name, though some once thought that Palmer was his wife's maiden name. Possibly he did use Parmenter but Yorkshire people misunderstood his pronunciation and translated it as Palmer.

After Turpin had been identified, he and two other prisoners tried to escape. The plan was to kill the turnkey and the porter and then to ride off on Thomas Griffiths' mare. However, they were detected and stopped. Turpin was a particularly popular – or notorious – prisoner and many people came to the prison to see him, after having paid a fee to Griffiths. Turpin was confident that his future would be rosy: 'He seems very sure that nobody alive can hurt him' and told Griffiths, with whom he used to hunt, that they would do so again on another day. However, every night he was put in the condemned hole which was a very secure place.[33]

There was talk that Turpin might be sent to Chelmsford prison from York Castle to be tried for the robberies he committed in Essex.[34] One newspaper even stated this as a fact and doubted he would reach Chelmsford in time for the assizes there.[35] However, his father, who was languishing in that gaol and who was served a bill of indictment in March, 'the old man's general good character and Innocency, of the fact laid to his charge, plainly appearing to the satisfaction of the Grand Jury' and Sir Charles Caesar, baronet and Grand Jury foreman, found the bill ignoramus and so the old man was released.[36] What convinced him of Turpin the elder's innocence was that the other prisoners tried to break out and the old man let the keeper into the secret, as he was not one of their group.[37]

Crowle later noted:

> 'upon the first discovery of Turpin's being in York gaol, it was the Attorney General's opinion that he should be brought up here [London] to be tried which would have been a great expense to the Crown, and then doubtful

119

whether he would have been convicted here, but upon the assurances that Mr Crowle gave the Attorney General that there was sufficient proof against him at York he gave it as his opinion and consented to his trial there, by which means a very large sum of money was saved to the Crown'.[38]

Therefore the trial went ahead at York. This could have been because most of the witnesses to his crimes in and near London were dead or transported, such as Wheeler and King, Jones and Rowden, and his crimes there had taken place some years ago so the recollections of others might be less reliable. Whereas the crimes of horse stealing had been recent and there were reliable witnesses. The crimes committed in and near London were more serious, but horse stealing could merit the death penalty as well as murder and robbery. A guilty verdict in York was more likely than one in London and the outcome would be the same, so the trial was held in York.

The assize judge was Sir William Chapple (c.1676–1745) of the Court of the King's Bench. He had been called to the Bar in 1709 and had been a Dorset MP from 1723 until 1737 when he became a judge. Thomas Place and Richard Crowle (1700–1757), barrister of the Inner Temple and younger brother of George Crowle, led the case for the prosecution. Defendants were not usually represented in court but could speak on their own behalf and question witnesses. They began by examining the first witness, namely Thomas Creasy, the owner of the mare allegedly stolen by Turpin. Thomas Kyll, a 'professor of shorthand' took the trial notes down and later published them.

The assize indictment of 1 March read:

'To wit the jurors for our Lord the King upon their oath present that John Palmer otherwise Pawmer otherwise Richard Turpin, late of the castle of York Labourer on the first day of March in the twelfth year of our Sovereign Lord George the second now King of Great Britain etc. at

the parish of Welton in the county aforesaid one gelding
of a black colour of the price of three pounds of the goods
and chattels of one Thomas Creasy then and there being
found did then and there feloniously steal take and lead
away against the peace of our said Lord King his Crown
and dignity'.[39]

The jury was made up of the following men, some of whom can
be identified using the 1741 York poll book: William Calvert
(joiner/carpenter of Jubbergate, Tory/Whig), Samuel Waddington,
William Popplewell, John Lambert, Robert Wiggins, William Wade
(woolcomber of Swinegate, Whig), Thomas Simpson (servant/
shoemaker of Lendale/Fossgate, Tory), George Smeaton, Robert
Thompson (whitesmith/miller of Colliergate/Goodramgate, Tory),
William Frank, James Boyes and Thomas Clarke (grocer/miller of
Coney Street/Skeldergate, Tory).[40]

The assizes began on 19 March. Of the twenty-five people on trial,
the first was Lawrence Roberts of York, accused of burglary in York.
He was found guilty and sentenced to death. Naomi Hollings was
found guilty of the same offence and was likewise sentenced. Thomas
Hadfield was found guilty 'for Robbery on the Highways'; perhaps
while in gaol he and Turpin compared notes. John Robinson and John
Monkton were also found guilty; all three were sentenced to hang
unless they could gain a pardon or a reprieve.[41]

On 22 March it was Turpin's turn. One of the two prosecutors
began to examine the first witness, Thomas Creasy:

'Where do you live?'

'At Heckington, in the county of Lincoln'.

'Pray sir, had you a mare and a foal?'

'Yes'.

'Where did they go for feed?'

'On Heckington Common'.

'When did you first miss them?'

'Upon a Thursday morning I was enquiring for them and they could not be found'.

'What day of the month did you think it might happen?'

'Upon the 18th or 19th day of August'.

'What month?'

'The month of August last'.

'You say you missed them on the 18th or 19th of August last pray then when did you see them last?'

'The Day next before I lost them'.

'When you then missed your mare and foal, what did you do to get intelligence about them?'

'I hired men and horses and rode 40 miles around about us to hear of them and got then cry'd in all the market towns about us'.

'How long was it before you knew of the mare and foal, or who told you of them?'[42]

'One John Baxter, a neighbour of mine, told me he had been at Pocklington Fair in Yorkshire, and lying all night at Brough, he happened to hear of a man that was taken up and sent to the House of Correction at Beverley for shooting a Game Cock who had such a mare and foal as mine: Upon which information I came to Ferraby near Beverley and put up my horse at Richard Grassby's, who keeps a publick house and began to enquire of him about my mare and foal, Who told me there was such a mare and foal in their neighbourhood; which I thought by the description he gave me, to be mine, so then I told him I was come to enquire about such a mare and foal'.

'Did you know the marks on the mare and foal as he described them to you?'

'Yes I did and I told him these marks agreed with my mare and foal, before I did see them'.

'Was it when your Neighbour came Home, you made this Inquiry?'

'Yes it was, and by this information of his, I went to Ferraby and give at the Landlord and people an Account of their marks'.

'Describe their Marks'.

'She was a black mare, blind of the near eye, having a little white on the near fore foot, and also the near Hind Foot, and scratched (greased) on both the Hind Feet, and the near Fore Foot, with I's, or marks, resembling that letter, burnt on the near shoulder, and a Star on the Forehead'.[43]

'How long have you had her?'

'I did breed her myself, and kept her till she was ten years old'.

'Did you give this account to Richard Grassby, before he shewed you her?'

'Yes, I did'.

'Had the foal any marks?'

'Yes it did, a black ball'.

'Where did you see her?'

'At the stable door, they fetched her out for me, and I knew her'.

'From all these marks you were very positive that the mare and the foal were yours?'

'Yes, I am sure they were mine'.

'Did you receive them at that time?'

'No, I did not get them then'.

'Are you sure the mare and foal were yours?'

'Yes indeed I am'.

'When you came to Ferraby, did you tell these marks, or the description of them, and to whom?'

'Yes indeed, I told them to Richard Grasby, the Landlord'.

The court then asked Turpin: 'Have you any Question to ask this Witness? You have heard what he has said against you'. Turpin then spoke for the first time in the trial.

'I cannot say any Thing, for I have not any Witnesses come this day, as I expected, therefore beg your Lordship put off my trial 'till another day'.

'We cannot put off this Affair: if you had spoke and desired a reasonable Time before the Jury was sworn and charged, it might have been[44] granted to you. Now you are too late – the Jury cannot be discharged. You have Liberty allowed you to ask any question of the Witness'.

'This Witness is wrong because on the 18th of August I was here in York Castle'.

This was a nonsensical lie; Turpin was not at York Castle until 16 October 1738 and was not even charged until earlier that month. In August he was still a free man and this was immediately pointed out in court. He clearly could not think of anything better to say. 'No sir, you were not here the 18th of August'.

Griffiths was then called and he stated that Turpin was not under his custody until October 1738.

Turpin then changed tack and referred to Creasy, saying: 'I never did see this man in my life'. He then addressed Creasy directly.

'Do you know one Whitehead?'

'Yes'.

'He's the man I bought the mare and foal off'.

Captain Dawson was then called as the second witness.

'Pray sir, inform us what you know of this affair?'

'I was one Morning riding to Welton, and met a Man leading a Mare and Foal, and asked him if that was his Mare and Foal. He told me No, but they belonged to one Palmer. I asked him if he would dispose of the Foal? He said Palmer was coming up the street. I turned about, and saw Palmer, who told me it was his Mare and Foal, and they were bred in Lincolnshire. I asked him if he would dispose of the Foal? He said he would rather sell the Mare with her. I reply'd, I had no occasion for the mare, only the foal, and asked him the price of the Foal.[45]

He said Three Guineas. I told him, it was too much to ask for the Foal, and offer'd him Two Guineas, and said I would not give him more, upon which I went about my Business, and afterwards I observed the Prisoner coming up a Hill with the Mare and Foal, and as I was going along, a Countryman said Sir, you have been bargaining and bid Two Guineas for the Foal, you'll see him come back again, and if you please, I fancy you may have it. I said, Let him come to my House, and I will pay him the Two Guineas: So about Three o'clock in the Afternoon, he came with the Mare and Foal, and I had them both put in a Stable; I went then to pay the Prisoner Palmer'.

'Pray who was it that brought the Mare and Foal to your House?'

'Nobody brought the Mare and Foal to me but himself. I went, and paid him for the Foal Two Guineas, and then he told me I might buy the Mare, for she was worth money. I told him, I had no Occasion for the Mare, but the Prisoner being a little pressing about it, I told him I had a horse of no great value, and if he would change, or let me have the Mare to nurse the Foal, I would rather do it. He did not like the first Proposal, but I told him I would not take the Mare except he would have the Horse, so I gave him Four Guineas, but being obliged to go to my Regiment, I left the Place soon after'.

'When did you leave the Country?'

'Soon after, I think, about October I went away[46] and gave Richard Grassby the care of the Mare, and he had the Liberty to work her'.

Turpin was then addressed.

'Have you any thing to say about what the Captain hath said against you?'

'Nothing at all'.

The third witness, Richard Grassby, was then called to the witness stand.

'What have you to say about the Mare?'

'I had Liberty to work her'.

'How long have you known the Prisoner?'

'I have seen the Prisoner several Times since, and I think, I have known him about Two Years'.

'What manner of Visible Living had he?'

'He had no settl'd way of living that I know of at all, tho' a dealer, yet he was a Stranger, and lived like a Gentleman'.

'Had you the Mare of Captain Dawson?'

'Yes, I had the Mare and Foal'.

'Did he give you the Liberty to work them?'

'Yes'.

'About what time did you work her?'

'About October 12th, I think'.

'Did you work her?'

'Yes, I did, for I had a Close belonging to the Captain'.

'Was the Mare challenged when you had her?'

'Yes she was. I had been drawing with her, when Thomas Creasy came to me, and gave me an Account very fully of all her Mark, before he saw her'.[47]

'Then when he saw her was that the very Mare and Foal?'

'Yes the very same'.

'Do you remember this Man?'

'Yes, for he offered to sell me Horses'.

'What do you know further about Palmer?'

'He was about two years at Welton'.

'Did you know him there?'

'Yes, he was reckon'd a Stranger'.

'In what manner of way did he support himself, or how did he live?'

'He lived like a Gentleman'.

'What time was it that you saw the Mare?'

'I saw the Mare in August in his possession'.

Turpin was then addressed by the court.

'Will you ask this witness any questions?'

'No, I have nothing to say'.

'Can you be positive that Palmer offered this Mare to sale?'

'Yes indeed I can and I am positive that this is the man' looking at Turpin.

George Goodyear was then called as the court's fourth witness.

'Do you know of a Mare and Foal that was lost near where you live?'

'Yes very well'.

'Do you know about what time this Mare and Foal was lost?'

'Yes I know and I remember the time they were missing, it was towards the latter end of August'.[48]

'When did you see the Mare?'

'In August'.

'Have you seen the Mare again?'

'Yes'.

'Was it the same you saw before?'

'Yes'.

'Are you positively sure?'

'Yes, I am perfectly sure'.

The court then turned to Turpin. 'Would you ask this witness any questions?' As on previous occasions he had nothing to say in his defence and made no effort at all. He replied, 'None'. Richard Grassby was recalled to the witness box.

'When did you see this Mare?'

'In August'.

Then James Smith and Edward Saward, who had been brought from Essex as witnesses, came forward, to identify Palmer as Turpin the highwayman. Why this was necessary is another question because Turpin was not on trial as a highwayman, but as a horse thief. However, their evidence would go to show that Palmer was Turpin and the jury may well have known that he was a notorious criminal; these facts would not inspire any of the jury to an acquittal. James Smith was the first to take the stand.

'Do you know the prisoner Palmer at the Bar? Look at him and tell what you know about him'.

'Yes I knew him at Hempstead in Essex, where he was born. I knew him ever since he was a Child'.

'What is his name?'

'Richard Turpin. I knew his Father, and all his relations. He married one of my father's Maids'.[49]

'What? Was you with him frequently?'

'Yes'.

'When did you see him last?'

''Tis about five years since I saw him'.

'Have you any particular Marks to show this is the man?'

'This is the very man'.

'Did you not teach him at school?'

'Yes, I did, but he was only learning to make Letters, and I believe he was three quarters of a year with me'.

'Do you think this is he?'

'Yes, this is the man'.

'As you lived there, why did you come down to this place?'

'Happening to be at the Post office, where I saw a Letter, directed to Turpin's Brother in Law, who, as I was informed, would not lose the Letter and pay Postage, upon that Account, taking particular Notice thereof, I thought at first I remembered the Superscription, and concluded it to be the Hand-writing of the Prisoner Turpin, whereupon I carried the Letter before a Magistrate, who broke the same open (the Letter was subscribed John Palmer) and found it sent from York Castle: I had seen several of Dick Turpin's Bills, and I knew his Hand'.

'Are you sure this is his letter?'

The letter was then produced in court.

'Yes I am sure this is his Letter'.

'Was that the cause of your coming down?'

'Yes'.[50]

'How happened you to take notice of a Letter?'

'Seeing the York stamp'.

'From these circumstances, did you come down here?'

'Yes indeed, I did come on this account'.

'When you came to the Castle, did you challenge him or know him?'

'Yes, I did, upon the first view of him and pointed him out from among all the rest of the prisoners'.

'How long is it since you saw him last?'

'I think about five years'.

'Do you know any thing more of him?'

'I think he might be about eleven or twelve years old when I went to the Excise and he worked with his Father, who was a Butcher'.

'Was he ever set up in the Butcher Trade?'

'Yes I know he was'.

'How long might he live in that way?'

'I cannot tell. He lived at (word unknown, possibly Buckhurst Hill) in Essex, and left it after about six years, then kept a publick house'.

'Did you afterwards see him?'

'Yes, I saw him afterwards, six miles from thence'.

'What became of him then?'[51]

'I do not know more, only the last time I saw him, I sold him a Grey Mare, about five years ago, before my Brother died'.

'Do you know no more of him?'

'This I know of him, and I have been many times in his company, and frequently with him'.

'Palmer, you are allowed the liberty to ask Mr Smith any Question'.

'I never knew him'.

Smith's words were the same as he previously gave to the JPs when arriving earlier at York Castle.

Edward Saward of Hempstead, Essex, was the next witness to be called.

'Do you know this Richard Turpin?'

'Yes. I do know him. He was born and brought up at the Bell, his Father kept a publick house'.

'How long have you known him?'

'I have known him these twenty two years; I cannot say I know exceedingly exact, but about twenty two years upon my soul (court then reproved him for not needing to swear again). I know him ever since he was a boy, and lived at the Bell'.

'How long did he live there?'

'I cannot exactly tell, he lived with his father and I was very great with him'.[52]

'Did you know him after he set up for himself?'

'Yes, I knew him perfectly well then, and I have bought a good many Joints of Meat from him, upon my soul'. Another reprimand, Saward was encouraged to be serious and not make rash comments.

'Did you know him since he left Hempstead?'

'I was with him at his house in Hempstead'.

'Did you see him there?'

'I saw him frequently, I can't tell you how often'.

'How many years is it since he left Hempstead?'

'He came backwards and forwards'.

'How long is it since you saw him last?'

'About five or six years'.

'And can you say this assuredly or firmly?'

'Yes, and I never saw him since'.

'Had he any settled dwelling?'

'Not that I know of'.

'Now look at the Prisoner, is this Richard Turpin?'

'Yes, yes, Dick Turpin, the son of John Turpin who keeps the Bell at Hempstead'.

Turpin denied he knew the man, but eventually claimed he knew Smith.

'Mr Smith, when you spoke to him at the Castle, did you know him?'

'Yes, I did and he did confess he knew me, and said unto me two or three times, Let us[53] hung our eyes in drink and I drank with him, which is this Richard Turpin'.

The court then addressed Turpin.

'There was a Mare and Foal lost, what account can you give, how you came by that Mare and Foal?'

'I was going up to Lincolnshire to see John Whitehead, there was a Mare and a Foal before his door, and I was there, drinking'.

'Does he keep a House and sell ale?'

'Yes'.

'What place was it?'

'Within a mile of Heckington. The man had been at a Fair and bought a mare and Foal, and he wanted to sell them again'.

'What time was this?'

'In August. I asked him the price and gave him seven Guineas for Mare and Colt; he gave me back Half a

Crown. I staid all night and came away next Morning. I went to all markets and whenever I went, I rode with them, without ever being challenged'.

'Have you any Thing more to say?'

I have sent a SubPoena, for a Man and his Wife, they were present when I bought them'.

'What was his Name?'

'I cannot tell, therefore I desire some longer Time that these witnesses may be examined. I also sent a Special Messenger with a letter'.

Mr Griffiths was summoned and said that the messenger had returned. 'What say you to that?' Turpin was silent.

'If you have any witnesses, you should have[54] had them before this time; have you any witnesses here present?'

'I have none at present, but tomorrow I will have them. I am sure no man will say ill of me in Yorkshire'.

'Have you any witnesses here?'

'Yes. William Thompson Esq, also one Whithead and a Mr Gill'.

All these were called by the court but none appeared.

'The jury cannot stay and you can see there is none to appear for you'.

'I thought I should have been removed to Essex, for I did not expect to be tried in this Country, therefore I could not prepare witness to my character'.

The Judge then gave the charge to the jury.

'The Reasons I had for changing my name were that I having been long out of my trade, and run myself into debt, I changed my name, to my mother's which was Palmer'.

'What was your name before you came to Lincolnshire?'

'Turpin'.

'Was it Richard Turpin?'

'Yes'.

'I thought I should have been removed and got my trial in Essex'.

'You have deceived yourself in thinking so'.

The jury then, without having to leave court for discussion, gave their verdict: guilty.[55]

Turpin was then indicted a second time, for having stolen a black gelding, the property of Thomas Creasy. The latter was called to the witness box.

'Was you in possession of a gelding, August last?'

'Yes I was'.

'About what time did you miss it?'

'The 18th day of August I missed this Gelding'.

'Where did you find him and what colour was he?'

'I found him at the Blue Bell in Beverley'.

'How came you to hear he was there?'

'Richard Grassby was the person who told me it was my Gelding'.

'Did you describe the Gelding to him?'

'Yes, and then he told me it was the same'.

'Upon that what did you do?'

'I went to the landlord of the house in Beverley and described him to him'.

'Do you remember what Description you gave him of the Gelding?'

'Yes, the Description was of a black Gelding with a little star on his forehead'.

'What did he (the Landlord) do then?'

'I went with him and he showed me the horse'.[56]

'Are you sure the gelding he showed you was yours?'

'Yes I am'.

'But are you very sure that was your Gelding?'

'Yes, yes, indeed I am'.

'Did you show him to any person?'

'Yes I did, I shewed him to Carey Gill, the constable at Welton'.

Gill was then addressed:

'What do you know concerning the prisoner?'

'He was taken up by me for shooting a cock, upon which I carried him to Beverley Sessions'.

'Which way did you carry him or how did he go?'

'He rode upon his own horse and I along with him'.

'What month did this happen in?'

'At Michaelmas Sessions, which was October the 6th'.

'Do you know what horse he rode upon?'

'He rode upon a horse which he called his own'.

'Did you see the horse?'

'Yes, it was the same horse he came from Welton on‘.

Creasy was then questioned.

'How did you get your horse again?'

'I got him from the Justice, by his Order'.

'How many miles was it from home, that you got this horse?'[57]

'It was about fifty miles from the water side to Welton'.

'Was that the same horse you heard described?'

'Yes it was'.

'What marks had he?'

'He was a black gelding with a little star on his forehead, and carried a good tail'.

The court then addressed James Smith.

> 'How long is it since you have known the prisoner at the bar? Look at him again'.
>
> 'I have known him from his infancy, these twenty-two years; and he is the very Richard Turpin which I have known at Hempstead and the very son of John Turpin in that town'.
>
> The court then addressed Turpin.
>
> 'Have you any more to say?'
>
> 'I bought this horse at Whitehead'.

The jury then brought in their verdict: guilty. It is not known if they needed to retire to another room to confer or whether their decision was made in court. The judge then addressed the prisoner, and before he passed the sentence he asked him if there was any reason why he should not do so.

'It is very hard on me my Lord because I was not prepar'd for my defence'.

'Why was you not? You knew the time of the Assizes as well as any person here'.

'Several persons who came to see me, assured me, that I should be removed to Essex to be tried there, for which Reason I thought[58] it was needless to prepare Witnesses for my defence here'.

'Whoever told you so was highly to blame, and as your Country has found you guilty of a crime worthy of death, it is my Office to pronounce sentence against you'.[59]

The trial proceedings probably took about an hour. This will sound very short by twentieth-century standards; the trial of John Haigh in 1949 lasted two days and that was short by the standards of that day – modern trials would take far longer. Yet eighteenth-century trials were usually far shorter and several would occur in a single day; sometimes criminals on trial for the same offence would be tried in batches, for example those of the Gregory gang in trial for the Lawrence farm.

A King's Messenger had been at York Castle, in case Turpin was not convicted, in order to have him sent to Chelmsford.[60] Newcastle had told Place that if Turpin was acquitted, he should be held at York Castle until there were further orders from the Attorney General.[61] Clearly the government was taking no chances; Turpin was in custody and he was not to slip away and would be tried again, on other charges, in another place.

It was recalled after the trial's result that 'the Fellow has made a great noise in the World, he'll now die like a Dog'. Many people had lost money, having made bets that Turpin would indeed be found not guilty.[62]

If Turpin's real identity had not been uncovered, would the result have been any different? Horse theft was a capital offence and the man Turpin was hanged with (John Stead) was another horse thief who had been found guilty of stealing a grey mare worth £3 from one William Hewittson of Sprowston on 1 February 1739. However, we do not know Stead's antecedents. If he had a criminal record and was a bad character he would be more likely to have been hanged, as indeed he was. If Palmer had been tried with an unblemished previous record he might well have been transported – such was the lottery of punishments at this time. Had this happened then the world would never have known the fate of Turpin and it might have been presumed that he had escaped justice, perhaps by escaping overseas, by turning his hand to an honest living, or by dying or being killed. Had this happened it is possible that his later reputation would never have been established. But we must return to reality.

Although there was no court of appeal, it was not uncommon for petitions to be sent to Secretaries of State, asking for a reprieve from the death sentence and for transportation instead. These appeals stressed the good character of the guilty man, his family and his standing in the community, and were often sent and signed by the local elite. This possibility was explored by Turpin, who wrote to his father on 24 March from York Castle, or so a letter published in a contemporary history claimed (the original does not survive):

'Dear and honoured father,

The Witnesses I call'd to my character was William Thompson Esq., Mr Whitehead and Mr Gill, who not being so kind as to appear, as expected, I have the Misfortune to acquaint you that I was convicted the Day before yesterday at the Assizes and am to suffer the 7th of April next for Horse stealing, if you have any love remaining for your once dear son, I hope either you or my brother will go to Colonel Watson and Madam Peck, and if possible prevail on them to intercede for me, that

I may get it off for transportation, I have no other hopes left but this and this is my last petition

> From your unfortunate son
> Richard Turpin'.[63]

On 29 March, Turpin's father wrote to him thus:

> 'I received you letter this instant with a great deal of Grief, according to your Request, I have writ to your Brother John and Madam Peck, to make what intercession can be made to Col. Watson, in order to obtain Transportation for your Misfortune, which had I £100 I would freely part with it to do you good; in the mean time my prayers for you, and for God's sake, give your whole mind to beg of God mercy for your many transgressions, which the Thief upon the Cross received pardon for at the last hour, tho' a very great offender. The Lord be your comfort, and receive you into his Eternal Kingdom.
>
> > I am your distressed, yet loving father
>
> > John Turpin
>
> > Hemstead
>
> All our love to you, who are in much Grief, to subscribe ourselves your distressed brother and sister, with relations'.[64]

John also wrote to his other son, also called John, on the same day:

> 'Dear Son,
>
> I received a Letter from your brother Richard, the 27th instant dated 24 March and he is to suffer the 7th April, which is on Saturday at seven night at York, on the suspicion of stealing a horse or a mare. And now his last

petitions are that I or you would go to Colonel Watson in order to obtain transportation. Tho' he has been remiss in many things yet let your Bowels of Compassion yearn towards him. I'd have you as above mentioned, and be as quick as possible. We are all at present in health but deeply concerned to acquaint you with this

From your dear Father

John Turpin'[65]

Colonel Watson was Jonas Watson (1663–1741) of the Royal Artillery and resident in Great Sampford. Madam Peck was the wife of William Peck of Sampford Hall. Both were prominent residents local to Turpin's father and brother-in-law, and who might well have been thought to be influential enough to assist Turpin, but there is no evidence that they were approached or any suggestion that if they had been they would have exerted themselves on Turpin's behalf.[66]

The author of a contemporary history of Turpin noted that few men, even among robbers and killers condemned to death, could look death in the face without making provision for the afterlife in which their souls would be judged, and a horrible fate in Hell for the unrepentant. Turpin's behaviour, he was shocked to note, was anything but repentant. He recounted:

'Turpin, being committed prisoner to York Castle… liv'd in as much pleasure as the liberties of the prison could afford, eating, drinking and carousing, with anybody that would spend their time with him. Neither did he alter his behaviour after his condemnation. After it was rumoured abroad, that he was the Turpin who rendered himself so notorious for his Robberies in the Southern parts of England, abundance of People from all parts resorted daily to see him. It being about that Time a subject very much disputed in all companies and conversations whether this man was the real individual Turpin, the highwayman or not, a certain young gentleman, who pretended to know him, went one day to see him, to satisfy himself if he was the very man as reported as having viewed him very circumspectly, he told the Keeper he would lay him a wager of half a guinea that this man was not Turpin. Which Turpin hearing, whispered to the Keeper, lay him the Wager, I'll go your halves.

He continued his mirthful humour to the last, spending his time, drinking, joking and telling stories. He seemed to pay little regard to the serious Remonstrations and Admonitions of the Reverend Clergyman who attended him, and whatever remorse he had on his conscience, for his past villainies, he kept it to himself, not expressing the least concern at the melancholy circumstances he was in'.[67]

It is not surprising that there were many visitors. The assizes were a major social season in York, accompanied as they were by horse racing at Knavesmire, just to the south-west of the city, from 1730 and a permanent theatre from 1734 in Minster Yard. Since 1732 there had been assembly rooms on Blake Street. The neighbouring nobility and gentry flocked to the city on these occasions.[68] And in 1739 there was a 'celebrity' criminal to be visited. However, Turpin was probably not in the same league in the popularity stakes as famed thief and gaol-breaker Jack Sheppard, who was visited in the condemned cell in London by 'hundreds of society tourists, missionary vicars, and even the fashionable portrait painter, Sir James Thornhill'. Visitors paid the turnkey 1s 6d each for the privilege of meeting Sheppard.[69] However, Sheppard was in London and Turpin in York; visitors to a London attraction would have been far more numerous than those in a provincial city.

Not all those on trial at the assizes were found guilty. Eight were acquitted and another ten who were accused of counterfeiting had their trial held over to the next assizes. Of those seven found guilty, Roberts was reprieved, and so was Naomi, who 'pleaded her belly'. Two of the remaining five, Robinson and Monkton, were, like Rowden and Jones in 1737, sentenced to transportation. Of the remaining three, Turpin's fellow highwayman, Thomas Hadfield, was let free on condition that he acted as hangman, which he assented to (there was then no salaried hangman and this continued well into the next century in provincial assizes, such as with the killers of Christine Collins at Stafford in 1840). Therefore, John Stead and Turpin were the only ones to hang.[70]

Turpin prepared himself for the end of his life on earth. 'A few days before his execution, he bought himself a new fustian frock and a pair of pumps, in order to make his leave of the world in as decent a manner as he possibly could'.[71]

This was typical behaviour for criminals who were about to be hanged. In September 1716 one Bean, a robber, was to hang at Tyburn and on the day prior to the execution, a woman visited him. Bean 'bid her be sure to send him clean linen, for he was resolved to die in clean linen'.[72]

Typical, too, was the fact that the condemned man received visitors who brought food and drink. James Woodforde recalled, in Oxford in 1763, 'Went with Dyer, Russell and Master after Dinner down to the castle to see the Prisoners, where we drank two bottles of port and for wine etc., paid 0.1.6. William Cartwright, a young good looking fellow, who is in the Castle for a High way Robbery, drank with us the last Bottle, and smoked a Pipe with us… We gave him between us 0.2.0.'[73] Some of the Jacobite prisoners in York Castle in 1746 were likewise treated liberally by visitors.[74]

There was discussion in 1888 about the shackles that Turpin was allegedly weighed down in. One correspondent, James Williamson, thought that the ones shown to him in the prison were too heavy. Another friend thought they were too light, having worn them at the museum in the York Philosophical Society's grounds, and so

Williamson wondered if those chains were actually worn by Turpin.[75] According to Harper, who may have been to York Castle to see them, the shackles were 28 pounds in weight.[76]

The sheriff of Yorkshire, Sir George Crowle, was responsible for the county gaol, the assizes and the disposal of the prisoners. At the end of each year he would submit his expenses to the Treasury for payment. On this occasion he claimed £20 'for conveying under a strong guard to the place of execution the most notorious highwayman Richard Turpin and John Stead (a horse thief) and for executing them'.[77]

The execution of a condemned felon was a big day, as Fielding noted a little over a decade later:

> 'The Day appointed by the Law for the Thief's Shame, is the Day of his Glory in his Own Opinion. His procession to Tyburn and his last Moments there; are all Triumphant, attended with the Compassion of the meek and tender hearted, and the Applause, Admiration and Envy of all the bold and hardened. His Behaviour in his present Condition, not the Crimes, however atrocious, which brought him to it, are the subject of Contemplation. And if he has sense to temper his Boldness with any degree of Decency, his Death is spoke of by many by Honour, by most of by Pity and with all by Approbation'.[78]

On the morning before his execution, Saturday 7 April, Turpin gave £3 10s to five men to be his mourners. They were to wear hatbands and gloves, probably all black in colour as was then typical for mourners, and would follow the cart taking him to the gallows and be present at the subsequent burial. He also paid several more to wear the same apparel. Some of these men appear to have been from his home county, which begs the unanswerable question, who were they? Furthermore 'He left a gold ring and two pairs of shoes and clogs to a woman at Brough, although he acknowledged he had a wife and child living', as we know he did. Who this woman was we shall never know, but clearly Turpin had abandoned his wife and son and had in more recent times enjoyed the company of another woman.[79]

It could well have been a day when the weather was poor. Jessop recorded, albeit two days later and at Holmfirth to the south-west of York, 'Strong blustering cold wind rain and hail'.[80]

It is possible that it was early afternoon when Turpin was taken in a cart, along with John Stead, aged thirty-eight from Pontefract, Yorkshire, also convicted of horse stealing and who appeared very penitent, to the place of execution, beyond the city walls on the road towards Tadcaster. This was at Knavesmire, Hob Moor and en route they may have stopped for a drink at the Blue Boar pub on Castlegate.[81]

A contemporary map suggests that the route from the gaol would have taken Turpin north along Castlegate, passing St Mary's church and then turning west into Ousegate, passing St Michael's church then west over Ousegate Bridge, on which were the city council chambers. The route was west up Micklegate – a contemporary historian marvelled at the 'length and spaciousness of it' – before passing another three churches until Micklegate Bar was reached.[82]

The procession passed out of the city southwards and along the Tadcaster Road for about a mile, passing St Katherine's Hospital before halting on the east side of the road, near to the race course where there was plenty of open space for the crowds. Apparently once at the wooden platform which held the gallows:

> 'Turpin confessed himself to be really the man made so notorious by for Robberies in the south; tho' he denied many Facts fathered upon him in the public Prints. When he came to the place of Execution, he stript off his Cloaths and dressed himself in a Suit of White Dimonthy; talked a good while to the Gaoler and spectators; and assured some of his Friends (who came out of Essex and attended

on him as Mourners) to take Care of the decent interment of his Body'.[83]

Another account noted:

> 'he behaved himself with amazing Assurance, and bow'd to the spectators as he pass'd: It was remarkable as he mounted the ladder, his right leg trembled, on which he stamped it down with an air, and with undaunted courage, looked round him, and after speaking half an hour to the topsman, threw himself off the ladder, and expired in about five minutes'.[84]

It should be noted that the hangman put the noose around the neck of the man about to die, who ascended the ladder and then jumped or was pushed off it, leaving him hanging from the rope by his neck. Death from strangulation often took several minutes or even longer (in comparison to the speedy deaths achieved by executioners in the twentieth century when deaths took seconds), but the man would remain there for some time to make sure. This would have been an unpleasant, painful and undignified death for Turpin and an unpleasant sight for the sensitive.

The alleged speech he made to the executioner has already been recounted, about being an apprentice in Whitechapel and falling into crime, about the deaths of Morris and King and various highway robberies, concluding:

> 'He also confessed the Facts of which he was convict'd, but said many Things had been laid to his Charge, of which he was innocent.
>
> Tho tis very probable he was guilty of several robberies not here mentioned, yet this was the whole Confession that the Topsman could get out of him'.[85]

How much of this alleged confession is true is another question, for it suggests that the bulk of Turpin's highwayman career took place after the murder of Morris, yet in reality it was coming to an end by then, as he fled to Yorkshire soon after. Likewise his alleged career as a horse thief seems to predate that in reality as it is only known to have occurred after he arrived in Yorkshire, not beforehand.[86]

It has also been alleged that Turpin gave the hangman or possibly the clergyman present a small gift. It was a whistle and had the figure of a man and a barrel on its top. This is not absolutely proven, but it is held at York Castle Museum, having been unearthed in 1939, and is labelled as such.[87]

Turpin's body hung for some time at the place of execution (Jacobite prisoners executed in York in 1746 were hung for ten minutes before being taken down), but was removed at three in the afternoon. It was brought to the Blue Boar in Castlegate and then at ten o'clock on the following morning it was buried in a coffin in the churchyard (described as a garden) of the former Anglican St George's church without Fishergate postern and not far from Walmgate bar. This place of burial had been commonly used for executed criminals since the seventeenth century and there was no funeral service and so no reference in the parish register for St Denys with St George. The coffin bore the inscription 'J.P. 1739, RT aged 28'. An elderly man told a young relative in the early nineteenth century that it was a few yards to the right of the entrance to what was then a graveyard, which is not where the much later gravestone now is.[88]

The grave was dug deep and the paid mourners attended the burial. However, at about 10am on Monday 9 April some people were found trying to remove the body from its resting place, having clearly taken it some way from the graveyard. Hearing of this a crowd assembled who, fearing the body was to be sold to the doctors for anatomising, went to the place where it had been subsequently placed and carried it through the streets in a form of triumphal procession, the corpse naked on a board covered with straw, on four men's shoulders, back to the same grave and then covered with lime.[89] This was not necessarily a show of sympathy for Turpin as a criminal or a hero, but an act of hostility towards the commonplace practice of doctors trying to acquire a newly deceased corpse to dissect for research purposes. There had been no report of any physical or even verbal demonstration at Turpin's execution on the part of the crowd. There were clear limits to what some of the crowd thought decent or would tolerate.

Several of those involved in the fracas were identified and brought before the city's quarter sessions court on 4 May. Bodysnatching was a felony under common law, rather than a criminal offence (so offenders could not be hanged or transported) and was often overlooked by the JPs. However, this very public incident could not be disregarded. Dr Marmaduke Palms, a city surgeon, was there 'for unlawfully causing to be taking up the body of Richard Turpin out of his grave'. In this Richard Hogg, labourer, had done the actual work of 'unlawfully and inhumanely assisting and exposing the corps'. James Fentiman, a porter, was accused 'for violently entering Dr Palm's Garden House and doing damage there' to retrieve the body. When the officers of the law intervened, such as George Shelton Esq, they were insulted by the likes of William Gregson, a labourer, and Christopher Jackson and John Flint assaulted George Hepworth, constable, and removed John Hornby from Hepworth's custody.[90]

There was an indictment at the York quarter sessions for several people for having stolen Turpin's body. Most were bound over in recognisances of £20 each to appear at the next court on 18 May. They did so and all save Dr Palms and Fentiman were then discharged. These two were bound over to keep the peace and had to appear before the court again on 13 July. Palms was then discharged but Fentiman was bound over yet again until his final appearance and discharge on 27 July.[91] It seems Palms left York thereafter as he is not listed in the 1741 York poll book.

It would seem probable that Turpin was interred in an unmarked grave; most burials had no headstone, so it is impossible to be certain

Above: The Bluebell Inn, Hempstead. (Author photograph, 2022)

Right: Sign on the Bluebell Inn commemorating Turpin's birth. (Author photograph, 2022)

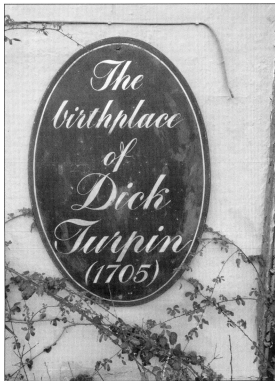

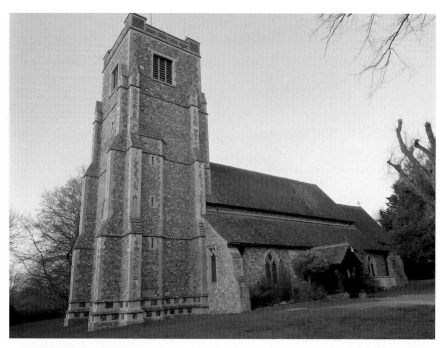

St Andrew's church, Hempstead. (Author photograph, 2022)

Exterior of school room at St Andrew's church. (Author photograph, 2022)

Above: Dick Turpin's Cottage, Hempstead. (Author photograph, 2022)

Right: Dick Turpin's Cottage, Thaxted. (Author's collection)

Left: Sign above door of Dick Turpin's cottage, Thaxted. (Author photograph, 2022)

Below: Dick Turpin's cave, Epping Forest. (Author's collection)

Near Dick Turpin's Cave, Epping Forest

Turpin shoots Thomas Morris, 1737. (*Newgate Calendar*, public domain)

Left: Duke of Newcastle. (Author's collection)

Below: Green Dragon pub (top right), Welton. (Author's collection)

Dudley Ryder. (Author's collection)

York Prison. (Author photograph, 2021)

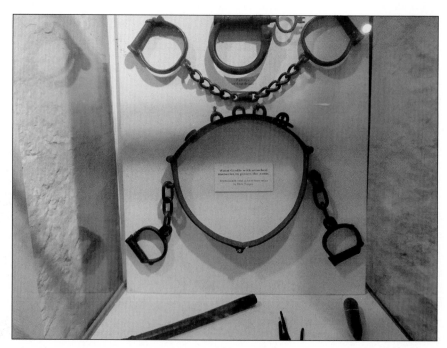

Chains allegedly worn by Turpin when at York Prison. (Author photograph, 2021)

Right: Prison cell, allegedly used by Turpin. (Author photograph, 2021)

Below: Turpin's Room, Blue Boar pub, Castlegate, York. (Author photograph, 2021)

Site of Tyburn, Knavesmire, York. (Author photograph, 2021)

Display board about Tyburn. (Author photograph, 2021)

Right: Whistle allegedly given by Turpin to the hangman. (York Castle Museum)

Below: Gravestone of Dick Turpin, York. (Author photograph, 2021)

Matheson Lang as Dick Turpin with a dead Black Bess, 1922. (Author's collection)

Victor McLaghlan as Dick Turpin, 1931. (Author's collection)

Bonny Black Bess. (Author's collection)

The Black Horse pub sign, Iver Heath. (Author photograph, 2021)

Above: Dorney Court. (Author photograph, 2021)

Left: Advert for York Dungeon. (Author photograph, 2021)

Poster advertising Dick Turpin pantomime. (Author photograph, 2021)

Poster advertising highwayman drama. (Author's collection, 2021)

Left: Sign concerning Turpin in Bostall Wood. (Author photograph, 2021)

Below: Street sign in Greenwich. (Author photograph, 2022)

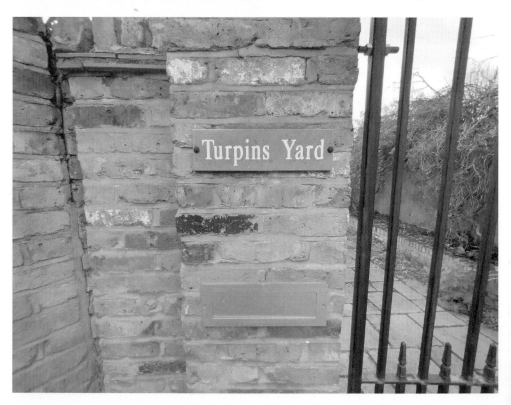

where his mortal remains lie (just as at Culloden Moor, it is unknown exactly whose remains are in the vicinity of the late nineteenth-century 'clan' gravestones). In the twentieth century a marker was erected in St George's churchyard bearing the words

'JOHN PALMER OTHERWISE

RICHARD TURPIN

THE NOTORIOUS HIGHWAYMAN AND HORSE STEALER

EXECUTED AT TYBURN APRIL 7TH 1739

AND BURIED IN ST. GEORGE'S CHURCHYARD'.

In 1979 a plaque was unveiled on a wall on Lead Mill Lane, adjacent to the cemetery, by the then sheriff of York. It is no longer there at time of writing (2021), but an informative display board about the life and crimes of Turpin has been erected nearby, and on a nearby map of the city there is a reference to Dick Turpin's grave.[92]

Presumably the corpse remained undisturbed after reburial, but in 1861 a newspaper claimed that the Morley family of York was putting goods up for auction. These apparently included the skull of Dick Turpin which had been in their possession for some time. The provenance of this item was not, however, revealed.[93]

It seems that contemporaries saw Turpin as being more than a run-of-the-mill criminal (no one ever published anything about John Stead, for example). One newspaper claimed, 'The noise this fellow made for some time is the only apology that can be given for troubling the publick with an account of so mean, and, from whatever appeared of him here, so stupid a wretch'.[94]

Turpin had evaded the law for three years following the breakup of the Gregory gang of which he had been a member and had frequently featured in the press in these years. There is a parallel with Ronnie Biggs, who was not a leading member of the Great Train Robbers of

1963, but who escaped from prison and evaded the law for longer (1965–2001) than any of his fellow gang members, living in South America, and his name as a criminal at large was often in the press, as was Turpin's, and in both cases these men became better known than perhaps their actual criminal exploits warranted.

Shortly after Turpin's execution, epigrams were published and reprinted in the press. One was purportedly from a Yorkshireman and another from a southerner. They were clearly capitalising on the fame of Turpin to make their own points.

The first was as follows:

> EPIGRAM ON TURPIN, by a Gentleman
>
> Full oft the south has sneer'd our <u>Northern Clime</u>,
>
> And Horsestealer, been call'd a <u>Country Crime</u>:
>
> But now no longer we will bear such Jokes,
>
> <u>This Rogue is theirs</u>; and we the Honest Folks.
>
> <u>Of knaves and Fools</u> we don't say we have neither
>
> But <u>knave and Fool</u> are seldom found together
>
> Our purer <u>Northern</u> Air's , too sharp by half,
>
> A <u>Yorkshire Tike</u> has bit this <u>Essex Calf</u>
>
> This dull-bred Rogue has found it to his cost,
>
> <u>A Fish out of its Element is lost</u>'.

The second was:

> 'When Turpin cruis'd near home, splendid he rolled
>
> In cash and rings, and watches cap'd with gold,
>
> Lean Yorkshire, chang'd the scene, his trade fail'd there
>
> In vain those roads he try'd above a year
>
> Till poverty reduc'd him to small-beer

What could he do, in that dire starving case

But take the trade peculiar to the place?

Turn Yorkshire tyke, and steal a horse or two,

So hanged at Tyburn, 'midst the jockey crew?

For boldest born, if with hunger stung,

Will feed on carrion, mix'd with poison dung'.[95]

Another result of Turpin's execution was that two farmers from Old Stamford, Essex, came to Yorkshire to recover the horses which had been stolen from them by Turpin, 'as successful in praties and horse stealing as he was before in highway robbery'. The newspaper thought that others would follow their example.[96]

Meanwhile, on 7 August 1739, there was a petition from Richard Grassby and others (Thomas Creasy, George Goodyear, George Dawson, Carey Gill, James Smith and Edward Sawood) to the Treasury; they were the men who had given evidence against Turpin at the York assizes, 'without which they apprehended that notorious offender could not have been brought to justice'. They asked the Treasury for £200 and £50 rewards for his apprehension and conviction as had been advertised in *The London Gazette* in 1737. They pointed out that Turpin was 'so desperate and notorious an offender' and that they had 'been at great trouble and expense (besides neglecting their several employments at their respective homes) on going to and continuing at York during the said trial'. On 26 February 1740 the petition was granted and the sum paid out. On 20 March 1740 there was also an order to pay George Crowle the same amount for his part in his expenses in taking 'that notorious offender, Richard Turpin'.[97]

In the immediate aftermath of Turpin's death, with the scourge of the highwayman still ever present, his name was still being brought before the public. Sometimes these villains were likened to Turpin. John Rattery, a horse thief, was executed at Aberdeen in June 1739 and was noted as 'seemed in some things to equal Turpin himself'.[98]

Another highwayman in Epping Forest was described, later in the same year, as being 'almost a second Turpin'.[99] In 1740 there were several instances where criminals were likened to Turpin. In November James Clarkson, 'a notorious thief and housebreaker' was hanged at Berwick and apparently he 'died with less intrepidity than the famous Turpin, not being daunted in the least'.[100] In the next month a robber who stole from the gentlemen near Durham was 'remarkably bold and not much unlike the late Turpin'.[101] Turpin was referenced in the first published novel of Henry Fielding, *Joseph Andrews*, published in 1742, where Fanny Goodwill is suspected of being a highway robber, 'He warranted she was a relation of Turpin'.[102] Much later he was referred to again. Lewis 'the noted highwayman' was taken at Uppingham in 1781 and it was said that he 'committed more Robberies than ever the famous Turpin did'.[103] In the next decade, in reference to a highwayman called Broadbent a text referred to 'the memorable days of Turpin'.[104]

Chapter 6

Evolution of the Turpin Myth

We shall now turn from Turpin the criminal to Turpin the mythical hero. Most historians writing about the former refer to Turpin the myth. No one does more so in this vein than Professor Sharpe, titling a whole chapter in his book 'Turpin Hero', and exploring the various manifestations of the myth of Dick Turpin. This follows a previous chapter about the novel *Rookwood* by William Harrison Ainsworth (1805–82), a Manchester lawyer turned novelist, who did more than anyone else to create the myth. As has already been noted, the factual record of Dick Turpin does not paint him in a very favourable light. Far from it. But several decades after his death he began to be seen differently. It is usually stated that the aforesaid Ainsworth is the man responsible for the origins of the Turpin myth, but, though he had an important role in propagating it, he was not the original source.

Leading Turpin scholars Derek Barlow and Professor Sharpe pinpoint the origin of one of the most popular myths, that of Turpin's ride from London to York on Black Bess (never referred to by any contemporary; Turpin's only ride to York was in October 1738, from Beverley, under guard as a prisoner) as first appearing in print in 1808.[1] While they are right in pinpointing the book, they are wrong about the year, because the book had first been published in 1800. Alarm bells about the accuracy of the book, including as it does *The Life of Sawney Beane, the Man Eater*, a fictional horror tale about sixteenth-century Scottish cannibals, should ring, but the relevant point here is

153

that it introduced the ride to York story as being an exploit of Turpin. According to the author:

> 'Early in the morning he [Turpin] set off, and robbed a gentleman of 50 guineas and a valuable watch in the environs of London. Apprehensive of being known and pursued, he spurred his horse and took the northern road, and astonishing to relate, reached York the same evening, and was noticed playing bowls in the bowling green with several gentlemen'.[2]

Black Bess does not feature here, however, nor does the (unnamed) horse die on reaching York, though the seed of the famous ride had been sown and would grow as the myth developed. As with the poem published in 1737, the story included material about Turpin's charitable nature. Despite his villainy, which at least the anonymous author did not conceal, 'he gave several proofs of possessing a heart capable of feeling for the distress of a fellow creature'. 'Proofs' of this was that on meeting a man on the Essex Road and about to rob him, the man said he had but 15s 6d in the world and Turpin next day gave him 10 guineas. On another occasion, meeting a woman who was in desperate need of money to pay her rent, Turpin found her the money she needed.[3] The veracity of the ride will be touched upon later in this chapter.

It is possible that the story of the ride to York and Turpin's benevolence derives from accounts of a late seventeenth-century highwayman. The earliest version of the story stated that Captain Richard Dudley, alias Swift Nicks, after a highway robbery, left Barnet at 5am and reached York at 6pm in order to prove he could not have committed the earlier robbery. Although no date is given as Dudley was hanged in 1682, it may have been in the previous decade. Another, lengthier, version is given by Daniel Defoe in the 1720s.

This is that a highwayman known as Nicks in about 1676 robbed a gentleman at Gad's Hill near Rochester, Kent, at 4am. He then rode to Gravesend, took a ferry across the Thames, then rode through Essex, Cambridgeshire and Huntingdon before taking the Great North Road, reaching York by 8pm that evening. Here he had words with the Lord Mayor. This was in order to establish an alibi for the crime on the grounds that he could not have committed a robbery in Kent and have been in York on the same day. Charles II referred to him as Swift Nicks. Turpin's 'charitable nature' may also derive from the first account of Dudley: 'whenever he had got any considerable Booty from Great People he would very generously extend his charity to such whom he really knew to be poor'. An early account of the life of highwayman William or John Nevison (hanged at York in 1685), also stated, 'he was charitable also to the poor; as relieving them out of those Spoils, which he took from those who could better spare it'. Nevison was also polite to ladies he robbed.[4] The stories about these highwaymen were thus incorporated by those later writing about Turpin (in the later nineteenth century Nevison was ascribed the ride to York).

There were also songs about Turpin in the early nineteenth century, pointing to popularity and fame. The first is from a collection of 1817:

'Of all the famous robbers,
That doth in England dwell;
The noted Richard Turpin,
Doth all the rest excel.

He is a butcher of his trade,
And lived in Stamford town;
And did eight men near Leicester rob
As is full well known'.

Another ditty was:

> 'For shooting of a dunghead cock
> Poor Turpin he at last was took
> And carried straight into a gaol
> Where his misfortune he doth dwell
> O rare Turpin hero
> O rare Turpin hero.
>
> 'Now some say that he will hang.
> Turpin the last of all the gang;
> I wish this cook had never been hatched
> For like a fish in the net he's catched
> O poor Turpin hero'.[5]

This song, '*O Rare Turpin Hero*' has been amended since 1817 and was sung (and recorded by) late twentieth-century balladeers such as Ewan MacColl.

Furthermore, from 1819 there were a number of plays performed in London which featured Turpin, always prefixing his name with Richard rather than Dick. Why this should have come about is another question; the book of 1800, reprinted in 1808, may have influenced the theatre impresarios of the time. Perhaps in the post-Napoleonic age, in which social, economic and political challenges were threatening to fundamentally change society, the public saw historic legends from the pre-industrial age as comforting, undemanding entertainment.

The plays were certainly popular, as a newspaper noted of a production at Atley's Theatre, 'The brilliant success of *Richard Turpin* has surpassed the manager's most sanguine expectations, complete ovations have attended each night's representation and thunderous applause follow the fall of the curtain'. Mr W. Barrymore played 'the notorious highwayman'.[6]

There were many more such performances in the following decade. At Davis' Royal Amphitheatre at Westminster Bridge in 1822, for six nights '*The Life and Adventures of Richard Turpin*' was performed, which also featured, curiously enough, a real bear and two dogs.[7] In Liverpool in the following year '*Turpin: the Yorkshire highwayman*', was staged, with panoramic views of the scenery.[8] Perhaps the first performance of the ride from London to York was at Davis' Royal Amphitheatre in 1823, as the Turpin play featured an attack on the York coach and the journey from London to York, and Turpin shooting his horse (perhaps the first time this was shown).[9] In 1827 at the Theatre Royal, Covent Garden, there was 'A melodramatic spectacle founded on the exploits of Richard Turpin the highwayman'.[10] A similar entertainment appeared at the same venue in 1830 with Mr Blanchard playing Tom King (a renaming of the real Matthew King, which was to become common).[11]

Even before the once-famous novel, there was a groundswell of popular enthusiasm for entertainment based on the alleged exploits of Turpin, but it had taken 80 years after his death for this feeling to exist at this level. Highway robbery was still a real danger in the later eighteenth century. However, it was on the decline by the beginning of the next century and non-existent by the 1830s.

The favourable cultural climate was important. The early nineteenth century was the peak of the Romantic movement in the arts. This highlighted emotion and individualism, glorified the past and was suspicious of industrialisation and science. It was a reaction to the modernisation of society. Therefore a hero taken from the past, who could not be seen as threatening to the present, was ideal. This was true of Sir Walter Scott's Jacobite Highland heroes, for example, and of Turpin.

The plays of the 1810s and 1820s had shown there was a demand for the dramatization of the exploits of a highwayman hero. This fed into the most important piece of Turpin fiction of them all. This was the novel *Rookwood: A Romance* by William Harrison Ainsworth, which was first published in 1834 and became a popular bestseller, being reprinted several times and winning critical acclaim: 'both readers and critics welcomed with acclamations this new bizarre romance... excited them with its inimitable narrative of the Ride to York'. More than any other single work it projected the image of Turpin as a heroic and gallant highwayman, despite being unoriginal, drawing as it did on previous work.

In the fourth edition, the author explained in the introduction why he adopted the approach taken in the novel, writing 'I have not, as yet, been able to obtain satisfactory evidence that the extraordinary equestrian fact [Turpin's ride on Black Bess to York] attributed to him by oral tradition, and detailed in this work, was ever actually accomplished'. Ainsworth did not invent the story; it pre-dated his book, and Ainsworth admits that Turpin was perhaps not even a good horseman and was merely 'an undoubted robber'. This seems reasonable enough.[12]

However, Ainsworth then throws out reason and gives vent to romanticism: 'Turpin, however, I take it, has met with imperfect justice at the hands of his Ordinary Biographers. He was a more important personage than they would have us believe... he played no unmomentuous part upon the stage of life in his generation'. He elaborates on this hypothesis, in that there was a reward for Turpin, that he inspired terror and that comparisons were made between him and Walpole. Reference is made to Turpin visiting Holland in 1736 and dealing with one Daniel Malden.[13]

Ainsworth continues in his account of Turpin's importance, 'Turpin's authenticated exploits bear no proportion to the reputation he enjoyed, in his own time, for unparalleled audacity – a reputation which the lapse of a century has not undimmed'. Ainsworth does not elaborate on this. He then explains why he has such an admiration for Turpin, 'Turpin, the hero of my boyhood. I have always had a strange passion for highwaymen and have listened by the hour to their exploits as narrated to me by my father and especially to those of dauntless Dick, that chief minion of the moor'. He recalled standing on the rural roadside and thinking of Turpin, so in his novel 'in selecting a highwayman for a hero, I should choose my old favourite,

Dick Turpin'.[14] To an extent Ainsworth was indulging in nostalgia for the legends of his lost youth, but was unknowingly setting up these legends as the basis for what would be taken as fact by later generations.

Rookwood is a gothic romance of mystery among an old gentry family in the north of England, about a disputed family inheritance. Turpin is not the principal character but he is a leading supporting one. He appears early on, as Jack Palmer, 'a good humoured, good looking man' and the novel is, as we shall see, meant to be set in 1737. Palmer and some other men are singing a song about highwaymen and one verse is as follows:

> 'Nor did highwaymen ever before possess
>
> For ease, for security, danger, distress.
>
> Such a mare as Dick Turpin's Black Bess, Black Bess'.

Palmer then adds 'The gentlemen I speak of never maltreated anyone, except in self defence'.[15] In their discussion of highwaymen the following lines are given:

> 'Who makes more noise than them all put together?'
>
> 'Who's that?'
>
> 'Dick Turpin… he seems to me'.
>
> 'They tell me Turpin keeps the best nag in the lot and can ride further and further in a day than any other man in a week'.
>
> 'So I've heard'.[16]

Already Turpin's character is being exalted before he has made his known entrance into the story, but the reader is being prepared for the fact that the author is to present Turpin as a hero. Those who know history will know that Palmer was Turpin's pseudonym, but only after he arrived in Yorkshire in June 1737.

There is then more of a discussion about Turpin. He is said to have haunted Epping Forest, but another speaker states 'The whole of the North Road from Tottenham Cross to York gates come within Dick's present range'. Coates, a lawyer, whom the reader is clearly not meant to like, is critical of this admiration for criminal exploits and he says 'It's a disgrace to the country that such a rascal should remain unhanged. Government should look into it. Is the whole of the Kingdom to be kept in a state of agitation by a single man?' Palmer sneers at Coates's attitude and there is a comparison of the stated description of Turpin and Palmer and some similarities are noted. Eventually Palmer reveals himself as Turpin.[17]

Turpin disappears from the book for a few chapters and then reappears to sing a song about himself and his horse, Black Bess (an invention of Ainsworth's, as is the replacement of Richard by Dick as Turpin's first name). He also rescues Luke Bradley and sexton Peter, and we learn Turpin is friendly with a group of gypsies who live in the forest.[18]

He is then absent for a few more chapters. We then are given some narrative which builds him up, both physically and morally: 'Turpin's external man, as we have before said, was singularly prepossessing. It was especially so in the eyes of the [fair] sex'. He is 'a fine fellow' and 'his high courage' is mentioned, as is 'his good breeding and his debonair deportment' and 'manly beauty'. He is provided with dialogue to boost his character, as he tells Eleanor Mowbray 'I'm the most humane creature breathing – would not hurt a fly – much less a lady'.[19] In this Turpin is posited as a romantic hero for the first time, which is an important facet of the myth, and this seems to be an original innovation of Ainsworth's as it is crucial to the development of Turpin as a ladies' man.

There are a lot more of such assertions in the next few pages. A coachman says 'he's as civil speaking a chap as need be, blow my boots if he ain't'. Turpin boasts 'When did Dick Turpin desert his friends?' As to his horse, 'No Bedoin arab loved his horse more tenderly than

Turpin' and the man himself said 'I would rather lose my right hand' than his horse. The narrator notes 'Dick was intrepid to a fault' and 'danger was his delight'.[20] The name Black Bess is first given (though as we shall see, the inspiration for the name was probably taken from a song of 1825) to Turpin's horse in the novel, and as with the famous ride, the name has endured. There are no contemporary records of the names of any of the horses Turpin actually rode.

We then have Turpin's famous exploit. He is to ride from Kilburn to York in order to help Luke Rookwood; the stories of the seventeenth-century Swift Nicks state he made the ride to establish an alibi following a robbery. However, before he can commence, Coates and a Chief Constable try to arrest him (no reference to Bayes here). At this time Turpin is with his friend and fellow highwayman Tom King. In the fight, King urges Turpin to use his pistol to escape and he does so, but in the confusion, Turpin shoots King by mistake and King is severely wounded in the chest. Turpin regrets what he has done and throws his gun away before riding off.[21]

The next few chapters detail the epic ride from London to York. Turpin rides Black Bess through Hampstead Heath, Highgate, Tottenham and Edmonton, all the time being pursued by the forces of the law. We are told that Turpin 'was the crack rider of England of his time, and perhaps any time'. Stopping off at an inn, the publican remarks of him 'He's a regular good 'un'. Turpin rides through the night, scarcely stopping. He rides by Coventry, Northamptonshire, Grantham and Newark and up towards Yorkshire. Eventually Turpin arrives in sight of York and his enemies damn him with faint praise, 'the fool rode her from London to York, last night, such a feat was never performed before'. However, it was at the cost of Black Bess, who dies and Turpin buries her.[22]

Ainsworth later wrote

'The Ride to York was completed in one day and one night [an evening until 6am the next day]. The feat – for feat it was, being the composition of a hundred ordinary novel pages in less than 24 hours – was achieved at the Elms, a house I then occupied in Kilburn. From the moment I got Turpin on the high road till I landed him in York, I wrote on and on without the slightest sense of effort. I began in the morning, wrote all day and as the night wore on, my subject had completely mastered me and I had no power to leave Turpin on the high road'.[23]

The author has it on good authority that this ride is physically impossible. Horses trained for endurance racing can manage 100 miles in 12 hours, the time allotted by Ainsworth; horses not trained for such feats could manage 40. We have no idea as to what training the admittedly fictional horse had, but even at best what Ainsworth writes is not only untrue, historically speaking, but would not be possible for any horse and rider. It is about 200 miles from London to York.

Later Coates and Sir Henry Rookwood discuss the book's real villain, with the former remarking that he is responsible for 'felony, burglary, murder, every description of crime under the Heavens. He's a devil incarnate'. Sir Henry Rookwood then observes, 'Turpin is as mild as milk compared with him'. Later, Major Mowbray, a man who has been robbed by Turpin and is later pursuing him, says 'I am not sorry for his escape. He's a brave fellow, and I respect courage'.[24]

In the epilogue, the author describes Turpin's execution, pretty much as was reported in the contemporary press and histories. He observed, 'He died not, as other men die by degree, but at once, without wincing, and quiet at his execution'. Ainsworth then sums up his opinion for his hero, 'he was a sort of hero. We have a singular delight in recounting his feats, and hair breadth escapes... Perhaps we may have placed him in too favourable a point of view – and yet we know not... many doubts rest upon his history'.[25]

The Turpin of *Rookwood* is as far removed from the Turpin of reality as it is possible to be. He is complimented and flattered by one and all. He never puts a foot wrong and one could be forgiven for believing that this is propaganda. He is handsome, brave, kind; everything that could be wanted for a fictional hero. Had Ainsworth created a purely fictional character he might have done better to have chosen another name. Yet this literary invention was to have a long life, despite the book from which he sprung and its author being mostly forgotten.

Rookwood was just one milestone in the progress of the myth of Turpin that grew in the nineteenth century. There were numerous 'penny dreadfuls', short stories, serials and comics about Turpin and other highwaymen aimed at increasingly literate young people. Turpin and his alleged exploits became very well known; far more so than they had in the previous century. Simple and exciting stories with a minimum of exposition and a maximum of action are always going to appeal to readers, especially if illustrated. This had some unfortunate and unforeseen consequences.

Charles Dickens was a friend of Ainsworth and in what became Dickens's first novel *The Pickwick Papers*, written two to three years after *Rookwood* was first published, there is a song, written in 1825, about Turpin and the Bishop, with Turpin on 'bold mare Bess' on Hounslow Heath, where Turpin robs the cleric. Interesting, the footnotes to the poem note that Turpin was 'a legendary highwayman'.[26]

More stories were written about Turpin in the nineteenth century. The 'history' behind some of these was doubtful in the extreme. In an anonymous pamphlet of the Victorian era, meant as a short biography of Turpin, there is a meeting between Turpin and King and a young man who turns out to be none other than Charles Edward Stuart. The highwaymen swear undying allegiance to the man they deem the rightful King, before he rides north to Scotland to begin the attempt to restore the Stuarts to the throne. This is presumably meant to be set in 1745 (six years after the real Turpin's death), and Charles's movements in that year are well known: in reality he was in France preparing for the journey to Scotland by sea. The pamphlet begins with Turpin's birth at Hempstead and ends on the gallows at York, as well as including the now obligatory ride to York.[27]

Another fragment of the myth can be found in a one-act play. Here King and Turpin are desirous of enriching themselves from a wealthy merchant, but not by highway robbery. Rather they insinuate themselves into the household and Turpin pretends to be in love with the daughter of the house, who has a dowry of £10,000. Eventually their true identities are discovered and they are arrested and taken away. In the final scene it is revealed that the so called law officers are actually members of their own gang and that they have got away with a diamond ring and a valuable snuff box.[28]

The alleged impact of these depictions was referenced in the press. In Wolverhampton it was noted that children of poor families were ignorant of modern historical figures such as Wellington and Napoleon and even Queen Victoria, but 'while of Scripture names I could not in general terms gain any rational account, many of the most sacred names never having even been heard, there was a general knowledge of the lives of Dick Turpin and Jack Shepherd'.[29] When Charlie Peace, a noted burglar, was gaoled in 1879, a journalist compared him to Turpin and Sheppard, and wrote 'the history of whose exploits, I regret to say, still forms so fascinating a literature for the boys of the lower classes'.[30] An East End teacher was telling his pupils about Shakespeare and his works and asking which play was each child's favourite:

'A little urchin in the class cried out that the play he loved best was Dick Turpin. There is at present, it ought to be explained, that there is a circus in the neighbourhood. "But who told you that Shakespeare wrote Dick Turpin?" "You told us yourself", answered the young playgoer. "Not I", cried the teacher, "Never". "You told us yourself" cried the unabashed youth "that Shakespeare wrote the best plays, didn't you?" "Well, what of that", demanded the other. "Dick Turpin is the best play that I have ever seen, and I thought he must have written it" said the youth.'[31]

However, the impact of these stories was apparently far worse than inculcating simple ignorance. Some young readers were inspired to embark on criminal careers. A newspaper article bemoaned the profits being made by the publishing of sensational tales aimed at young people, 'calculated to lead the juvenile mind'; these included those featuring Turpin, Sixteen String Jack, Claude Duval and other criminals as models of gallantry and pluck.[32]

The name of the long-dead highwayman clearly struck a chord with more than one young tearaway. In 1877, Inspector Rowe was driving a cart along Coombe Lane in Surrey when a young man jumped out of a ditch and held onto the horse and shouted 'Hold hard! I am Dick Turpin'. Rowe identified himself as a policeman and the man and two companions ran away. He managed to catch hold of one of them, a seventeen-year-old youth employed in a factory, who said it was 'only in fun'.[33] Other young offenders were similarly inspired to attempt burglary and it was noted that they had read 'the adventures of Dick Turpin or something of that sort'.[34] Horace Wright was another youth with a desire for a criminal life. He was described as a highwayman and labelled 'A Modern day Dick Turpin'. On horseback, wearing a mask and pointing a gun at a coachman, he obtained a sovereign in Cambridgeshire.[35] Eight years previously, young criminals had been arrested in Hull: 'The prisoners are said to have been led to this extraordinary course of crime by reading the lives of Dick Turpin, and such characters, and they had determined to become burglars, highwaymen, and to crown all, murderers'.[36] Henry Howley, the fifteen-year-old leader of a gang of thieves in Marylebone, went by the name of Dick Turpin and his younger brother as Tom King; others went by the names of Sixteen String Jack and Claude Duval.[37]

Peter Sheldrake, a London lad, had tried to steal a cash box and it was said of him 'he was a good boy until he started reading

Dick Turpin and Jack Shephard and other penny awful literature'.[38] Thomas Walton, a fifteen-year-old from Leeds, had been found on enclosed premises with pistols and ammunition and had been reading *A History of Dick Turpin*.[39] In Manchester it was found that the motivation for another gang of young criminals was 'their present position was entirely owing to their having read cheap literature, and having assumed the characters of Claude Duval, Dick Turpin and other criminal notorieties'.[40]

There was worse to come. John Brigden, a thirteen-year-old of London, shot dead a younger boy, James Baze, a fellow chorister, with a pistol as he refused to give him his orange. The Revd William Scott 'said that the occurrence all arose through the boys playing "Dick Turpin the Dashing Highwayman" in consequence of reading a vile romance of that name. The boy Brigden... was going to have a play at Christmas of Dick Turpin and he and his playmates were practising highway robbery of one another in sport to get their hands in. That mischievous kind of play was made popular by the penny gaffs of the East End'.[41]

As to Henry Westby of Nottingham, accused of shooting his father, 'there had been no doubt that the accused had been reading sensational literature. The walls of his bedroom were embellished with pictures from the life of Dick Turpin and many newspaper cuttings were found in his office desk with accounts of marvellous adventures'.[42]

This concern about the consumption of fictional crime fuelling real-life crime has parallels with late twentieth-century fears about 'video nasties' and also the more general effects of viewing sex and violence on the screen (whether TV, film or increasingly online) as entertainment and this translating to reality, with the allegation that it may have an effect on impressionable minds, especially those of the young.

It was not only youths who adopted the *nom de plume*. One Wing Farley tried to hold up a mail coach near Ramsgate in Kent in

1887 by shouting out that he was Dick Turpin when confronted by Robert Turtle, the mail coach driver.[43] James Brown, a hen stealer of Hounslow, was known, for no obvious reason, as Dick Turpin.[44]

Reference was made to Turpin in an article about Greek bandits holding up passengers on a train in Turkey: 'Indeed, but for the resistance made by certain of the passengers, the robbers would have displayed all the courtesy and consideration of Dick Turpin, Gentleman Jack Claude Duval and other eminently polite thieves of our own country'.[45] Likewise, when a farmer was robbed near Driffield in 1848 he pleaded that some of the money stolen from him was intended for his mother, 'The robbers – Dick Turpin like – had the generosity to return Jones his watch and half crown'.[46]

Francis Gardiner, an Australian bandit who was executed in 1864, was likened to Turpin by a York newspaper: 'whose career so much resembles that of the description of the celebrated Dick Turpin... that in sketching his history we seem to repeat the well-known feats of 100 years ago... like Turpin he had an eye for a good horse'.[47] Two Australian bandits in 1854, it was said, were 'two of the most daring characters that ever lived, and who, in England, would rank with Dick Turpin and Jack Shepherd'.[48]

More innocently, in 1893 at a fancy dress party for children in York, one child came as Dick Turpin and it was remarked that the others came as 'other personages dear to nursery and legendary lore'.[49] It was not just the lower classes who had formed an affection for Turpin; a man attending a Colchester fancy dress ball came dressed as him.[50] Likewise, at the parade to mark the 700th anniversary of Colchester's charter, one man dressed as Turpin.[51] At a carnival in Feltham, a couple came as a cavalier and Dick Turpin.[52]

Turpin was also referred to in more derogatory terms at a meeting of Hull Council in 1875 when criticism was being made of the Dock Company, as a councillor noted, 'Dick Turpin would have been ashamed to acknowledge such acts as the Dock Company and the Railway Company were guilty of'.[53] In the following year, in a discussion of bookmaking in France, 'It is pleaded in his behalf that he exercises an anxious and laborious vocation, and so he certainly does. As much might be said for Dick Turpin, but the state and society do not encourage... the exercise of vocations... which have a tendency to demoralise the population'.[54] At a meeting of the Edmonton Social Democrats, one man said 'Dick Turpin and the other old road rogues were honest men compared to the modern rogues who served the people as he had been describing'.[55] A Bush Hill Liberal claimed in an attack on the Conservative government, 'It was said that Dick Turpin robbed the rich to give to the poor'.[56]

Plays and circus acts featuring Turpin continued. These and the cheap stories were the principal means of conveying the myth in the nineteenth century. At Scarborough in 1880, Hengler's Grand Cirque performed 'The Favourite Hippodramatic Spectacle, Turpin's Ride to York and the death of Black Bess'. Dick Turpin was played by Mr F.C. Hengler himself in 'faithfully portraying all, the most notable incidents of that celebrated historical event'.[57] In 1876 at the Volunteers' fete in Hounslow, one Mr Albert de Noye, comic vocalist and mimic, performed his comic medley 'the Life and Death of Bold Dick Turpin'.[58]

Harmston's circus, in 1884, performed at York, and 'always highly appreciated in this city' was their adaptation of the ride to York; 'the well-known story drew enthusiastic applause'.[59] At Scarborough in 1892 there was a circus and one performer there was a Mr Croueste, who 'also appeared later in the evening in the character of Dick Turpin, whose ride to York was cleverly reproduced'.[60]

There was also a report of a circus in 1891 at which the ride to York was performed, with James Powell riding a black mare. He apparently did so with such sympathy that the audience was convinced that the horse had really died at the end of the ride. 'It has been said that Dick Turpin never did this ride to York, that it was someone else. If the facts be so all we can say is, so much the worse for the facts. It seems a pity to have so romantic legend spoiled'.[61]

In the Thomas Hardy novel *Far from the Madding Crowd* (1874), the roguish Sergeant Troy plays the part of Turpin in a country fair and there is the following exchange of dialogue with Bathsheba Everdene:

> 'Have you ever seen the play Dick Turpin's Ride to York? Turpin was a real man, was he not?'
>
> 'O yes, perfectly true, all of it. Indeed, I think I've heard Jan Coggan say that a relation of his knew Tom King, Turpin's friend, quite well'.
>
> 'Coggan is rather given to strange stories connected with his relations, we must remember. I hope they can all be believed'.
>
> 'Yes, yes, we know Coggan. But Turpin is true enough'.[62]

More respectably, but in a similar vein, Lord Halifax, in a speech glorifying Yorkshire and Yorkshiremen, in 1900, remarked: 'Dick Turpin, I was told, was also a Yorkshireman, and of him, too, we must be proud, if for nothing less than his ride to York. ...How much more exciting must travelling have been in those days'.[63]

Interest in Turpin as a figure grew and a history of the parishes of West and East Ham, by Dr Pagenstecher, in 1887 included a section on him as 'he was a resident of these parishes' and so it was thought that this would be of interest.[64]

Other entrepreneurs, as well as publishers and circus owners, cashed in on Turpin and so contributed to the myth. A place called Turpin's cave at High Beech, Essex, advertised that schools, societies, beanfeasts 'and every person seeking pleasure' should come along there. There would be drink, tobacco, accommodation' at lowest possible prices, but the novelty was that 'Visitors will see Dick Turpin's sword, spurs, etc, that were dug out of the old cave; a sight worth seeing'.[65] A few years later a Yorkshire farmer told a journalist as a matter of fact that 'You see that white building there, that's where Dick Turpin got into after Black Bess died at Dringhouses, and he jumped out of the window nearly over the door there, and got away, when the London detectives broke into the house.'[66]

There was more scholarly tourism, too. In York the Richmondshire and North Riding Naturalists' Society visited the prison and were shown by the governor 'the condemned cell, with the identical waist band, leg manacles and hand cuffs worn by Dick Turpin'.[67] In 1891 the British Archaeological Association visitors were also shown the dungeon where Turpin was said to have been held.[68]

Given Turpin's predilection for pubs in real life it should come as no surprise that many claimed to be connected to him. One in Highgate, the Flask Tavern, South Grove, 'was popularly supposed to have been one of the haunts of Dick Turpin, the notorious highwayman'. There was a stable nearby where Black Bess sheltered and the place had numerous secret passages and places to hide.[69] In 2022 the pub still prominently advertises this association. The Wake Arms on the Epping Road was claimed as a frequent place visited by Turpin.[70] Similarly, the Nag's Head in Hounslow, which claimed to be a haunt of Turpin's, 'where in the rear of the premises, a decayed stable, called "Turpin's stable" is shown, where it is authoritatively stated the daring chief of highwaymen lodged his bonny Black Bess'.[71] There was also a pub in Black Bull Court, Wych Street, London, haunt of Turpin, Sheppard and others of their ilk, which was to be demolished.[72] None of these have any known link to the authentic Turpin.

It was not just pubs which were reputed to be linked with the long-dead criminal. One journalist claimed, without irony, that 'The average south Londoner is not aware that Dick Turpin once lived in a romantic cottage of Thornton heath not far from the Crystal Palace'. Apparently he 'emptied many a well packed purse in the district – in his day a desolate region'. It later became a farmhouse and was up for demolition.[73] Likewise, a house in Long Sutton, Lincolnshire, was said to have been a residence of Turpin with a secret cellar and a stable for Bess; the real Turpin did have a connection with Long Sutton in 1737–38 which has presumably led to this myth.[74]

There seemed no end to the Turpin mythology. One literary effort was *The Ballad of Dick Turpin* by Alfred Noyes (1880–1958).

'The daylight moon looked quietly down
Through the gathering dusk on London town

A smock-frocked yokel hobbled along
By Newgate, humming a country song.

Chewing a straw, he stood to stare
At the proclamation posted there:

"Three hundred guineas on Turpin's head,
Trap him alive or shoot him dead;
And a hundred more for his mate, Tom King".

He crouched like a tiger, about to spring.
Then he looked up, and he looked down;
And chuckling low, like a country clown,

Dick Turpin painfully hobbled away
In quest of his inn – "The Load of Hay"…

Alone in his stall, his mare, Black Bess,
Lifted her head in mute distress;
For five strange men had entered the yard
And looked at her long, and looked at her hard.

They went out, muttering under their breath;
And then – the dusk grew still as death.

But the velvet ears of the listening mare
Lifted and twitched. They were there- still there.

Hidden and waiting; for whom? And why?
The clock struck four, a set drew nigh.

It was King! Dick Turpin's mate.
The black mare whinnied. Too late! Too late!

They rose like shadows out of the ground
And grappled him there, without a sound.

"Throttle him quietly – choke - him dead!
Or we lose this hawk for a jay, they said".

They wrestled and heaved, five men to one.
And a yokel entered the yard, alone;

A smock-frocked yokel, hobbling slow;
But a fight is physic as all men know.

His age dropped off; he stood upright.
He leapt like a tiger into the fight.

Hand to hand, they fought in the dark;
For none could fire at a twisting mark.

Where he that shot at a foe might send
His pistol ball through the skull of a friend.

But "Shoot Dick, shoot" gasped out Tom King
"Shoot! Or damn it we both shall swing!
Shoot and chance it!" Dick leapt back.

He drew. He fired. At the pistols crack.
The wrestlers whirled. They scattered apart.
And the bullet drilled through Tom King's heart…

Dick Turpin dropped his smoking gun.
They had trapped him five men to one.

A gun in the hand of the crouching five.
They could take Dick Turpin now alive;

Take him and bind him and tell their tale
As a pot house boast, when they drank their ale.

He whistled, soft as a bird might call
And a head rope snapped in his birds dark stall

He whistled, soft as a nightingale
He heard the swish of her swinging tail.

There was no way out that the five could see
To heaven or hell, but the Tyburn tree;

No door but death, and yet once more
He whistled; though at a sweetheart's door.

The five men laughed at him, trapped alive;
And – the door crashed open behind the five!

Out of the stable, a wave of thunder,
Swept Black Bess, and the five went under.

He leapt to the saddle, a hoof turned stone,
Flashed blue fire, and their prize was gone…

He rode for one impossible thing; that in the morning light,
The towers of York might waken him
From London and last night

He rode to prove himself another,
And leave himself behind.
And the hunted self was like a cloud;
But the hunter like the wind.

Neck and neck they rode together;
That, in the day's first gleam,
Each might prove that the other self
Was but a mocking dream.

And the little sleeping villages, and the
Breathless country side.
Woke to the drum of the ghostly hooves,
But missed that ghostly ride.

They did not see, they did not hear as the ghostly
Hooves drew nigh,
The dark magnificent thief in the night
That rode so subtly by.

They woke, they rushed to the way-side door,
They saw what the midnight showed
A mare that came like a crested wave,
Along the Great North Road.

A flashing spark in the formless dark,
A flash from the hoof-spurned stone,
And the lifted face of a man
That took the starlight and was gone.

The heard the sound of a pounding chase
Three hundred yards away
There were fourteen men in a stream of sweat
And a plaster of Midland clay.

The starlight struck their pistol-butts as they
Passed in the clattering crowd
But the hunting wraith was away like the wind
At the heels of the hunted cloud.

He rode by the walls of Nottingham,
And over him as he went
Like ghosts across the Great North Road,
The boughs of Sherwood bent.

By Bawtry, all the chase but one has dropped
A league behind,
Yet one rider, haunted him, invisibly as the wind.

And northward, like a blacker night, he saw the moors
up-loom

And Don and Derwent sang to him, like a memory in the
gloom.

And northward, northward as he rode, and sweeter than
a prayer.
The voices of those hidden streams
The Trent, the Ouse and the Aire.

Streams that could never slake his thirst.
He heard them as he flowed
But one dumb shadow haunted him along the
Great North Road.

Till now, at dawn, the towers of York rose on
The reddening sky.
And Bess went down between his knees,
Like a breaking wave to die.

He lay beside her in the ditch, he kissed her lovely head,
And a shadow passed him like the wind and left him with
his dead.

He saw, but not that one as wakes, the city that he sought,
He had escaped from London Town, but not from his own
thought.

He strode up to the Mickle-gate, with none to say him nay.
And there he met his Other Self in the stranger light of day.

He strode up to the dreadful thing that in the gateway
stood
And it stretched out a ghostly hand that the dawn had
stained with blood.

It stood as in the gates of hell, with none to see or hear
"Welcome," it said, "Thou'st ridden well, and outstript all
but me".'[75]

As a piece of pro-Turpin propaganda this is excellent. The poem's sympathy is entirely with Turpin as the pursued man; no hint of his previous crimes is alluded to. Noyes was a poet, playwright and short story writer. He clearly had an interest in and sympathy with highwaymen, as his most famous poem is 'The Highwayman' (1906), in which a highwayman is riding into a trap, believing that his love (by the name of Bess, probably an allusion to Turpin's alleged horse) is awaiting him at a remote country inn. However, she is being held by soldiers and sacrifices herself to try and save his life. Noyes also wrote about Robin Hood and Sir Francis Drake. 'The Highwayman' is still a very popular poem today. The poem about Turpin selects two aspects of *Rookwood*: the attempted arrest of Turpin and the ride to York. The sting in the tail lets the reader know that Turpin's life will not be long after the end of the ride and infers that his death will be at York. The 300 guineas reward is fictional.

'The Highwayman' may well have been the inspiration for another piece of Turpin mythology that relates to the entrance to Bostall Woods in Plumstead, not far to the east of Charlton, Kent. Apparently there was a place in the wood called Turpin's cave, where he would hide from pursuing soldiers. Fanny, a barmaid in a nearby hostelry, would warn him of their arrival in the district by lighting a lamp that he could see from a distance. A sign relating the story also notes that Turpin was a notorious highwayman and was hanged at York in 1739.

In 1931 the then well-known singer Roy Leslie performed Dick Turpin's ride to York, claiming it to be factual 'we all learned that at college'. The song includes contemporary references to platinum blondes and a holidaymaker fresh from Blackpool as well as Turpin's committing a number of bloodless robberies en route from London to York. There is also a folk song about the ride, with different lyrics, in which Turpin shoots at the 'chief of the police' and his bullet strikes King instead.

Another early twentieth-century Turpin enthusiast, of the same generation as Noyes, was Mr G. Coleman Green, born in 1878 and living in Bayswater, London, in 1922. He read a poem he had written titled 'Dick Turpin's Ride to York' at the Marylebone Central Evening Schools. The scene was the Spaniard's Inn, Hampstead. The main character in the poem is instantly recognisable by his description:

'With white peruke, and shaved chin

Three cornered hat, and sabre bright'.

Turpin tells the pub landlord that he will tell him and the gathered company 'How I took the road to York'. It seems that Turpin is a ghost and that:

'I was but known through fame of Bess

All knew her by her great black coat

I, Turpin, loved her none the less'

He then tells the gathered pub customers, 'with Turpin, King of the highwaymen' he will begin his story. He starts at Edgware Mill, being pursued by Bow Street Runners (who never existed in Turpin's time, but are often portrayed as his main enemies). He rides over Hampstead Heath, to Biggleswade, Huntingdon, Grantham, Newark, Retford, Gainsborough, Doncaster, Snaith, Selby and then is spotted by a patrol of dragoons. Eluding them, the Ouse is crossed, and Fulford is reached. Then, within sight of York, Black Bess dies. The poem takes much of its matter from *Rookwood*.[76]

Green gathered together a whole scrapbook of cuttings and his jottings about Turpin. A little concerned his birth and death, but most was about his career as a highwayman and places and objects possibly connected to it. Much of this was fiction and wishful thinking on Green's part. For instance he states that Turpin stole from the butcher he was apprenticed to, that the Essex gang was broken up by dragoons in Epping Forest, that King was an aristocratic young man and that the fight in which the latter died was with the Bow Street Runners.

The collection included notes on how Green had it on the authority of Judge Parkes that Turpin's Oak in north Finchley was Turpin's observation post, and that he and Bess passed it on the ride to York. A field near Hampstead church was where, said an elderly man, Turpin cleaned Bess's bridle and saddle. There were pictures and notes of places where Turpin was said to have stayed or hidden, such as an old coaching inn in Little France, Westminster, Hartsbourne Manor in Bushey Heath and a toll house in Highgate. A resident in an old cottage on Harefield Lane in Uxbridge told him that a long-dead owner of the property had once helped Turpin. Green even rode part of the route to London and asked people he passed by about it, but few could usefully help him.

Green writes, 'Some people say that Turpin was a myth, but we cannot ignore many of the details contained in these Notes which have been collected from many independent sources'. He later states that the 'Fact remains' Turpin did ride to York to escape arrest. Of Turpin's character, Green observes:

> 'Turpin seems to have indulged in a series of daredevil adventures, such as delaying coaches, robbery under arms.
>
> It should be noted he WAS NOT HANGED FOR MURDER but for horse stealing.
>
> His love for Black Bess in my opinion is a great English epic and I certainly think there is considerable basis of Fact about it'.

Later he adds: 'Dick Turpin, who seems to be appreciated for his fine qualities as a horseman and whose daring points to the conclusion that he would have been more successful as a cavalry leader'.[77]

In 1939 there was an exhibition in York to mark the bicentenary of Turpin's death. Two relics shown were a leg brace girdle and an iron leg bar. There was also a carved ivory whistle allegedly given by Turpin to the clergyman who attended him on the gallows. The chains weighed upwards of 28 pounds. It was stated that it was in 1379 that the place in Knavesmire was chosen as the York Tyburn.[78] The exhibition tried to demythologise him: 'Turpin was never more than an ordinary rogue… Turpin had few friends even among the gentlemen of the road'.[79]

It appears there was a radio drama by Colin Simpson in 1952 about Turpin, which was reviewed thus:

'I liked Colin Simpson's Turpin for its realism and lack of sentimentality. Legendary haloes for highwaymen derive more from tale tellers and romantic rhymsters than from the populace, though an occasional spectacular generosity with other people's money would be popular from the beneficiaries. Mr Simpson showed us the "immortal outlaw" as he would be seen by his victims and the public generally, that is to say, as a sordid criminal who did not stop at murder and for whom the gallows at York was a fitting end. The story was not less but more interesting for being divested of a false romance and presented as a straight period piece'.[80]

Political capital was still being made in reference to the long-dead bandit, as it had been before, 'The only difference between Dick Turpin and the socialist group which control Durham County Council is that the Councillors do not wear masks'.[81] A trade union meeting advocated Dick Turpin tactics for wage negotiations.[82] More recently, a newspaper reported tax demands so swingeing that 'they would make Dick Turpin blush'.[83] Banks overcharged, it was claimed, like Dick Turpin.[84]

References to criminals as being Dick Turpins continued to be made, as in 1924 when a thirteen-year-old lad stole a horse by riding it away in Hull.[85] Ambrose Benson, a seventeen-year-old printer from

Ripon, a burglar, was apparently led into crime by reading a life of Turpin and watching cinema films.[86]

A new legend was also written off as fact. This was 'one of Dick Turpin's lesser known exploits', robbing the Duke of Portland in his own grounds at Bulstrode in Buckinghamshire. Turpin rode up to the carriage bearing the Duke holding what seemed to be a roll of paper, but actually concealed a pistol and demanded the Duke's watch. Once the watch was handed over, Turpin nodded and bowed as he departed the scene.[87]

Actor-producer Billy Rhodes bet a fellow producer 5s that he could not copy Turpin's ride from London to York on his horse Ralph, wearing eighteenth-century garb. He left London at 2.30pm.[88]

The Turpin myth had been much spread about via comics aimed at boys; this had occurred in the Victorian era (there was a 254-volume series in the 1880s titled *Black Bess: The Knight King of the Road*), in the 1920s and again in the 1950s. These gave Turpin entirely invented adventures, and there was little about the original man therein. Riding Black Bess, this capable horseman, swordsman and all-round action hero did battle with a variety of enemies, acting generally for the common good. In the 1950s *Dick Turpin Thriller Library*, Turpin is referred to as Captain, acquires allies in the shape of a comic Irishman, a subservient Black man and a woman named Moll Moonlight, and their adventures become increasingly bizarre. In one story they battle a Count Vronsky and a monstrous defrosted Siberian giant with the strength of twenty men. Turpin was increasingly merely a name and a very few selected characteristics on which to hang a series of exciting adventure stories.[89]

There are also memorabilia and items featuring Turpin, which do not exist for most criminals. In the nineteenth and twentieth century Royal Doulton Potteries made character jugs showing the head of Turpin, wearing a tricorne, sometimes moustached and sometimes masked. They also produced figurines of him on Black Bess. Staffordshire Potteries produced similar figures. Coach House

Breweries called one of their cask ales Dick Turpin. A railway locomotive was named *Dick Turpin*. There is a Dick Turpin jigsaw and a Dick Turpin boardgame. A punk T-shirt has an image of the highwayman and the motif 'God save Dick Turpin'. There are also Dick Turpin pantomimes. Race horses in the mid-nineteenth century were called Dick Turpin.

There are a number of pubs called Dick Turpin. This is interesting because few pubs are named after murderers. There is The Burke and Hare in Edinburgh, and from 1976–88 the Ten Bells pub in Spitalfields was named the Jack the Ripper, and even had alleged memorabilia (it no longer does). Apart from these, there are, fortunately, no known pubs named after the Krays, John Christie or John Haigh or other well-known killers.

Turpin-named pubs are found in Wickford, Essex, in Newcastle under Lyme in Staffordshire, and in Redbridge. Other pubs have alleged associations with Turpin; almost all of these links are entirely spurious. The Plough in south Ealing is one, as is the Old Hats in west Ealing and the George in Acton. A Mr Haynes wrote of the former:

> 'It was said to have been kept at one time by an uncle of the celebrated highwayman, Dick Turpin. When pursued he generally disappeared in this direction, but his hiding place remained a mystery until the old Plough inn was pulled down to make way for the present modern day hotel. A small room was then found concealed in a mass of masonry, and in it were a table, a bedstead and a pistol with Dick's initials on the handle. The landlord had not the slightest suspicion of the existence of this little chamber'.[90]

When the author visited this pub in 2021 he found that the young man behind the bar had not heard of the Turpin connection before that day, but that the author was the second person to have mentioned it to him. There is no reference to Turpin in the pub.

A similar story is recounted by Charles Harper concerning the Coach and Horses tavern in Hockley in the Hole in north London. A portmanteau was discovered bearing the words, on the inner side of the lid, 'R. TVRPIN'. The portmanteau was large enough to contain a suit of linen.[91]

There are other accounts of similar relics. The Spaniards pub on Hampstead Heath had Turpin's pistol, bloodstained sword and the knife he ate his last meal with.[92] Another pistol, a double barrelled flintlock, allegedly owned by Turpin, was found at the White Bear inn, Drury Lane, and was marked 'Presented to Dick Turpin'.[93] The Reindeer pub in Banbury also had a pistol with an inscription to him.[94] Dick Turpin's wallet, marked R. Turpin, was acquired by the Yorkshire Philosophical Society in 1911.[95] A Southwark firm of costumiers lent Turpin's boots and hat to a Peterborough music hall proprietor.[96] A Cambridge gentleman bought a velvet coat, mask, spurs and yet more pistols belonging to Turpin which had been left at a Cambridge pub. Some of these relics were patently fake; the items at the Cambridge pub were stated as having been left by Turpin in January 1739, yet he had been incarcerated in York for three months by then and was never released.[97]

Another pub with alleged Turpin links was the Mother Redcap in Upper Holloway. The stable there sheltered Black Bess before the ride to York. The author of the report was not one for fiction, referring to 'the notorious and cowardly cut throat that Harrison Ainsworth attempted to transform into a gay and gallant cavalier' and noted there was no evidence to support any link between the pub and Turpin. Interestingly enough, however, 'The belief is, however, fondly entertained by old dwellers in Holloway'.[98]

The Bell, the pub in Hempstead where Turpin was born, also made use of his links there. In 1899 it was stated that some years ago the wall of the pub had been adorned recording the fact.[99] In 1950 the landlord, a Mr Collings, had a sign over the front door that read 'Dick Turpin's birthplace'. Officials from the town planning department ordered him to remove it. Major General Skinner, chairman of the parish council, said it was 'ghastly' and the chair of the local Women's Institute agreed that it was a disgrace. However, Collings stuck to his guns, 'The most famous highwayman in history was born under this roof and they want to stop me saying so. Hempstead is a historic village and I want to put it on the map'.[100] Decades later advertising for the pub stated 'Dine where Dick Turpin was born' and there was a 'Dick Turpin's charcoal grill bar'. The newspaper advert also showed a silhouette of a highwayman.[101] The pub still proudly announces on an exterior wall that Turpin was born there. Its name was changed to the Rose and Crown in the nineteenth century and later it became the Blue Bell. Apparently in the 1980s there were memorabilia, relics and even a Turpin family tree down to 1971 there.[102] Regrettably the pub, which was reopened in 2003, is, at time of writing, closed. It is a Grade II listed building.

The Blue Boar pub in York also makes the most of its Turpin connections, for he rested there for a day as a corpse in 1739. In 2021 the author visited and saw that inside there is a notice pointing the visitor to a lower room, named the Turpin room. There are faux notices 'Dick Turpin – Notorious Highwayman and killer – 1705–1739 – Laid out in these cellars after being executed for the crime of horse theft'. A tricorne hat, pistol and purse are also featured. Nearby is another poster 'Dick Turpin wanted for highway robberys Reward by Order! Dead or Alive'. There is also a coffin with the legend 'Here lies the body of John Palmer formerly Richard Turpin'. Finally, there is a black plaque to Turpin. Apparently the staff at the York Dungeon provided guidance for this room.

Less well known is the Red Lion on Merchantgate in York, which also makes allusions to its Turpin connections, but this is fantasy. Exterior signs at the pub claim that Turpin patronised the inn and escaped from enemies by leaving via the priest's hole and chimney: 'It is rumoured to have been an escape route used by the infamous highwayman Dick Turpin. The pub may have been one of his favourite haunts'. However, the only time that Turpin is known to have been in York was as a prisoner in 1738–39. Possibly his actual connection with the Red Lion in London's Whitechapel has been confused with the York pub. The Three Legged Mare pub in High Petergate in York refers (correctly), in its interior, to Turpin being hanged on such a device in 1739.

The centuries-old George and Dragon pub on Acton High Street in west London also has laid claim to an association with Turpin. An article stated:

> 'Infamous Dick Turpin drank at the George and Dragon and some say he still haunts its rambling corridors. Acton's oldest pub played host to Britain's most famous highwayman who preyed on unsuspecting travellers on the Uxbridge Road. Black Bess, his trusty stead, bedded down in the horse's stables. Today, landlord Mick Newman recounts tales of sightings of the legendary figure but has yet to see him for himself'.[103]

However, the establishment was not a public house until later in the century, according to Dr and Mrs Harper-Smith, late Acton historians.

The Temeraire, in Saffron Walden, on one of its boards, provides local history information, as this chain of pubs usually does. It refers to Turpin being a highwayman, housebreaker and horse thief, but unfortunately it repeats the mythology begun by Bayes in stating that Turpin was a cattle lifter and smuggler. It adds a new myth of its own: that he was hanged at York 'for murdering an Epping innkeeper'.

Both the Flask on Highgate Hill and the Spaniards still (2022) feature references to Turpin. At the entrance to the former is a sign stating that Turpin 'the famous highwayman', stabled Black Bess there and that this 'may be true'. It also states 'it is said' that Turpin rode Black Bess to York to escape capture for a murder he may have committed but was taken in York. At the entrance to the Spaniards and on the front page of the drinks menu, the reader is told that Turpin's father was landlord of the pub and Turpin 'was said' to have hidden there, and that his ghost and that of Black Bess have been seen there.

The Chandos Arms in Edgware (not far from the scene of one of the gang's last notorious housebreakings) was another pub allegedly patronised by Turpin.[104] A cottage in Buckden Hill was claimed as a home of Turpin.[105] A house in Long Sutton with a secret chamber was claimed as Turpin's house.[106] A cottage in Edlestone was also claimed as a hideaway of Turpin.[107] The Green Man in Epping had a 'Dick Turpin chamber', a room in which there was a chest large enough to conceal three or four men.[108] The 'Dick Turpin' cottage on Stony Lane in Thaxted was, in the 1930s, a shop selling ladies' underwear.[109] It is now a private residence but still has the legend 'Dick Turpin's cottage' over the door lintel and on the window sill can be seen Turpin memorabilia (in 2022). A thatched cottage opposite the Blue Bell pub in Hempstead has the name 'Dick Turpin's cottage' affixed to its exterior.

However, the White Hart pub on Drury Lane, from where Turpin and his fellow thugs rode in 1735 to attack Farmer Lawrence in his home, has nothing in the pub to mention this. Ironically it has signs telling the customer to beware of thieves and has some prints from Hogarth's Beer Street and Gin Lane on its walls. At least this was the author's experience in September 2021.

Stories of Turpin abound. One Percy Talaman, resident of Hanwell in Middlesex, recounted the following tale in a collection of the locality's oral histories in about 1980, referring to his youth decades earlier:

'I remember going to Stud Farm on Monday evenings…
the "round house" in the garden which Dick Turpin
was alleged to have used as a hideout when chased by

the bailiffs. A brace of pistols and a horse harness hung on the inner window walls supposedly to have been the property of the farmer of that period aiding and abetting him in this matter'.[110]

The only other known criminals celebrated at present by a pub sign in Britain are Burke and Hare at 2 High Briggs in Edinburgh. In 1828 they killed sixteen poor people to sell the fresh corpses to doctors who did not ask questions. It is hard to justify why these two murderers are worthy of such commemoration, and compared to Turpin they are both more recent and killed far more people. If the Jack the Ripper pub in Spitalfields had to change its name (to the Ten Bells), as it did after twelve years in 1988, then surely this should too.

There were also a number of people who claimed personal connections with Turpin. A Mr Gee's father knew Turpin and helped him on Helpstone Heath.[111] Charles Mortlock, aged eighty-six 1928 was from Hempstead and claimed he was descended on the female side of his family from Turpin. Today the web site Ancestry.co.uk lists over 230 family trees which claim Turpin as one of their own; an archivist at Essex Record Office told the author that a researcher there had claimed descent from Turpin, a man he admired[112] Mrs Emma Whitaker of Colchester, aged ninety-three in 1931, said that her father-in-law knew Turpin well.[113] More bizarrely, a Mrs Elizabeth Freeman, aged ninety-two in 1950, said that she once served Turpin beer at the Bell and Swan pub in Stamford.[114] Another elderly woman was a fan and the centenarian declared that she only put the radio on to listen to tales of Turpin, 'I never tire of reading of his exploits'.[115]

Turpin was certainly excused or seen as a hero by others. A socialist from a farm workers' union was at a meeting of the union in Hempstead and, noting his pleasure to be at Turpin's birthplace, added 'the reason Turpin and many other men became highwaymen was not because they were wicked, but because it was the only possible life for a man of spirit in the age in which they lived'. He added, though, that he did not want to see more Dick Turpins.[116] One man, recounting his youth, recalled that after pleading with his father to let the family visit the circus, he eventually went and admired Black Bess. He then wrote, 'If Black Bess made me enthusiastic, Dick Turpin mounted on her almost sent me wild with admiration. His scarlet coat, how gorgeous. His lace cravat, how graceful'.[117]

It is hard to think of any other criminal in England, with the exception of the semi-mythological Robin Hood, who would be treated in such a way. John George Haigh stayed at the Onslow Court Hotel in London for five years and was a regular at the George in Crawley but neither acknowledges a connection with the acid bath murderer. Even the Great Train Robbers and the Krays of the 1960s, who have their admirers, have not been celebrated. However, in 2015 the Nag's Head pub in Knightsbridge did have a reference on its wall to the fact that two notorious murderers of the 1940s, Neville Heath and John Haigh, were both regulars there.

Could this be because Turpin existed in the far distant past? This cannot be the only answer. Jonathan Wild is from the same era and is now almost forgotten. Claude Duval and Sixteen String Jack were both once well-known highwaymen, but again they are virtually forgotten. Turpin's antiquity is one factor, but it cannot be the only one. Luck and Ainsworth perhaps help to supply part of the answer.

This being said, there is no statue of Turpin (though in 1912 there was a reference to a suggestion that one be put up to commemorate the ride to York), whereas in Nottingham there is one for Robin Hood and at Derby there is one for Bonnie Prince Charlie. Rob Roy MacGregor has a statue in Stirling and another in Aberdeenshire. There are, at least, some limits to the kindly posthumous treatment of Turpin.[118] Yet there are streets named after Turpin; none, surprisingly perhaps, in York, but there is a Turpin's Yard in Greenwich and more appropriately a Turpin's Lane in Woodford, not far from some of the crimes of the Gregory gang. In Long Sutton, Lincolnshire, there is a Dick Turpin's Way and a York Ride.

It may be instructive to compare Turpin with a Scottish and an Australian equivalent. Rob Roy MacGregor (c.1671–1734) was a cattle raider, operated a cattle protection racket and was an outlaw as well as taking part in unsuccessful rebellions against the Crown. In later life he was pardoned and died peacefully in bed. However, a biography issued in his own lifetime, a novel by Sir Walter Scott in 1817 and several films in the twentieth century have created for him a daring and heroic image. There was poetry and music celebrating him. More recently, statues have been erected of him in Stirling and in Peterculter, Aberdeen. The statue in Stirling was put up in 1975 and there was no controversy about the figure it depicted; he was celebrated as a legendary hero and the 1950s Walt Disney film fantasy about him was cited with approval. As the 1962 film *The Man who shot Liberty Valance* notes, 'When the legend becomes fact, print the legend'.

Australia's Ned Kelly (1854–80) is a similar case. He became involved with crime as a teenager and served time in prison for robbery. Along with three other men he later shot and killed three policemen and so was declared an outlaw. There were more raids and another killing, but in 1880 after a shoot-out with police he was captured, tried and executed. Since then there have been many ballads, books and films about Kelly, mostly very favourable to him, and he has become a national icon. In part because of his manifesto, Kelly has been seen as a political and social revolutionary, a friend to the underdog and an enemy to the oppressive police and their masters. There is even a statue to him, six metres high, showing him in his home-made armour and holding a gun, unveiled in 1992 at Glenrowan, scene of his final skirmish with the police. Proprietors of a local tourist shop paid $12,000 to erect it. It helped put the town on the tourist map and that was presumably its intention. This was controversial for the local police and descendants of those officers killed by the Kelly gang were understandably offended by what they saw as the celebration of a murderer (one stating 'It glorifies a murderer and a terrorist, what kind of that message does that give to society?') and they wanted it taken down. They thought the true hero of the Glenrowan siege was the teacher who warned that the Kelly gang was planning to derail a train whose arrival was imminent, thus saving lives.

In all these instances men who were once viewed as criminals are now largely seen as heroes, transformed by the power of the press and the moving image. The question must be why this has occurred. One answer is that these figures from the past are important for what they represent and what they symbolise, not necessarily for the men themselves or their actions. All criminals are inherently anti-authority, as they are breaking the law in the commission of their crimes. Authority and the law can be seen as being corrupt, incompetent and oppressive. Therefore those who oppose it can be lauded as being heroic, standing up for their less heroic, i.e. law-abiding, peers. The passage of time also serves to reduce the perceived criminality of their actions; very few people have heard of Thomas Morris, the man Turpin shot dead, or the policemen killed by Kelly and his gang. And fiction lets the writer use their imagination and dispense with tiresome facts and controversies to provide an entertaining experience for the reader/listener/viewer.

This seems to be a fairly universal experience, certainly in the English speaking world (American outlaws of the late nineteenth century 'Wild West' are sometimes seem in such a light too), and these three criminals are sometimes referred to as 'Robin Hood figures'. Robin Hood is the famous legendary English outlaw who began to be written about in the fourteenth century. Although it is possible that there was a 'real' Robin Hood, the character in the stories is fictional. He is an outlaw who robs the rich to give to the poor, a great archer and swordsman, lives in Sherwood Forest and, with his faithful companions, is beset by enemies such as the Sheriff of Nottingham.

There are many books, films and TV series about Robin Hood, and even a statue in Nottingham to his memory. Yet 'he' is different from the others for he is purely fictional and new writers are free to embellish the story, add characters and shape them to meet the perceived needs of the present-day viewer. The myth of Robin Hood is strong and he is cast as a heroic ideal; there is no need to have any qualms about messy historical reality in his case. Later criminals have been likened to Robin Hood, often to the benefit of their public image.

However, some saw through the veil of myth cast over common criminals. One Fitzwilliam, writing in 1888, complained 'Mr Harrison Ainsworth and a host of Grub Street imitators, have endeavoured to cast a halo of romance, which, when stripped of its trappings of fine language, and romantic surroundings, leaves us with a poor specimen of depraved humanity'.[119]

Still the mythologising persists. Professor Sharpe discusses a Turpin pantomime in his work of 2005, set in and around a dairy farm, but this was not the only one. In 2001 a pantomime was written 'loosely based on the famous tale of Dick Turpin and his ride to York'. Turpin is meant to be played by the principal boy. The performance includes songs from the 1960s musical *Oliver*, and even more bizarrely, songs by 1970s Swedish group Abba and from the film *Ghostbusters*. The story is set in York in 1732 and Turpin is in Newgate, awaiting imminent execution. The common people trumpet his virtues, with lines such as 'That's not fair. Dick Turpin was a good man' and 'He's helped many a poor person in his time'. The rich mayor, to reinforce this point, counters this by replying 'And stolen from the likes of me'. Later a character says 'He never hurt anyone. It's just that he sometimes takes from those who have got too much to give to those who haven't got anything'. Just to ensure the audience has got the message, Turpin himself says 'Like Robin Hood I rob the rich to give to the poor'. Turpin escapes Newgate and the incompetent lawmen fail to take him. He steals 200 guineas from the mayor and all ends happily as he and his girlfriend, the improbably named Cindy, plan to marry and with the 200 guineas buy a pub in Lincoln.[120] The Turpin pantomime continued to be staged in 2021 with adverts for a performance at the Grand Opera House, York, of *Dick Turpin Rides Again, The Legend Returns*, though the posters do not obviously show anyone decked out as a highwayman.

Turpin is also a figure in the tourist trade, nowhere more so than at York where he died. The York Dungeon is a tourist attraction in the centre of York, established on Clifford Street in 1988, clearly imitating the London Dungeon. This is a showcase of history and entertainment, displaying elements of the city's gory and criminal past, including Guy Fawkes, witches, the plague, torture and execution. One of the 'attractions' is Dick Turpin. Initially the exhibits were static displays, but now actors in costume engage with visitors in entertaining dialogue. In order to publicise the opening of the Dungeon, a man dressed in eighteenth-century costume was to recreate the ride from London to York, but over three days and stopping off at various locations en route.[121]

In 2021 the York Dungeon's promotion leaflet showed a highwayman on horseback with pistol and money bag, in eighteenth-century garb, next to two modern tourists on an open coach. The text stated 'Live Actor Shows including the Vikings, Guy Fawkes & Dick Turpin'. Inside, the eleventh of eleven attractions is the highwayman with his money bag and gun with the text, 'Dick Turpin. Look out for Dick, he'll take your money, valuables and your life!' On the exterior of the York Dungeon, in a window, are two images of figures, one of which is a villain with a gun and the words 'Look out, Dick's about'.

More soberly, Turpin is also prominent in the York Castle Museum, based in the former prison. The promotional leaflet mentions him twice. In the illustrated York timeline near the beginning of the museum, his stay in the prison and execution are both mentioned, although both occurred in 1739. In a display of porcelain are two figures of Turpin and one of 'Tom' King. In the prison section of the museum is a display of handcuffs and various restraints, including 'waist girdle and attached manacle to pinion the arms. Traditionally said to have been worn by Dick Turpin'. Then there are the cells, mostly about six feet wide and eighteen feet long, with a barred window to the exterior, the adjacent cell and the wall facing the corridor. These each have a prisoner's name on the entrance and one is Richard Turpin. Visitors can sit on a bench and a hologram of a well-dressed man purporting to be Turpin appears and tells of his hopes and fears, hoping to be sent to America where he envisages there are horses and, though admitting his guilt, he wishes to be tried in Essex where he is sure he will not be convicted. Finally, there is a room where the fates of the prisoners are detailed on a large wall. For Turpin there is an E-Fit by Ian Greaves of the North Yorkshire Police based on descriptions of Turpin as given in his lifetime.

A mile out of York is the place where Tyburn was located. The site itself is commemorated by a small monument with 'Tyburn' written on the top. Nearby is an explanatory board about the site and some of the notables hanged there, including the Jacobite rebels of 1746. Turpin is given a prominent place, but his birth year is given as 1706 and a note states that he 'was not famous in his lifetime', and that the legend was created by Ainsworth, so there is room for error. Turpin's grave, not far from the museum, is also highlighted.

York tourist guides note the city's Turpin connections and try to dispel the myth with a more factual account. Yet inadvertently errors have crept in. One guide refers to Turpin as having 'committed several murders' (as well as that of his 'accomplice Matthew King') and again gives his birth year as 1706.[122] Another states that Turpin in prison wrote to his brother and that Smith was a teacher.[123]

In contrast to York, Essex makes little of Turpin. The nearest museum, at Saffron Walden, has only one item in its collection which is Turpin related and that is only a news cutting. In 1899 a sign adorned the pub in Hempstead denoting his birth there, and it was described as 'a picturesque timber plaster and framed cottage', dating to about 1480. It was also said that there is a group of nine trees in a circle near the pub known as Turpin's Ring and it is alleged that the young Turpin indulged in cock-fighting there.[124]

Another attempt at capturing the tourist trade that employed Turpin's name was a three-day coach tour of 'Epping Forest and Dick Turpin country'.[125] Essex Tourism also produced a leaflet titled 'Dick Turpin Country' in 1986, giving a mix of historical information and places of tourist interest, as well as places to stay and eat. Much of the history was erroneous: Turpin's date of baptism was given as his date of birth, he was said to have been arrested in York, and to have tortured a woman to death, and poaching was said to have been a capital crime.[126]

Ghosts are a popular phenomenon and there are numerous stories of alleged sightings of Turpin as a ghost. One historian of ghosts wrote 'The King and Queen of British ghosts are Dick Turpin and Anne Boleyn... Dick Turpin haunts as many pubs as Anne Boleyn does palaces and stately homes'.[127] Likewise Richard Jones wrote 'The ghost of Dick Turpin must be one of the busiest in England. For that matter, with the number of pubs that claim his living self as a previous customer, it's a miracle he was able to stay upright in the saddle'.[128] Many of these sightings refer to Turpin's horse as Black Bess, showing that the myth predominates even here.

Unsurprisingly, many ghosts emanate from pubs. Some are in London. Jones states that the Flask in Highgate has a ghostly Turpin as a pub customer.[129] However, he details the Spaniard's Inn, Hampstead, as the most haunted Turpin pub, with Black Bess being stabled there and people hearing ghostly hoofbeats in the car park at night-time and the horse's master being seen in the pub itself, cloaked and disappearing through a wall as well as his presence being felt by customers.[130] It has been alleged that Turpin's father was the publican and his son used it as a hideout. There is a ghost in an upper room and a mounted ghost has been seen nearby.[131] The Rose and Crown in Clay Hill, allegedly kept by Turpin's grandfather Mr Mott, is another haunted Turpin pub.[132] Clarke refers to a Turpin haunted pub in Shoreditch.[133]

It was also alleged that the property in Epping Forest next to Turpin's cave was haunted. One author of a ghost book was told by the owner that there was a carved, cruel face on the cave wall. Her daughter said that she had seen a ghost at the nearby High Beech, a white misty shape on horseback. She had also seen a figure by the front garden gate near to the cave and felt a cold sensation in a room in the house.[134]

There were also alleged ghostly hauntings. Apparently Turpin's ghost rode from the Horse and Wells in Woodford to Knighton Woods at night.[135] It was claimed two weeks later in the same newspaper that a rook had seen Turpin ride through an Essex forest, and that a highwayman swung from the gibbets there.[136]

The Chequers Inn at Smarden, Kent, dates back to the fourteenth century. Apparently staff and guests there have seen 'a roughly handsome man dressed in green velvet, a tricorn hat and riding boots'. He has also been seen at a writing table, with a quill pen, and riding outside on Black Bess.[137] The Bell Inn, Stilton, in Cambridgeshire is also allegedly haunted by Turpin. Apparently he stayed there for nine weeks when he was on the run, jumped out of a window and onto Black Bess and then took the Great North Road. The ghost has been seen riding through the streets and a guest woke up one night to see a hooded figure in his room.[138]

Turpin is also said to haunt his final physical resting place, St George's Fields in York, where on a path nearby, 'Many claim to have seen the spectral figure of a rider, sitting astride a black horse, dressed in a tunic and a black tricorn hat. He is said to remain quite still, partly obscured by the trees'.[139] At Heathrow airport, built partly on Hounslow Heath, airport employees feel or hear him behind them, breathing on their necks, barking or howling, and when they turn round, no one is there.[140]

The Cock Inn at Sibson is another alleged Turpin haunt. Apparently he lived at his parents' cottage in nearby Hinckley and kept Black Bess in nearby Lindley Wood. Turpin's ghost is seen in the deserted village of Streeton Baskerville, where he is seen in black tricorn hat, a coat with red sleeves and riding a phantom horse.[141] The Old Swan in Wroughton, Buckinghamshire, is another of Turpin's haunts, and the large stone outside is known as Turpin's stone for mounting Black Bess.[142] On the Loughton Road in north-east London on Traps Hill a ghost on a black horse is seen riding down with a woman clutching his waist, feet dragging on the ground and shrieking piteously. This is meant to be the ghost of Mrs Shelley, a rare example of one ghost tormenting another.[143]

Woodfield House in Weathercock Lane, Apsley, Bedfordshire, was a place where a farmer killed his daughter and her lover. Turpin supposedly found the bodies and blackmailed the farmer into giving him shelter when he needed it. Subsequently there have been claims of phantom horses and a man dismounting there.[144] Oddly enough none of the haunted pubs have any factual links to pubs associated with the real Turpin and his fellows.

A television programme, *Most Haunted Live*, ran a three-part Dick Turpin special at the end of December 2003. Three locations were investigated for paranormal activity: in York at Knavesmire, the churchyard and the York Dungeon, on Hampstead Heath and at Epping Forest. The conclusion was that the latter was the most haunted, 'that's where his energy was, more so than any other location'. This is a conclusion that could just as well be reached by reading contemporary histories and newspapers about Turpin's crimes. A more recent paranormal investigation came out with nothing new and ironically scuppered its own claims to veracity when the investigators asked the alleged ghost of Turpin what the name of his horse was and the voice replied, somewhat indistinctly, 'Black Bess'.

Some myths are palpably false. One is that Turpin stole a silver plate from the parish church of Walthamstow and then ransomed it.

Alas, this and other items of church silverware went missing in 1674, over three decades before Turpin's birth.[145]

In 1985 there was a computer game for the Spectrum 48K titled *Dick Turpin*. As was then customary, there were basic static graphics and text descriptions where the player, who played Turpin, had to type in their decisions, being prompted by the message 'What now Dick?' The player had to retrieve various artefacts in order to reach York and outwit the soldiers who were seeking him. Apart from the York reference there is a nod to reality when the hero is confronted in his cave by Thomas Morris. There is also a screen showing a highwayman holding up a coach. Apart from this there is virtually no criminality in Turpin's actions and so Turpin the hero is here far removed from the real man.

A recent (2021) novelisation using Turpin as its main character is that of Richard Foreman, a historical novelist, in *Turpin Assassin: Hero, Highwayman, Legend*. This incorporates some facts: Turpin is married to Elizabeth, is a butcher's son from Essex and uses a pseudonym, John Palmer, albeit when posing as a gentleman in London's high society. However, this is also historical fiction, though it uses a real figure as its main character rather than having real figures as subsidiary characters, as in Bernard Cornwell's *Sharpe* series. Dr Samuel Johnson (who never met Turpin) also features. Turpin is given a fictional accomplice, Nathaniel Gill, and a fictional enemy, an aristocratic French assassin, and the plot is, of course, the fruit of the novelist's imagination. As with much of the fiction involving Turpin, character and plot are adapted to suit the needs of the story. Turpin, with a modicum of historical reality, may not be the parfait gentil knight of *Rookwood*, but he is still a recognisable hero for a modern readership. The book was clearly popular, as a sequel appeared in 2022, and there are other modern Dick Turpin novels in which Turpin is a hero, righting wrongs and generally very unlike the real man. The public demand for Turpin as gallant hero is as strong as it has been in the two previous centuries.

It can be argued that the main purpose of fiction, for viewers, tourists and readers, is to provide entertainment, not education. The former can serve to double as propaganda, as unconsciously or not, the reader can be beguiled into the truth of the author's creations and thus beliefs can be implanted or reinforced. Even if we do not imbue fiction with a necessarily sinister intention, in the light of any historical grounding the reader can certainly be led astray. The fictional Turpin and his exploits are entertaining – there can be no doubt about that. Daring deeds cannot but win admiration. In the twentieth century and beyond, the screen, whether large or small, dominated mass entertainment and it is to this that we shall now turn, for it has helped foster the myth of Dick Turpin. Turpin in fiction is a highwayman, but his criminality is minimised. He is never vicious or cowardly, but brave and a first-class horseman. He helps the downtrodden and takes on evildoers. He is without doubt a hero.

As Hagger concludes:

> 'But like the multi-slice image of a cultural scan three centuries, an attentive examination still reveals much about the physiology of article and enduring myth. From England's most wanted gangster to literary object of desire, to pulp fiction swashbuckling hero to pop culture heart throb he has survived these disparate stages of postmodern commodification with his enigma intact. A Dick Turpin for the twenty-first century can now come out of hiding'.[146]

Unlike the fictional Bulldog Drummond and Dick Barton, whose heyday of popularity is long gone, but like the equally fictional James Bond and Sherlock Holmes, the fictional Turpin is a figure who can be endlessly modified to suit the demands of the contemporary world, despite, or perhaps because, he is stuck in the historically unfashionable eighteenth century.

Chapter 7

Turpin in Film and TV

Books, and especially fiction, are a prime way of familiarising the public with a particular historical event or personage. Theatre and circuses in the nineteenth century popularised Turpin, especially with their dramatization of the ride to York. But in the following century and beyond, to ensure continued fame, exposure on the big or small screen is an even better way of bringing characters to the public's attention. As popular as Ian Fleming's *James Bond* novels of the 1950s and 1960s were and are, the subsequent films based on the character and his exploits are even more so. This is surely true of Dick Turpin too. Watching a film or TV show is undemanding in both time and intellect compared to reading even the best of books. It can also be a sociable activity rather than a solitary one.

Some books about Turpin refer to the films and TV series, but their examination is generally limited. There has been a brief survey of Turpin depictions in film and TV in the last major work covering Turpin, focussing on *Carry on Dick*, in an examination of Turpin as a cultural phenomenon. It seems that there was a Turpin film in about 1912, as a cinema in Lincoln was showing *The Adventures of Dick Turpin*, but there is no more known about this film and it probably no longer exists.[1] Then there was the 1922 film, *Dick Turpin's ride to York*, starring Matheson Lang and made by Stoll Studios. It was 80 minutes long and the only other character in the film known to history was 'Tom' King. Only part of the film now survives.[2]

Perhaps the first full-length Dick Turpin film which wholly survives is a 'silent' film of 1925 that is 69 minutes long (now available on the internet and on DVD) starring Tom Mix, then a well-known actor in cowboy films, as Turpin and titled simply *Dick Turpin*. Alan Hale, better known as Errol Flynn's co-star in many later films, plays King and these are the only characters based on real people. It was partly filmed on location in Epping Forest. The introductory text tells us that Turpin 'looted the lords' and was a hero to the common folk; that he 'loved the lonely and downtrodden', and that he was a 'sinner with a warm heart whose kindness outweighed his knavery'. We are told that 'ruthless history' had been harsh to him, but legend, 'Kind Fiction' had not. Black Bess is noted as being Turpin's horse. This uplifting text is a taste of what is to come; the audience has already been told what to think by this introduction to the film's hero if they were ignorant of it beforehand.

The initial scene has Turpin on his horse riding through the forest and he spies a coach. He has a black mask as a disguise. Holding the coach up with the words 'stand and deliver' he is treated to a harangue by the Bishop of London and Turpin instantly gives the clergyman a small purse of money to use for the poor, before letting the coach go on its way. He then meets Tom King, a fellow highwayman and friend. They first try to hold one another up, but when they recognise each other they are amicable and King tells Turpin he is backing a boxer from Devonshire in a bout in London.

Turpin then spies another coach and chases it. The occupant, Lord Churlton, asks his coachman to stop and prepares to fight, but he is overcome. Hearing a pistol shot, a patrol of Bow Street Runners, 'the police of the time' on horseback, ride to the coach but Churlton is forced by the hidden Turpin to deny that anything untoward has occurred. Turpin leaves them and then comes across two footpads who are attacking another coach. He disperses them and finds that he has rescued Squire Crabtree and his niece, Lady Alice. He escorts them to the Red Lion inn, near Cambridge. He finds that Lady Alice is to marry Lord Churlton. Turpin treats Lady Alice with much courtesy and gallantry.

Churlton arrives and he and Crabtree try to apprehend Turpin, aided by the Bow Street Runners. Turpin escapes with the aid of Black Bess and rides to London, pursued by his enemies. He is joined by Lady Alice and her maid, Sally. The former says to him, 'It is noble of you to risk so much for me – a stranger' and Turpin is described as a 'gallant highwayman'. They meet up with King and discuss what to do.

In London both the Bow Street Runners and soldiers try to find Turpin. They see Bully Boy, the boxer, about to take part in the match as arranged by King. Thinking the boxer must be Turpin, they arrest him and he is thrown into Newgate Prison. Knowing this, Turpin and King decide to have Turpin impersonate the now-gaoled boxer and he takes part in a boxing match. While this occurs, Crabtree and Churlton go to Newgate and state that the prisoner there is not Turpin and deduce that the man taking part in the bout might be Turpin. He escapes and goes to Epping Forest, where he declares his love for Alice and promises to marry her and 'give up the road'. However, an old woman tells him that a child is hurt and so Turpin goes to help. This is a trap and he is arrested and put in Newgate. We are shown that he has the support of the crowd who endeavour to hinder the forces of the law.

In the condemned cell, Turpin only has a few days before he is executed and he is in despair. When the chaplain enters he prays and refers to his mother 'I tried to spare her this'. Sally arrives and tells him that King will try and rescue him. She also tells him that Alice will be forced to marry Churlton at York. On the day of the execution, Turpin is taken out of the prison to be hanged, but the crowd jostle with the guards and King, who has exchanged places with the hangman, tells Turpin, 'The mob is with us'. Turpin escapes and he, King and Sally ride away, reaching the Red Lion pub. There Turpin cares for his horse.

In the pub, Sally and King are together, when an unknown man raises his pistol and for no obvious reason, shoots King, who soon dies in Turpin's arms, 'God be with you' he says before he expires. Turpin then mounts Black Bess and rides to York, being pursued by the Bow Street Runners. Eventually the pursuers drop off and by the time he arrives in York, he is alone. However, a watchman shoots Black Bess dead and the grief-stricken Turpin is shown mourning his beloved horse.

Turpin then enters the castle where Lady Alice is staying. Turpin shoots Churlton and he and Lady Alice leave together. We are told that they flee to France and presumably live happily ever after. Throughout the film Turpin is shown as being brave, kind and gallant, popular among the people. He is not responsible for King's death and the ride to York on Black Bess and the horse's death all feature, the latter two elements taken straight out of the novel *Rookwood*. Epping Forest and the Red Lion pub also feature, though the latter is not shown as being in London.

Apparently Mix was 'undoubtedly amongst modern film artists, and one would naturally expect that he would be chosen to play Dick Turpin'. One contemporary review praises his work, 'Mix has many opportunities to display his superb horsemanship'.[3] Another newspaper praised it, 'the author of this romantic tale of the road has invested Dick Turpin with all the heroic qualities with which legend has gilded his memory... We see him despoiling the rich to bestow charity on the poor, a form of Socialism which meets with general approval when committed in a scarlet coat'. Mix is 'in his element as a genial and dashing highwayman'.[4]

The film has gone down well with recent reviewers and none of the admittedly few reviewers had any observation to make about its factual accuracy.

In 1933 the first 'talkie' Turpin film starred Victor McLaglen, then a major Hollywood star who would go on to feature in films such as *Gunga Din*. It was made by Cricklewood Studios and was 79 minutes long. No copies of the film are thought to exist.

As with the earlier film, this was loosely based on the *Rookwood* novel, and featured Frank Vosper as Tom King. Again he is the only character apart from Turpin who is based in reality. McLaglen's performance was hailed, 'An expert horseman, a hearty fighter, a jolly laughing hero, he dominates – as it is right he should – is exhilarating'.[5] One lengthy review notes:

'The exploits of the gallant outlaw and his faithful black horse have become, by popular acceptance, sanctified with the odour of acquired respectability, and by long established fact, transmuted into a semblance of historic accuracy. Happily the picture does no more, and no less, than to gloss over his more nefarious activities, and as the popular conception of fact and fiction. He is shown as a chivalrous rascal, who protects the fair sex, succours the oppressed with his equally acquired gains, delights in leading his pursuers a merry dance... the process lets Dick Turpin out comfortably and gives the modern motor bandit a decidedly bad break'.[6]

Another newspaper heralded the film thus, 'Dick Turpin, ever popular English highwayman'.[7]

Another Turpin film appeared in 1951, titled *The Lady and the Bandit*, also known in Britain as *Dick Turpin's Ride*, starring the handsome American actor Louis Haywood as Turpin and one Patricia Medina as his rather socially exalted wife. The film's opening titles show crossed pistols on a reward poster for Turpin of £100. There are sentences on the screen to further introduce the viewer to the film's hero, 'England – the eighteenth century, a lawless age of lawless men – and among them one man lives on in song and legend... Mounted on his legendary horse, Black Bess, Turpin and his partner Tom King terrorised the English countryside'. The words then liken Turpin to Robin Hood and Captain Kidd. The implications of the word 'terrorised' are never realised in the film, and perhaps this is an unintentional allusion to harsh reality. It serves the same purpose as did the text at the beginning of the 1925 film.

Turpin and King ride through the countryside, holding up stage coaches and tearing down reward posters that they see posted on trees. They hold up the London postal stagecoach with the words 'stand and deliver', with masks as disguises. Inside the coach are two gentlemen, an elderly woman and a young woman, who are relieved of jewellery and money. The old lady says 'This rascal must think himself a gentleman' as Turpin bows to the ladies. However, soon after, a party of dragoons spy the highwaymen and Turpin allows King to flee while he draws off the pursuers, and he soon outrides them.

We then see Turpin and King in a pub, which they have made their base, paying the landlord who knows their true identities. Turpin declares his wish to ride to London to buy fine clothes and is shown as a jovial character. Then King asks him if he is really interested in taking his revenge on Lord Willoughby. The lord gave false evidence leading to Turpin's saintly father being hanged for theft twenty years earlier and the orphaned Turpin was left to starve in a workhouse. King remarks that he and Turpin are 'common thieves'. The two of them have been friends for twenty years.

Meanwhile in London Sir Thomas du Veil (a real character, 1686–1746, chief magistrate at Bow Street), 'chief constable of Police' in Bow Street is meeting Hedger, a known criminal and fence, and in return for Hedger's life he agrees to help trap Turpin on his next visit to Hedger. Turpin arrives at Hedger's before the trap can be sprung and eludes his enemies, fleeing into a theatre on Drury Lane where David Garrick (1717–79, but not a professional actor until 1741) is acting in *Julius Caesar*. To escape his pursuers, Turpin persuades Garrick his name is Palmer and that he is an admirer of his. Garrick allows him an empty box at the theatre and there he meets Lady Greene and her daughter, Joyce.

Turpin charms the ladies, has supper with them and then escorts them back to their lodgings. Lady Greene says 'You have a certain virility about you' and he chats amicably with Joyce. After he has left a man calling himself Dick Turpin tries to rob him, and this turns out to be an unemployed valet by the name of Archibald Puffin. Turpin takes him under his wing and returns to his home.

There, to King's disgust, Turpin announces his wish to cease his criminal life. He has Puffin teach him how to be a gentleman as regards kissing, speech and wine. Turpin goes to St Albans to the home of Lady Greene and Joyce and they are revealed as gentlewomen in distress. They invite him to supper and believing him to be Richard Palmer, gentleman, he marries Joyce after a short courtship. He renounces crime and breeds horses, plants fruit trees and employs Puffin as his valet.

King interrupts this life with news that Lord Willoughby, British ambassador to Austria for seven years, is returning to England. King wants Turpin to return to life as a highwayman. Turpin explains that he desires nothing but a peaceful existence. Yet the news of Willoughby leads Turpin to ride to Dover to confront him. At Dover, Turpin goes to an inn to find the lord's coachman. He is recognised and some of the customers try to catch him but he escapes.

Next day Turpin holds up Willoughby's horse and is given the man's money and jewels. Yet Turpin finds an important document implicating Willoughby and Countess Margaret of Luneburg, mistress to the King, in treason. Turpin explains to Willoughby that he had his honest father, John Turpin of Newport Street, Hempstead, hanged in 1715 and himself 'dragged away' by the 'police'. Willoughby is unsympathetic and unrepentant. Turpin offers to fight a duel with the lord but the latter refuses. In the next scene we see the two high-born conspirators express their fear of discovery by Sir Robert Walpole, the 'Prime Minister'.

At Turpin's home, Lady Greene has found out that her son-in-law, Richard Palmer, is in reality Turpin. She persuades a reluctant Turpin to leave her daughter forever for the latter's good and he agrees, and on leaving we see a distraught Joyce. Turpin suggests that he inform Walpole of Willoughby's dastardly plans.

Reunited with King, Turpin returns to being a highwayman and we are shown a reward poster for £100, and then another, with the sum raised to £300. We are told that they commit robberies on Hounslow Heath. The two men argue in the inn that is now their base once again. As they do so, a stage coach stops outside, containing the King and Countess Margaret. Needing another horse, they buy Black Bess from the landlord. When Turpin finds out he is enraged and goes to recover the horse. The countess's maid, Cecile, confronts him and suggests that they go into partnership, with her providing information about wealthy victims and sharing the loot with Turpin once he has stolen it.

Turpin agrees and he and King rob the countess of her jewels, sharing them with Cecile. She also suggests another target, a more dangerous one, a coach carrying freshly minted coins which is sure to be heavily guarded. The two men rob the coach, but are in turn ambushed by a party of dragoons, who arrest King and he is thrown into prison. Turpin bluffs his way in and rescues his friend. Although they escape, Turpin is wounded by a shot fired by one of the soldiers.

The two men return to Turpin's marital home where his wife binds his wound. They discuss booking passage to America or the West Indies to start a new life. Turpin says he wants a peaceful death in bed. They also discuss the conspiracy hatched by Lord Willoughby in detail; apparently he is planning to invite Austrian troops to invade Britain, overthrow Walpole and start a war.

King and Cecile are proving troublesome. The former is in drink and argumentative and the latter is unhappy that Turpin is planning to leave the country without her. Meanwhile, Turpin enters Walpole's house late at night and gives him the incriminating document. Cecile betrays Turpin to her mistress, while Puffin tells Turpin, now back at his marital home, that he has booked them passage to America.

They learn that the house is surrounded by troops and that Joyce is in danger of being implicated as Turpin's accomplice.

Turpin decides that to save his wife he must ride to York in less than a day and be known there, thus proving he could not have been at Joyce's house. With Black Bess, it is possible, he reasons. There is a firefight with the troops and the two men ride away; King is shot dead in the process. We are then shown Turpin's ride through the night to York, while Joyce is questioned by du Veil and told that unless her innocence can be proved she will be sentenced to life imprisonment in Newgate.

Turpin eventually rides to York and to prove he is there, holds up the London to York coach. A man says 'I thought Epping Forest was his hunting ground'. Garrick is in the coach and he declares he knew who Turpin was when he met him in the theatre. Black Bess dies and Turpin is arrested.

At Kensington Palace, the King declares that Willoughby will be tried for treason and the countess will be deported. Walpole asks the King a favour, and the latter already has a pardon for Turpin, which is what he wanted, but it is pointed out that Turpin will be hanged in York the next day, following a trial and conviction, and that it is impossible for anyone but Turpin to ride to York in time to stop the execution, especially as the bridge at Doncaster is down and the journey is now an extra four hours.

Turpin is then shown on the scaffold, saying 'I've had an appointment with the gallows for 10 years'. He is then hanged and a spectator says 'He sure died brave'. This is the only screen depiction of Turpin's execution. The final scene shows Joyce and her mother on board a ship which is about to set sail. With them is Walpole, who tells Joyce 'His ride to York and its purpose. It was to save you'. Walpole praises Turpin for his patriotism and says that his service to the country was far greater than many others.

This is another film that shows Turpin as hero. It is the first of several to refer to his background and to the injustice that he and his

206

father suffered at the hands of an unscrupulous upper-class figure. It shows him using his pseudonym Palmer and that he hailed from Hempstead. As in the plays, the novel *Rookwood*, the 1925 film and Noyes's ballad, the ride to York and the death of Black Bess plays an important part in the film. Turpin is an avenger of past wrongs, a gallant gentleman, attractive to the ladies and a friend to the lowly, in this case Puffin.

Of course most of this is myth. Turpin's father was not hanged and there is no evidence his son was ever in a workhouse or victimised by a nobleman. Turpin never met Walpole nor Garrick; the characters of Lady Greene, Joyce, Lord Willoughby and Countess Margaret are fictitious. He never rode from London to York, nor alerted the government to a wholly invented conspiracy for an invasion. King was shot in Whitechapel not St Albans and not by troops; his death occurred nearly two years before Turpin's.

One newspaper was mildly scathing about the film. It noted that the film 'presents him [Turpin] in a light which may be startling to some people'. Turpin is 'a most worthy character… At heart he was a gentleman… He had little chance you see, as he was brought up in an orphanage… Dick was very strong on patriotism'.[8] Another newspaper highlighted Turpin's character, 'a romanticised yarn about the famous highwayman… it concentrates on the better side of Dick's character and shows him as a devoted husband and an ardent patriot. Believe it or not, his regard for the King's safety costs him his life'.[9]

There was a 25-minute short film made at Bray Studios in 1956 titled *Dick Turpin the Highwayman*, the first Turpin film in colour. It stars Philip Friend as Turpin and introduces him by having him riding through a forest and holding up a coach, telling the audience 'My name's Dick Turpin. My profession is highwayman'. Wording on the screen explains that most highwaymen were 'coarse bandits' and worthy of the gallows. The next screen tells us, however, that 'A few were gentlemen, bold, gallant adventurers' and Turpin was, of course, one of these.

The short drama depicts Turpin as a gentleman in every sense of the word. He is handsome, too, and goes by the name of John Palmer, which the real Turpin adopted in his post-highwayman career. This Turpin robs the rich in order to prevent the impoverishment of indebted small tenants. He robs the wealthy merchant, Hawkins, and when a young woman protests, 'Dick Turpin doesn't rob women', he answers that the money – £2,000 – is a dowry and thus belongs to the father prior to his daughter's marriage and to her husband thereafter. Yet the money is stolen by other robbers. Turpin fights the men and restores it to the rightful owner and then gives £500 to Sally, a maidservant, whom he also suggests could betray him for the £200 reward, but she answers that she would not do so for £2 million. Black Bess is shown as Turpin's horse. A later review of this drama, when it was shown on TV many years later, was discouraging, stating that it was a 'short adventure comedy of no possible interest to anyone. Very horrible' and awarded it one star.[10]

In 1965 Walt Disney made an 89-minute-long colour film for TV titled *The Legend of the Young Dick Turpin*, clearly aimed at being a film suitable for the whole family, billed as 'Exciting, exhilarating entertainment'. It starred British leads such as David Weston as Turpin, George Cole (then well known as the shady but jovial spiv Flash Harry in the *St Trinian's* films) as Evans, Bernard Lee (better known as James Bond's boss, M) as Jeremiah and Maurice Denham. The film began with Turpin as a young man, suffering at the hands of an oppressive squire and turning to crime only as a necessity (shades of the 1951 film here).

The film opens with the masked highwayman riding through a forest, an image that appeared often in previous films. He holds up a coach in the forest. There is also a song over the opening sequence, in a jaunty tune, similar to that of a Wild West cowboy film, highlighting Turpin's bravery and sense of justice (it was later released as a record). As with the 1925 film we are introduced to Turpin as being daring, a great horseman, a robber of the rich and feared by the gentry. We are told that the story of his youth has never been told before. Turpin is seen riding past a gallows.

A young boy is poaching in a lord's wood but is arrested by a gamekeeper. This is seen by the young Turpin, who is a tenant farmer of Dale Farm, Essex, one of a long line from the same district. He defends the lad and legitimises poaching as being an economic necessity for a family that will otherwise starve. Turpin goes into the wood and disables the mantraps. He is then arrested by two gamekeepers and taken before the forest's owner, Lord Carlsham, who is also a JP. He is irredeemably awful, greedy, arrogant, unmerciful, unpopular; he has no positive virtue whatsoever. He gives Turpin the choice of a fine of 50 guineas or two years in prison. Turpin cites the popular protest, 'These are hard times for some of us' and when being told that what he did is illegal, replies 'Then the law's wrong'. As ever, Turpin is standing for the rights of the common man against the injustice of the law. He also loses his beloved horse, Black Bess, which he protests strongly about.

We learn that Turpin is an orphan and has no family; his mother is long dead and his father died in the previous year. Mr Evans, Lord Carlsham's 'legal expert', defends Turpin, but to no avail. Turpin tries to prevent his horse from being taken, but is unable to do so and is knocked down. He pleads before Carlsham but without success. 'Farming's all I know' he states as he is thrown off the land and claims that he knows no other trade. Evans helps him with 12 guineas and suggests he see a man called Fielding in Aldgate, London. Turpin thanks him and then takes his horse, fighting Carlsham's servants in doing so.

A warrant for Turpin's arrest is formulated by Carlsham. Meanwhile, Turpin meets Fielding and agrees to rent accommodation from him. A young lad called Jimmy tries to steal from Turpin and when he tries to run from him is arrested by watchmen. Turpin has him released and the two become friends. Jimmy thinks Turpin is 'a country bumpkin' who needs safeguarding from thieves. He is a pickpocket and takes Turpin to a thieves' kitchen which is presided over by a Fagin-like figure called Jeremiah who seems benevolent enough.

Here Tom King, 'the famous highwayman' meets Turpin and challenges him to a dice gamble. Unlike the previous screen Kings he is no friend of Turpin. Turpin loses all his money as King has loaded dice. Turpin threatens to fight him, but King agrees to let him come with him and hold up a stagecoach as highwaymen. They seek to hold up Lord Carlsham's coach en route to Newmarket. Carlsham's obnoxious nature is highlighted as he appears far less favourably than his fellow passengers. Sir John, apparently a model landlord, refers to crime being a symptom of poverty, oppression and unjust landlords. Carlsham merely sneers at him. Lord Humphreys, a judge, is also present.

King holds up the carriage and demands the purses of all three men and after being given two, Carlsham manages to overpower him. Turpin then appears and turns the tables once again, taking King's purse and Carlsham's before thrusting the latter into a lake. He gives the purses to Sir John and Judge Humphreys as he states he has no argument with them. 'What kind of highwayman is this?' King threatens to kill Turpin and rides away.

At Jeremiah's, King tells how his attack failed, through no fault of his own. Turpin reappears and there is a fight. After giving King his purse back, less the 10 guineas he had been cheated out of, King again threatens to kill Turpin and departs. Turpin then offers to take Jimmy away with him, and he goes, despite Jeremiah trying to persuade him not to.

Evans has another scene with Carlsham, accusing him of turning Turpin to crime when he has him raise the reward for Turpin to 200 guineas. We see posters being displayed and more of the jaunty song about Turpin being a highwayman. Jimmy talks about Turpin, whom he admires intensely, and wanting to be a highwayman. However, Turpin states that he has no intention of being a highwayman and intends to emigrate now that he has the money to do so. He tells Jimmy that the two of them can go to France or Holland and then goes to a tailor to buy him a new suit. Jimmy twice tries to steal from the tailor but Turpin returns the booty on both occasions. There is also a comic song elevating Turpin and denigrating Carlsham.

Jeremiah reveals his true nature now that the reward has been upped to 200 guineas and his men seize Jimmy and try to force him to tell them where Turpin is. They fail but pursue him. Fielding and Turpin discuss going into partnership in the highwayman business but we sense that Turpin is only playing for time. Fielding contacts Carlsham and the latter's men seize Turpin.

We then see Turpin in court, presumably the Old Bailey, is accused of horse-stealing and taking Carlsham's purse on the road. Evans speaks up for Turpin, describing him as 'a hard-working, decent God-fearing man' (though there has hitherto been no evidence of Turpin having any religion) and explaining that he was 'an honest man goaded beyond endurance'. However, Turpin is found guilty and sentenced to death, stating 'I don't consider myself a thief' and Evans tries to show that Carlsham was the real thief for taking Turpin's farm.

Turpin is next shown in Newgate awaiting execution with resolution, being described as 'a model prisoner'. Evans and Jimmy visit him and the former says the appeal was dismissed, but the latter hinted that a rescue will be made. Turpin, who will be executed the next day, says to Evans 'Look after the boy and pray for me'. That night Jimmy rescues Turpin in a dangerous exploit and Evans explains he has an estate in Virginia and the three can sail from Greenwich that very morning.

Initially Turpin refuses to accompany them as he has a score to settle with Carlsham, who is at his London home. Turpin forces the villain at gunpoint to write a statement withdrawing any charges against him, not wishing to see him hanged and apologising for 'my injustice to him'. Turpin escapes and then finds that the watchmen have captured Evans and Jimmy and are waiting for him. Turpin outwits them and saves his two friends and gives them time to take their ship while he holds the watchmen at pistol point. Evans and Jimmy sail away without Turpin who is last seen riding away on Black Bess. There is a final burst of song, declaring Turpin is 'an outlaw from injustice' and that 'ahead of him the gallows and the rope on which he'll die'.

Val Doonican sang the ballad to accompany the film and the recording talks of Turpin's being a farmer who had his land stolen from him, then of his high courage 'no braver man than he', that he never robbed from a lady (except to steal a kiss) and that by 'cowardly informers in York he was betrayed'. We are told that he robbed the landed gentry and of his ride to York. Yet demanding 'your money or you die' with 'a pistol in his hand' does not obviously indicate courage on Turpin's part.

Some recent online comments about the film claim that it is fun, and one states 'Justice of that day has not changed all that much. There are still many people wrongfully committed'. However, two are somewhat critical of it, referring to Turpin's real life 'maybe not that glamorous' and another 'in real life he was a total c—t'.

The film has some similarities with the earlier films: Turpin is a hero, up against despicable upper-class villainy, and cares for Black Bess. He is arrested and faces execution, spends time in Newgate and is associated with King. Yet there are also differences. In the 1925 and 1951 films Turpin and King are friends; in this they are sworn enemies. In the 1965 film Turpin commits only one act of highway robbery and is morally upstanding and honest to a fault, and devoted to his friends.

Much of the film veers away from history as might be expected. Turpin was a butcher and publican not a tenant farmer; his father outlived him. Apart from King all the other characters are fictional. King was his friend in later life. Turpin was never in Newgate nor was ever tried at the Old Bailey. Other aspects of the film owe more to perceptions of the 1960s not the 1730s; though a magistrate could indeed sentence minor offenders singlehandedly (petty sessions), gamekeepers could set traps on their masters' lands.

Turpin's character is a rather dull, but decent young man, free from any charisma of the cinematic rogue as played by the likes of Errol Flynn. Unlike the earlier films there are no female characters and no romance. There is an extremely despicable villain, as with the 1951 film, which is not really the case in the 1925 version, and this creates sympathy by default for the film's hero. The contemporary press had little to say about the film, but were generally approving in a low-key way.

It should be noted that in the 1950s and beyond there was a slew of films and TV shows about pirates and outlaws, such as *The Buccaneers* and *The Adventures of Robin Hood*. These portrayed the pirates and outlaws as heroes, helping victims of corrupt officialdom and coming out victorious. Viewers were thus accustomed to seeing these characters in a favourable light, but it is important to note that these dramas were set centuries in the past, thus removing any hint that criminals were dangerous figures. This is exactly the same as the depictions of the nineteenth century.

The *Carry On* series of British low-brow comedy began in 1958 and ended in 1992, though most were produced from the 1960s to the mid-1970s. The films often had stories set in the past, from Roman to Victorian times. One of the later films, number 26, in 1974, was *Carry on Dick*. It was the final *Carry On* film to star series stalwarts Sid James, Hattie Jacques and Barbara Windsor, who had appeared in many of the preceding films. It was shot between March and April 1974 and exteriors were filmed near to the studios at Iver Common, Black Park, the Jolly Woodman pub, St Mary's Church, Hitchin Lane and at Stoke Poges Manor. It was 91 minutes long and cost nearly a quarter of a million of pounds to make.

The timeline is brought forward to 1750 and the Bow Street Runners are founded to deal with rising crime. The three main Runners are Sir Roger Daley, Captain Desmond Fancey and Sergeant

Jock Strapp. They are generally successful but when the former is robbed and stripped by highwayman Dick Turpin, they focus their attentions on his capture.

Turpin, played by Sid James, is the improbably named Reverend Flasher, vicar of Upper Dencher, and is aided in his crimes, all of which occur locally, by his two servants, Tom (a reference to 'Tom' King, perhaps?) and maid Harriet. His housekeeper, played by Hattie Jacques, is not privy to their designs until towards the end of the film. Unlike all other cinematic Turpins, here the character is elderly; James was then aged 60 and his age certainly shows.

As with the earlier films we are introduced to Turpin as a masked highwayman riding around woods; this time with two accomplices, and they hold up a stagecoach, Turpin using the words 'Stand and deliver'. They rob the occupants of not only their money and jewels, but also their clothes (implied nudity, though no actual frontal nakedness, is a common occurrence in the *Carry On* films). We are then introduced explicitly to Turpin as 'the notorious highwayman, Dick Turpin, better known as Big Dick, owing to the size of his weapon'. The shot then focusses on Turpin's pistol. Turpin is often referred to as Big Dick in the film; the *Carry On* films are known for their *double entendres*.

There is another highway robbery, this time of a coach load of female entertainers, but the robbers are nearly taken by a group of Bow Street Runners, hiding in ambush. They manage to outwit them and escape in the coach. The Runners are instructed to capture Turpin and Captain Fancey and Sergeant Strapp are sent by Sir Roger Daley to take him. As all the thefts have occurred within 20 miles of the village of Upper Dencher, which is a day or two's ride from London, they conclude that they should begin their investigations there.

Fancey and Strapp visit the church and meet the Revd Flasher, the rector, who is none other than Turpin, and see the collection of pistols in his vestry, but see nothing suspicious. They trust him and confide their intentions to him. The next scene is set in the local pub, the Old

Cock, where they are fed false information and both law officers are humiliated. The reward for Turpin is said to be 100 guineas but later is stated as being 300 sovereigns. In church the rector cites the book of Galatians and addresses his congregation as thieves and fornicators.

Fancey and Strapp are inveigled into another trap by Turpin and his accomplices, which results in them being arrested by the constable and his men, thinking they are Turpin and another, and put in the stocks and later gaoled. This is where Sir Roger Daley sees him, after having been robbed and stripped again. Meanwhile Miss Hoggett, Turpin's housekeeper, and Harriet both have designs on him, though Miss Hoggett is increasingly suspicious of her employer's nocturnal activities.

Harriet is identified of one of Turpin's accomplices, arrested and gaoled. The Runners plan to catch Turpin as he tries to rescue her, and they confide their plans to him. He outwits them as he and Tom dress up as women and bring drink to befuddle Fancey and Strapp. They succeed and take Harriet away. The Runners conclude that Flasher is really Turpin and plan to arrest him, but find he is conducting the sermon in church and so they must wait until the service is over before they can do so. Turpin extends the sermon as long as he can and has the congregation sing 'O God our help in ages past' on more than one occasion, as Miss Hoggett plays the organ despite having to recommence on numerous occasions. Strapp and the constable separately try to arrest him but fail and eventually Turpin, Harriet and Tom escape in Sir Roger's coach. They eventually 'cross the border' and deem themselves safe. Then a Scottish highwayman approaches the coach with his pistol, but seeing a somewhat undressed Turpin and Harriet peering out of the carriage window he leaves them to their pleasures.

There is little that can be said about the character of Turpin himself. He is played as an elderly bachelor vicar who is attractive to both his mature housekeeper and his younger housemaid. There is no reason given for why he is a highwayman nor what he does with his monetary gains (the clothing stolen from his victims is given to the church jumble sale). No background is given to Turpin. He is apparently affable to the Bow Street Runners and as a clergyman prone to making sermons about the sinful nature of his congregation. He is crafty and daring in creating trouble for his pursuers and in rescuing Harriet. Apart from Turpin there is no real character depicted in the film. The idea for the highwayman/vicar is doubtless taken from the fictional Dr Syn books and films in which a clergyman is also the leader of a band of smugglers in the eighteenth century and popularised by books and films, some as recent as the 1960s. Like the fictional Turpin this character is represented as a hero for the common man.

Historical inaccuracy and anachronism can be taken as read in the 'historical' *Carry On* films and this is no exception. Several shots of the churchyard show what is clearly a First World War memorial, and a character talks about fingerprints, which were not discovered until over a century later. And, of course, Turpin had been dead for eleven years in 1750 and had no connection with the Bow Street Runners, led then not by Sir Roger Daley but by the Fielding brothers. The notion that King George's writ did not run in Scotland would have seemed ridiculous to contemporaries in post-Culloden Scotland. Yet sharp-eyed viewers may have seen in the title sequence the note 'Any similarity to events or people alive or dead is purely coincidental' and in the trailer the phrase 'it may not be historical but is hysterical'.

A film review of the time said:

> 'In the hands of the Carry On gang the exploits of the celebrated highwayman Dick Turpin take on new proportions and new meanings... The Gang, one of the country's most beloved rep companies, wins through under Gerald Thomas' direction, even if there is a tinge of blue about the things they do and say. But it's good honest vulgarity'.[11]

A tribute to the film and its star is to be found in the Black Horse pub in Iver Heath, Buckinghamshire. On the pub sign outside is a picture of Sid James as Big Dick on his black horse. James lived in a house in Iver at this time.

Curiously there was a Spanish film called *Dick Turpin* which came out in the same year as the *Carry On* film. It starred Cihangir Ghaffari as Turpin and ran for 94 minutes. It was a swashbuckling adventure that, judging by the fact that none of the characters, except Turpin, actually featured in his life at all, was presumably utterly fictional. Turpin is shown as a hero to the common people in fighting upper class oppression

From 1979–82 London Weekend Television broadcast two series and one five-episode story, amounting to thirty-one 24-minute long episodes in a series titled *Dick Turpin*. It was heralded thus:

> 'Richard O'Sullivan stars as Dick Turpin in this action-filled adventure series chronicling the exploits of England's most celebrated highwayman. Along with his trusted young sidekick Swiftnick, Turpin dodges the ever-present threat of capture, doing some good deeds along the way and evading the attentions of the villainous Sir John Glutton, who tracks his every move'.

These were shown in the early evenings on Saturdays and were aimed at the children's market, though one series featured slightly more adult themes. The first series was of thirteen episodes and was shown from 6 January to 24 March 1979. The first seven episodes of the second series were broadcast from 16 February to 29 March 1980. Then there was titled *Dick Turpin's Greatest Adventure*, a five-part story, shown from 16 May to 13 June 1981. It featured only one of the usual supporting characters and each episode began and ended with a slightly different sequence. The final six episodes of series two were shown from 30 January to 6 March 1982. Most of the stories were standalone, except for the five-part story, but both tranches of series two opened with the first in a two-part story.

The creators and producers were Richard Carpenter, Paul Knight and Sidney Cole. Significantly perhaps, Carpenter and Cole also produced TV stories about Robin Hood. Richard Carpenter wrote most of the episodes; every one of series one, eight of series two and all of *Dick Turpin's Greatest Adventure*. John Kane wrote three episodes of series two. Charles Crichton and Paul Wheeler wrote one story each from series two. There was also a relatively small pool of directors: Charles Crichton directed three from series one and two from series two. Gerry Poulson directed three episodes from series one and two and all of *Dick Turpin's Greatest Adventure*. James Allen directed five episodes from the first series, and four from series two. Finally, there was Dennis Abey, directing one episode from series one, and two from series two.

Sidney Cole was a veteran producer of films and TV shows since 1928 and was a man with left-wing sympathies, helping found a film technicians' union and working on propaganda documentaries for the Spanish Republic during the Spanish Civil War (1936–39). From 1955–60 he produced the *Robin Hood* TV series and worked with many people who had been blacklisted from Hollywood because of their Communist views. He saw parallels between Robin Hood and Dick Turpin. His politics explained the thinking behind the *Dick Turpin* series, as he noted in an interview in 1979: 'They were lawbreakers but were the real moral guardians of the time. The law, you see, was wrong, and those in authority were real baddies. Most people can identify with this'.[12]

The episodes' introductions show the silhouette of a stage coach travelling at night and a gallows, and then Turpin pulls his scarf up to conceal his lower face (previous celluloid Turpins had worn a black mask over the top part of the face), and draws his guns. He then rides off and holds up the stage coach – all on board surrender. The audience is given an instant introduction to the main character. The ending shows several men on horseback riding about at night.

Richard O'Sullivan starred as Turpin and he is the only identifiable character from reality to appear in these stories. None of the Gregory gang nor King appear, and Turpin never goes anywhere near Yorkshire. Instead Turpin is paired with a teenager, a character called Nick Smith, but Turpin gives him the alias Swiftnick (clearly a reference to the highwayman known as Swift Nicks who allegedly rode to York in the previous century). The son of a widowed female publican, he is played by Michael Deeks. Turpin acts as a father figure to the young man. Other regular characters are Turpin's principal enemies, the grossly overweight Sir John Glutton, High Sheriff of Hertfordshire and sometime Jacobite, played by Christopher Benjamin, and Glutton's steward, Captain Nathan Spiker, played by David Daker. There are other semi-regulars, allies of Turpin such as Isaac Rag, played by Alfie Bass, and the publicans, Big Noll and her henpecked husband. Some well-known actors also appear in guest roles in *Dick Turpin's Greatest Adventure*, including Diana Dors, Patrick Macnee, Wilfred Hyde White and Donald Pleasance. Joan Sims was the only actor to appear in two versions of Dick Turpin, *Carry on Dick* and an episode of this series.

As in the films, Turpin is a completely different figure from that of reality, save for being a highwayman. In this story we learn from episode one that before the stories begin, his parents were small farmers, cheated out of their land and then dying of starvation. This was Glutton's work and Turpin vows to see him ruined in revenge. Turpin has served a brief spell (three years) in the ranks of the British army, at Gibraltar, in the 13th Battalion of infantry, a regiment officered by the madman Colonel Tobias Moat and the bullying Captain Spiker. He experienced men dying of the plague and learnt Spanish. Spiker says to Moat, 'There was one man you couldn't break no matter how many lashes he gave him', meaning Turpin. He is a bachelor and childless. We later learn that he hated life in the army. 'Not enough action?' a Hanoverian officer asks. 'Too many officers' he replies. We also learn that Turpin likes *The Beggars' Opera*, a popular and satirical musical piece by John Gay in 1728, which features highwaymen. Turpin can also cite the Bible, as when he bandies words with Mr Nightingale in 'The Champion' and can play the harpsichord in 'Pursuit'. In 'Jail Birds' he is shown reading a book, *The Lives of the Highwaymen,* and later signs his own name. He is also an excellent swordsman, fighting the champion of Hanover to a draw in 'The Turncoat'. However, his motivation is often left vague, and no reason is given for why he helps Jane Harding in *Dick Turpin's Greatest Adventure.*

We also learn in episode one that a man called Dick Turpin has been recently hanged in York ('He's dead and in Hell, robbing the Devil'). It is explained that this was another man going under his name (not the case; Turpin was masquerading under the name John Palmer), thus establishing the show's Turpin as an established highwayman and getting around the fact that a man called Turpin was executed at York in 1739. We later learn in 'The Thief Taker' that Turpin has been a highwayman for at least six years.

Character-wise, Turpin is a combination of Robin Hood and, more bizarrely, a proto-Marxist. He makes a few speeches to Swiftnick about the criminality of the law, designed to help the ruling classes as represented by Glutton. He tells Swiftnick's mother that there is no justice and refers to a ten-year-old being hanged for stealing 'a bit of bread', which in reality never happened. In 'The Judge', Glutton seeks to illegally enclose the common land so as to enrich himself, stating 'I'm the law around here... No property, no rights'. A villager says 'The gentry they're grabbing everything they can get their hands on... squeezing out the small farmer'. In 'The Hanging', Turpin denounces the law as being like a spider's web, catching the minor villains and letting the larger ones escape. He states that 'if there was any justice', Glutton, Spiker and Lord Harrington would be hanging, not him. In the opening episode and in the *Greatest Adventure* he talks about there not being any justice.

Most of the adventures do not revolve around Turpin being a highwayman. Although the title sequences show him holding up a stagecoach, the episodes show very little of this. In series one, the episode 'The Whipping Boy' is a rare example of Turpin holding up the stagecoach of the Duke of Hertford and in another series there is a reference to selling stolen jewellery to 'the best fence in Hertfordshire', Harry Sims. There are occasional references to coaches being held up and noblemen, rich lawyers and farmers being robbed of their money and jewels, but we see very little of his criminality.

Instead we see Turpin and Swiftnick being pursued by the agents of the law, usually those employed by Glutton and Spiker, by soldiers or by other villains, often in the employ of the rich and powerful, though not always. In series two, seven episodes feature the two heroes fleeing their enemies. One example comes in 'The Secret Folk', in which Spiker and his men pursue our heroes into a wood where gypsies rule. The other type of episode is where Turpin and Swiftnick come to the aid of someone in need. For example, in episode three of series one, 'The Champion', they find that the village of Mudbury is being terrorised by Nightingale and his bully Hogg, so Turpin comes to the villagers' rescue and defeats Hogg in a boxing match. In another, 'Turncoat', he comes to the aid of a young woman who is embroiled in a Jacobite conspiracy and incriminating evidence has come to light which Turpin has to fight a Hanoverian officer to reclaim. In 'The Upright Man', Turpin helps the widow of a recently executed highwayman and in 'The Hero' he helps a weedy young gentleman become a hero to woo his lady love. In both 'The Thief Taker' and 'The Judge' in series two, Turpin gives generous sums of money, once to a couple who have lost their livelihood to Spiker and again to a poor man wishing to emigrate to the American colonies. In 'The Judge', Turpin succeeds in ensuring the villagers' common rights are saved, 'Everything we must do must be done legally', he says. In 'The King's Shilling' he rescues a young woman about to be drowned.

Turpin is the hero to the common man, and unsurprisingly he is shown rescuing people in many episodes. In 'The Imposter', Glutton refers to Turpin as 'the people's hero'. Swiftnick says 'He meant freedom, a chance to hit back against injustice'. In an earlier episode he says 'He's the king of them all – Dick Turpin'. In 'The Hanging', Swiftnick organises a mob of 100 to storm Hertford Gaol where they believe Turpin is being held prior to execution.

The common people are shown as being very supportive of Turpin. In 'The Judge' he and Swiftnick arrive at the Black Swan and there are cheers and welcomes all around. The quack mystic in 'Elixir of Life' is their friend, as are all others. Even when he is not recognised, as by the signposter in 'Blood Money', the man has no bad word to say against him. Only his enemies are hostile, with Spiker referring to Turpin as 'a braggart, a coward' who preys on 'unarmed citizens and defenceless widows'; as a reference to the real Turpin this is very accurate.

Towards his enemies, Turpin is magnanimous. Even though he has some, such as the murderous Moat, at his mercy, or Lord Manderfell, and Spiker on several occasions, he never kills them, only leaving them unconscious or unable to immediately pursue or harm him and his friends. In 'The Poacher', Turpin tells Swiftnick to aim low when shooting to avoid being hanged for murder. In 'Sentence of Death', Turpin shows his abhorrence of murder when coming across the bodies of Lord Falmouth and his servant and referring to the killers as 'mad dogs'. Big Nell later announces that Turpin would never kidnap nor kill.

Turpin is also highly attractive to the opposite sex, regardless of their social class, including a maidservant, a female thief-taker and a countess. In *Dick Turpin's Greatest Adventure* he has two bedroom scenes with Lady Melfort and later Jane Harding. There are many other episodes in which he is helped by female admirers, such as Lady Harrington in 'The Hanging', and he often kisses the young women in other episodes. However, in 'Deadlier than the Male', he explains to Catherine Langford his attitude to women: they are like fine claret, and that too much is not what he wants.

Turpin is willing to sacrifice his own life to spare Swiftnick, as in 'The Hero' he suggests to Spiker that he let the lad go in return for him turning his back on Spiker to be shot dead. In 'The Hanging' he urges Swiftnick to escape.

There is even 'evidence' in the series that Turpin is viewed as a romantic hero by the gentry. In 'The Hero', in which a weak young gentleman attempts to woo a young lady, both are taken in by the highwayman legend. The young man believes that if he acts like one and even uses the name Turpin, his beloved will adore him. She, in turn, when captured by Turpin, says she has read all about him in the press, 'I've read all the stories about you'. To which Turpin remarks 'You mustn't believe all you read in the broadsheets'. He denies the story of the ride to York (which never surfaced in relation to him until 1800), holding up a stagecoach on Hounslow Heath and dicing with a duchess, attributing these to Nevison and Claude Duval. However, not all legend is disposed of; Turpin's horse in the series is Black Bess.

Although there are chases and sword fights aplenty, and numerous damsels in distress, there is virtually no killing or sex. Only in *Dick Turpin's Greatest Adventure* (certificate 12) is a villain killed and then not by Turpin, and there are two modest bedroom scenes.

Turpin's principal enemies are Sir John Glutton and Captain Nathan Spiker. The first is the owner of Rookham Hall (an allusion to *Rookwood*, perhaps), a manor house in Hertfordshire. He is also the High Sheriff of the county, a post that the series seems to believe is a long-term appointment rather than an annual one as in reality. Glutton is the archetypal Tory squire of fiction, in the same mould as Squire Western in Henry Fielding's *Tom Jones*; stupid (though Eton educated), vicious, greedy and at first a Jacobite, later betraying his allies when convenient to do so. He is fond of hunting and music. Physically and intellectually he is negligible, but he devises plans to capture Turpin and employs rogues and sadists to do so. Spiker, a former army officer, is his loyal henchman and slightly more intelligent and is vehement about wanting to capture Turpin. These characters appear in nine of the thirteen episodes in series one, but only five in series two, and not at all in *Dick Turpin's Greatest Adventure*. Oddly enough, in three later episodes of series one these two villains and the two heroes are working together in an uneasy alliance against mutual enemies.

Reference to and inclusion of real characters was minimal. Lord Harrington (Secretary of State 1730–42) appeared in the final episode, 'The Hanging', billed as 'special envoy to Sir Robert Walpole', a cold-hearted individual, and Walpole and the King are occasionally referred to. Nevison is likewise referred to at least twice, as Turpin explains how Nevison's ride to York has been attributed to him. In one episode, Turpin tells Barnaby Rusk that he was in fact betrayed by 'Gregory' who was later hanged. There is a reference to a character called Palmer. The Duke of Cumberland is referred to twice as commander-in-chief of the army (a post he was not nominated to until 1745), as is Charles Edward Stuart. *The Grub Street Journal*, a newspaper which in reality occasionally reported Turpin's crimes, is also referred to.

There are inconsistencies enough in the series. Dorney Court in Buckinghamshire is used as Glutton's home, Rookham Hall, but in series two it is used for the homes of other nobility and gentry, such as Lord Manderfell in 'The Fox' and that of Edward Faversham in 'Deadlier than the Male'. In the third episode of *Dick Turpin's Greatest Adventure*, Jane Harding looks at a coin with the legend 'Jacobus Rex' on it and Turpin says that's the King's head; yet James II had been deposed fifty-two years earlier. In series two he is shown making his return and making his peace with the authorities; in a later episode in the same series he and Spiker are working together. Yet in the last episode we are shown Spiker welcoming Glutton back to Rookham Hall and he no longer works for Glutton, as if previous episodes had not happened. Nor were assize courts or hangings conducted in the grounds of private houses, as in 'The Judge' and 'The Hanging'.

The series ends on no conclusive note; it could have been the ending to any episode. Turpin has been rescued by Swiftnick and Lady Harrington from the gallows. Conveniently forgetting her lover, whom Spiker was blackmailing her over (let alone her husband), they pretend that the noblewoman is being kidnapped and she asks 'How long will I be "kidnapped" for?' and Turpin answers 'How long do you want?' And so the final series story ends.

The show was aimed at children and featured heavily in the magazine *Look In*, an ITV house magazine aimed at children. There were also spin-off *Dick Turpin* annuals (1979–81) with word and picture stories and features, and illustrations from the series. Richard Carpenter wrote a collection of short stories based heavily on episodes from series one, which were published in two books. Ironically, given the character of Turpin portrayed in the series, in one of the annuals Carpenter described the real character of Turpin in a manner that was historically accurate and thus far removed from his creation. The question has to be, why did he choose to mythologise such a man? Presumably the answer is that a children's TV show cannot have a downright villain as a central character. The author recalls watching and enjoying this series when it was first scheduled, aged between nine and twelve, the target range of the programme. It was teatime telly and entertaining enough. It certainly introduced a generation of children to Dick Turpin, or at least to a reinterpreted version of the legend. In 2017–18 The Grub Street Lodger website provided critiques of the first few episodes of the series.

Perhaps this TV series inspired Adam and the Ants to perform *Stand and Deliver* in 1981, in which a rather postmodern eighteenth-century highwayman accosts wealthy travellers in their coach and later escapes the noose. Turpin was not explicitly mentioned in this song but the performance in turn inspired the *Horrible Histories* Dick Turpin song. *The Lady and the Highwayman* romantic film of

1989 depicted a brave and heroic gentleman highwayman fighting villains, giving money stolen from evildoers to their rightful owners and saving a fair lady. Fiction of this type naturally rebounded to Turpin's posthumous benefit.

The depiction of violence on the screen and public tolerance of it has changed over the years. There is now a perceived demand for darker themes. In the 1950s and 1960s *Dixon of Dock Green* was a popular and rose-tinted view of police work and crime, but in the 1970s *The Sweeney* gave a rather different and grittier portrayal and was no less popular. The screen Turpin from the 1920s to the 1970s, admittedly as much aimed at children as adults, had shown him and his crimes in a benevolent light. All this was to change.

A radically different showing of Turpin's adventures appeared in the next century. In 2015 Dale Nichol, an actor who had played Turpin in the York Dungeon, finally managed to have the first instalment of a proposed trilogy about Turpin produced by English Cinematic Pictures, based in Doncaster. This was an attempt at a more realistic Turpin and the first part, about Turpin's involvement with the Gregory gang, *Dick Turpin and the Gregory Gang Part 1*, was rated 18 as it showed brief nudity and sexual violence. This was the first time that the cinematic Turpin had been featured as being involved with this violent gang of housebreakers. It was a radical departure from the previous dramatizations. Many of those featured in the drama were from Yorkshire and Nichol played Samuel Gregory. Turpin was played by Alex Petreae, Mary Brazier by Aysen Hulusi and Constable Pullen by Hugh Leadon. Nichol and Leadon directed the 65-minute drama. It was a low-budget show, costing £250,000, about the same as the *Carry On Dick* film four decades earlier, and that was considered low-budget then. There does not seem to have been a cinematic release, nor was it broadcast on TV. Nichol stated that 2,000 copies of the DVD had been sold shortly after its release.[13] Its impact was thus much less than the 1970s TV series.

Three years later part two was released, *Dick Turpin – The Highway Man of Essex II*, dealing with Turpin's time as a highwayman in 1735–37, with the character of Constable Pullen, the Westminster constable instrumental in the arrest of some of the gang in 1735, being given additional prominence as Turpin's nemesis, and a fictional 'Lady Fountayne' played by Robyn Walton being introduced, presumably to add some fictionally necessary romantic interest. Matthew King (for once in film given the correct Christian name) was, naturally, the other prominent character, played by Gunalp Kocak. It was less violent, too, than its predecessor, though it earned a 15 rating due to sex and violence. At time of writing the third part, presumably dealing with Turpin's time in Yorkshire and his arrest, trial and execution, is in the making. This is titled *Hang Pawne, not Turpin*.

The series is far grittier than anything seen previously and those knowing Turpin only by the myth and earlier TV and film shows will find it shocking. Turpin and the rest of the Gregory gang; namely Samual (sic) Gregory and his lover Mary Brazier, are violent in speech and action and all three participate in robberies. The episode begins with Turpin in prison, sharing a cell with John Stead and being visited by Smith, Pullen, a solicitor and a journalist from *The York Herald*, and then goes back to his earlier life. They enter an old woman's room and steal her money; Turpin threatens her to have her surrender the remainder. They then enter the house of a married couple, Peter Lawrence and his wife. Turpin whips Lawrence and then Gregory strips and rapes their female servant in front of Mary. Turpin then does likewise. Gregory fights and kills a rival gang leader, Rowden, by a canal. After committing two robberies (one against an unnamed old woman, presumably Mrs Shelley, and one against Peter Lawrence, his wife and their female servant), Turpin and Gregory part amicably.

In part two, Turpin and the Gregory gang are operating independently. Turpin, as a highwayman, robs people while on foot. On one occasion he has an unnamed accomplice. Two victims are Dr and Lady Fountayne. In contrast to his behaviour towards the old woman and the maidservant in episode one, Turpin acts politely towards both his female victims; not robbing one and exchanging compliments and kisses with the second; she even gives him a black mask. An unnamed lord, badgered by 'the Prime Minister', urges Pullen to use any means possible to have the Gregorys and Turpin hanged. A reward of £200 is offered for the latter. Morris and his son then try to arrest Turpin, but he ties up Morris and shoots him in the head with his own blunderbuss. Pullen arrests Wheeler and he agrees to inform on the Gregorys. Turpin meets King and after some dialogue and Turpin's recounting his exploits with Gregory (shown in flashback and expanded; we see him roast the old woman over the fire to force her to reveal her money, which she does, and in another we learn that Wheeler is homosexual and a fence), King relates how the Gregory gang has broken up and Pullen is on their trail. This is the end of episode two.

The accuracy of the series is open to question, quite apart from the introduction of a fictional titled lady and the expansion of the role of Constable Pullen, who is shown having jurisdiction in Essex and meeting Turpin in York Castle. Gregory states that there is a political motivation in their crimes to send a message to the government to turn back from its taxes on drink and tobacco, a reference perhaps to the unpopular Gin Act of 1736, which increased taxes on this most lethal of drinks. However, despite crying for an attack on the nobility and gentry, they do no such thing. Samual Gregory is middle aged, the Gregory gang numbers but three people and Mary goes with them on raids. None try to hide their identities when committing their crimes. The murder of Morris predates the meeting with King. The nobleman's library has twentieth-century books on the shelves and the phrase 'son of a bitch' was not commonly used in 1730s England. In reality Rowden outlived Gregory and was transported, not killed by him, and Wheeler was not a fence.

Furthermore, there are at time of writing, at least two other attempts to bring to the screen versions of the life of Turpin. Time will tell whether either project will succeed. One is for a TV series of four parts to show a more historically accurate picture of Turpin, scripts of which have been offered to two companies. Another is *English Outlaw: The Story of Dick Turpin*, aimed at being 3 hours 22 minutes long and was optimistically envisaged as being available in December 2022. It is noted as being 'a swashbuckling dramatization of the life and exploits of notorious highwayman Dick Turpin', starring Carl Wharton (as Ben Cobbler) and Swaylee Loughlane (as Sam) and Steven Eljay (as Bill). It is written by Danny Fraser and Lynne Hambrey and directed by Bob Jordan. However, in the cast of characters there are only three which are based in reality, John Turpin, Thomas Rowden and King, while the Revd Millington and Sanne Millington may represent Turpin's father-in-law and wife. None of the other characters are known to history and so this rather casts a doubt on its accuracy.

In April 2022 there was an announcement that Apple TV+ was to produce 'the true story of the eighteenth-century villain', but the remainder of the promotional article suggested that it would be anything but. Comedy actor Noel Fielding, also known as a co-presenter in a popular cookery programme, was rather improbably cast as Turpin: 'Noel will bring his own interpretation of the criminal legend, combining Turpin's traditional tricorn hat and guns, with his own trademark bodysuits, make-up and jewellery'. An anonymous insider stated that though Turpin was a criminal, 'he also developed a sexy appeal all of his own. That's something Noel is going to play on in his own interpretation'. He added 'This is a very irreverent retelling of the story'. It is described as being a comedy adventure series with Turpin and his 'gang of loveable rogues' being pursued by 'the Thief Taker General'. This would appear to be as far removed as possible from the more realistic thug of English Cinematic Pictures.[14]

In May 2022 a DVD was on sale titled *The Highwayman: The Legend of Dick Turpin*. Apparently Turpin attempts to rob a coach and fails but takes the young lady passenger away with him. Meanwhile a murderous villain is bargaining for her hand in marriage with her father in exchange for wealth. Most of the story is in the form of conversations between two characters and there is a minimum of action. It seems that once again Turpin is (factually inaccurately) portrayed as a highwayman and nothing else, that he attempts to rob the rich travelling in a coach, that he is attractive to ladies and has an evil enemy to contend with.

In most of these film and television dramas, there is never any doubt that Turpin is the hero and this is heightened by his enemies being despicable in the extreme and/or being very foolish. They only focus on Turpin the highwayman, not Turpin the member of a gang of housebreakers or horse-stealer. These reinforce the longstanding myth originating from the early nineteenth century. However, it is refreshing that in more recent years a more realistic account of Turpin's life and crimes has been released, though its audience may well be limited by its relatively limited exposure to have a significant impact on the general public perception of Dick Turpin. Nichol's films do not make pleasant viewing and this may not appeal to a wider public. As Oscar Wilde remarked, never let the truth get in the way of a good story. However, as the 1925 film notes, history treats Turpin rather differently, as we shall now see.

Chapter 8

Turpin and the Historians

Unlike the purveyors of popular fiction, authors of non-fiction from the eighteenth century onwards have never mythologised Turpin, though not all were strictly factual, especially in the nineteenth century. The interest in the subject was explained in one of the very first histories of Turpin. Kyll wrote as the preface to the fourth edition of his book (now complete with Bayes's *History*):

'It is suppos'd the world naturally enquires after persons that have in any manner been render'd either Famous or infamous for which Reason we think the Account of a man who for some time past hath been not only the Terror but the Talk of a county the considerable figure in the Nation, cannot be disagreeable... Essex has been lately well alarmed at the crimes of Turpin, several families suffered by him, and others of Gregory's gang, as our ensuing Narration will relate'.[1]

Richard Bayes, the Essex innkeeper who was involved in the fatal shoot out in which King was shot, published his *Genuine History* of Turpin and Kyll, who had taken a shorthand account of Turpin's trial, published the *Trial of the Notorious Highwayman Richard Turpin*. It is noteworthy that Kyll emphasised Turpin as a highwayman, not as a robber or horse thief, presumably because the former appellation would be more appealing to his intended market.

There were, then, two contemporary publications attempting to capitalise on the resurgence of interest in Turpin, following his execution. Ward and Chandler of Coney Street, York, who also published *The York Courant* and advertised Kyll's booklet in their

231

newspaper, published an account of the trial to be sold at their shop outside Temple Bar, London, as well as selling it in shops in Leeds, Wakefield and Hull. It sold for sixpence.[2]

It sold very well and by 1 May 1739 the publisher was advertising the fourth edition. Three weeks later the fifth edition was being advertised. This edition appended Bayes's *Genuine History*, described as 'a large and genuine History of the Life of Richard Turpin'. They assured 'Those who have bought former editions of the Trial, may have Turpin's Life and the History of all his Robberies, singly for two pence'. It was still being advertised for sale in their York newspaper until at least 5 June 1739.[3]

Bayes sold his booklet for sixpence and it was printed by J. Standen at D'Anver's Head opposite Serjeant's Inn, Chancery Lane. On the cover was the appellation 'The Whole collected from well attested Facts, and Communicated to Mr Richard Bayes, at The Green Man on Epping Forest, and other persons of that County'. Next year was published *A Select and Impartial account of the Lives, Behaviour and Dying words of the remarkable convicts from the year 1700 down to the present time,* and this included 'Richard Turpin, for divers Robberies'.[4]

Bayes's *History* introduced a number of aspects to the tale which were untrue, such as referring to Turpin's wife's surname as Palmer. Other aspects were certainly suspect and not backed up by any other source, such as his apprenticeship in Whitechapel, being a smuggler, the description of the meeting with Turpin and King. Some elements of the story were taken out of chronological order, such as the attack on Mrs Shelley's household. Yet they were mostly faithfully copied by later authors and so gained, through repetition, the status of facts.

The *Reading Mercury* published a version of the trial on the front pages of three of its editions, explaining at the outset, 'The villainies of the famous, or rather infamous, Turpin, having made a great noise in the World, we have been persuaded to insert his Trial, which we hope will be agreeable to our Readers'.[5]

In 1740 there was published a general history of criminals, with a second edition in 1745 and a third in 1760. Turpin featured in these. The author wrote 'it deserves extraordinary notice so as no man ever lived more like a rogue, so no man ever died, more like a fool, as this fellow did'.[6] What followed was an almost word for word copy of Bayes's *Genuine History*, complete with printed letters, without any original matter at all.

These accounts of Turpin accord with other accounts of infamous criminals which were published shortly after their executions, which tended to be a mix of fact and fiction, with a dose of morality thrown in for good measure.

How does this compare to other well-known highwaymen and criminals such as Claude Duval, John Nevison, Jack Sheppard and Jonathan Wild? Seventeen pamphlets were published about the latter in the months following his execution, not just two as in Turpin's case. There are at least six about Sheppard published in the eighteenth century. Likewise, *The Lives of the Highwaymen* republished in 1742 mentions these first three villains but not Turpin. This is interesting, because Turpin had only been executed three years previously and he had garnered coverage in the press from 1735–39, so his omission seems odd. On the other hand neither Duval nor the others seems to be mentioned in the later eighteenth-century press as Turpin was. Possibly the book, which was a reprint, was not updated to include more recent villains such as Turpin. Nor did the *Lives of the Noted Highwaymen*, published in 1750, include him, though Duval was there. *Anecdotes of the remarkable highwaymen* (1797) ignored him too, though not Sheppard. Yet Turpin was not entirely forgotten, as we shall see, and was to eclipse all his peers in posthumous fame.

A later history was largely a repeat of those already published, but it added speculation, for instance on the character of King. Turpin 'was enlivened by the drollery of his companion, "Tom" King, who was a fellow of infinite humour, in telling stories, and of unshaken resolution in attack or defence'. It adds that King was killed in

Braintree, yet this is untrue. It also adds, without any foundation, that the Gregory gang stole from churches in Barking and Chingford. History was becoming increasingly merged with myth with the reader not necessarily able to differentiate between the two. This book also, as noted in an earlier chapter, introduced the story of the ride to York and Turpin being a kindly helper of the poor, and so history and myth were being served up together.[7]

The *Newgate Calendar* was a continually amended book/s chronicling notorious criminals in the eighteenth and nineteenth centuries. In a volume published in 1824 there were ten pages about Turpin. His upbringing was described, referring to him being the son of a Thaxted farmer and having 'a common school education'. Otherwise the account is fairly straightforward and adheres to Bayes's *History*. It states categorically that Mrs Shelley was placed on the fire and that Turpin shot King. The section ends with the following verdict, following an account of Turpin's reburial:

> 'It is difficult to conceive the reason of all this concern and sympathy: for surely a more heartless and depraved villain than Turpin never existed. Independent of the brutal murders perpetrated by him, it is impossible to overlook the mean rascality of his robbing the two country girls (which even his fellow thief refused to do) or the barbarity of placing an old woman on the fire, because she refused directing the gang to the little hoard, which had probably been laid by to support her in her declining years'.[8]

A later history was a short pamphlet, published in 1825 by an unknown author, which added unsourced information to Turpin's story, beginning after a brief relation of his early life, thus:

> 'his master discharging him from his house for his brutality and the egregious impropriety of his conduct

generally, which was not a little encouraged by his parents' indulgence in supplying him with money whereby he was enabled to cut a figure in town, among the blades of the road, and turf whose company he effected to keep'.

We also learn that he was poaching on the grounds of Sir Litton Weston, a gamekeeper provided evidence against him and he was remanded for future examinations.[9]

Turpin returns to Hempstead and finds Dennis, the gamekeeper, against whom he has sworn revenge, and kills him. He returns to London and joins a gang of thieves who break into homesteads to terrorise and steal from the inhabitants. On his way to Cambridge after the gang has been broken up, he meets King and Bayes' version of the meeting is repeated.[10]

The two commit crimes on the highway. Turpin shoots Morris dead, but in a scuffle in London with Bayes and others, Turpin shoots King in error and then rides away. It is then that 'thoughts of executing his extraordinary ride to York first washed across him; his bosom throbbed high in rapture, and he involuntarily exclaimed aloud, as he raised himself in the saddle "By Gad I will do it"'. He rides towards Hempstead but is pursued, he and Bess jump over the Hornsey toll bar, and ride through Tottenham and Edmonton, eventually reaching York. This is a variation on the ride to York tale, as had already been recounted in print.[11]

Once again there is a mix of fact taken from earlier writings, and fiction.

There were two booklets published in the mid-Victorian era about Turpin's life and these are remarkably similar in content. One begins 'The transactions of this most notorious offender made a greater noise in the world, than those of almost any other malefactor previous to his time'. It then uses phrases copied from the 1825 booklet about Turpin's early life. It also, like the previous booklet, relates the ride to York, using the version in the 1800 book as a model.[12]

Both this booklet and the other copy the sections first published in 1800 about Turpin's charitable nature.[13] These books did not deny that Turpin, as a member of the Gregory gang, participated in appalling deeds, but they softened his character by introducing unsourced 'information'. Myth was being written as history. One booklet finishes with some moralising, 'the young, the thoughtless and all those whose dispositions may tempt them to acts of dishonesty, should learn the high value of an unblemished reputation'.[14]

Turpin is one of the few criminals (Jack the Ripper was excluded) who has an entry in the late Victorian *Dictionary of National Biography* (the *Oxford Dictionary of National Biography* of 2004, aiming to be more inclusive, has entries on many more women, people of colour and criminals, though admittedly many of these were alive after the original *Dictionary* was compiled). The author of the entry on Turpin gave his year of birth as 1706, a common enough error, but was otherwise careful to stick to the information in the contemporary histories as to his life and career. He suggests that Turpin's flight to Yorkshire in 1737 may have inspired Ainsworth's novel, and tells the reader that the ride was actually the work of William Nevison in 1676, though earlier accounts attributed this myth to Richard Dudley. He discounts other stories relating to Black Bess, Hounslow Heath, Finchley and Enfield, classing him as a 'robber' and 'a very commonplace ruffian'.[15]

Over a century later, the *Oxford Dictionary of National Biography (DNB)* included an article about Turpin was written by Derek Barlow, whose book on the subject had been published in 1973. Instead of describing Turpin as a 'robber', Barlow uses the term 'highwayman', which perhaps subtly repositions Turpin in the reader's mind in a more favourable light. He gives a summary of Turpin's life and criminal career and his posthumous favourable reputation from the nineteenth century onward, citing *Rookwood*. He concludes, 'Turpin therefore is the classic example of the criminal who metamorphoses into mythical status as hero by perpetuation in entertainment and legend, achieves immortality'.[16]

Numerous references in the press concurred, describing Turpin as a real figure as an antidote to the myth. One noted that 'His deeds were most dastardly', though the piece becomes rather inventive when it claims that Turpin nearly burnt a woman to death to find where her money was and beat one Mason to death.[17] John Avery's lecture on Epping Forest was summarised in a local newspaper and he stated that Turpin was but 'a cowardly thief'.[18] Another stated that he was 'an unqualified villain'.[19]

There were pieces in the York press which tried to put the record right and focussed on Turpin's terror and housebreaking: 'Such was the real character of the man around whom has been weaved an almost unrivalled atmosphere of romance'.[20] Another stated:

> 'No literary legend of recent years has been more difficult to kill than that about Turpin's famous ride to York. Since Harrison Ainsworth adapted the story in *Rookwood*, it has formed the basis for attractive equestrian feats in every travelling circus and made the name Black Bess one of the most popular in our history. Yet as Major Griffiths asserts in his recently published book, Turpin never took such a journey as the novelist describes'.[21]

Thomas Secombe, who had written the *DNB* article about Turpin, wrote a lengthier piece in the *Essex Review* in 1902 and this was reprinted as a standalone booklet. It was an attempt at covering Turpin in both fact and fiction, regretting that 'It is one of the big verities of fiction... what is so far greater and stronger than Truth'. He also tries to identify some of the real places in the Turpin story, identifying Mrs Shelley's home in Loughton as Traps Hill Farm.[22]

Another attempt at serious history was made by Charles Harper in his book about highwaymen. He has no sympathy with the myth-makers and his chapter on Turpin asserts, after referring to the innumerable stories:

'the student of these things smiles a little sourly as he traced the quite unheroic doings of this exceptionally mean and skulking scoundrel and fails all the time to note anything of a dashing nature in his very busy but altogether very sordid career'.[23]

Harper notes that it is difficult for the historian to demolish the myths of the highwaymen wholesale without offending many, but even so, he feels that in one case he must do so, 'Only in respect of the great figure Turpin has always made, has it been found really necessary to seriously consider and restate the career of that much overstated scoundrel and put him in his proper place, a very much lower one that he usually occupies'.[24]

Unfortunately much of Harper's lengthy chapter on Turpin is taken uncritically from Bayes's *Genuine History* with some anecdotal evidence thrown in. The character of 'Ned Rust' as one of the Gregory gang is taken here as being factual, for example, but nowhere does this name appear in any contemporary record.[25] The shooting of Morris here predates that of King.[26] Harper provides good service in identifying the origin of Black Bess, having verses about 'Turpin and the Bishop', including the line 'His black mare Bess', although not quite the alliteration that Ainsworth was to establish a decade later.[27] He also suggests that social resentment may have led to Turpin being made into a martyred hero, given a mentality in which anyone rich is wicked and anyone poor is virtuous. Harper notes, 'We may readily imagine the ill-treated Mr Lawrence of Edgwarebury, rubbing his roasted posteriors and vehemently dissenting from that estimation of Turpin'.[28]

Gerald Oswald Rickword (1887–1969) lived in Colchester, Essex, and worked as an insurance clerk in 1911. He was also a would-be Turpin historian and in the 1930s amassed a large amount of research notes and newspaper cuttings about Turpin. Much of his information came from contemporary newspapers and other sources. Unlike the

London Turpin enthusiast mentioned in an earlier chapter, Rickword had no illusions about Turpin. He wrote a draft of his book, running to about 250 pages. In the preface he explained that he sought to explore 'the real man as divorced from the creation of the novelist… to portray Turpin as he really was, neither glossing over his faults, nor embellishing his virtues'. He wanted to tell how the Turpin story had been made into legend and how the memory of him had been kept alive, acknowledging that the eighteenth century was a time of irreligion, heavy drinking, immorality and poor behaviour.[29]

Rickword included both fact and supposition, for example supposing that when Turpin was in London in the 1720s, 'Turpin was present, no doubt, on that November morning in 1724, when the daring young prison breaker, Jack Sheppard, was turned off at Tyburn'. He agreed with Bayes's *Genuine History* that Turpin was a member of a smuggling band and later took to highway robbery prior to joining the Gregory gang.[30] In 1938, anticipating the bicentenary of Turpin's death in the next year, he began to approach publishers and there were some encouraging reports. However, the war intervened, but Rickword persevered in 1946. However, though one publisher praised the book as being 'painstaking in the extreme', they regretted that it was 'not quite enough definite material to make a book' and therefore it could not be published in its current state. It seems that Rickword's book was never published.[31]

Twentieth-century published books of substance about Turpin numbered two. There was *Immortal Turpin*, which was not unsympathetic to its subject:

> 'Turpin was an unconscionable rogue, but he could by no means have been without some virtues, for otherwise he would not have become a hero in the eyes of the common people of this time'.
>
> He was one of the products of his time, driven by circumstances rather than inclination to prey upon society

as it then was. The harsh inequalities of eighteenth century justice, when laws were framed more for the protection of property than of human life'.[32]

The author here is making assumptions and passing them off as fact. There is no evidence that Turpin was a hero to the common people and there is no way of ascertaining Turpin's motivations, yet the author does not make this clear. However, it is a rigorously researched and sourced book, the first ever to be published.

Then there was Derek Barlow's *Dick Turpin and the Gregory Gang*, published in 1973 and the most heavyweight of all books on the topic. Using sources from the National Archives, the Middlesex Record Office (now part of the London Metropolitan Archives), numerous contemporary newspapers and magazines, the author covers in minute detail the life and careers of not only Turpin, but the numerous members of the Gregory gang, and the latter had not hitherto been attempted. It is a narrative history in chronological order. Lengthy quotation is made from trial and other contemporary documents. He is critical of the factual accuracy of Richard Bayes's contemporary biography and of the letters purportedly written to and from Turpin when in prison. There is also a great deal of discussion and commentary about the possible reasons for various actions. He makes some comment on the Turpin mythology following his death, but unlike a later author, dwells on it for a relatively short time. He does not come to any explicit conclusions, but condemns the brutality of the gang in their later attacks and is equally hard on the 'treachery' of Wheeler in informing on his fellows.[33] The book lacks an introduction and a conclusion and this does not make the narrative an easy one to follow.

York Castle Museum put together a four-page illustrated pamphlet about Turpin, which stuck to facts and showed pictures of places and artefacts in the museum and tried to debunk the legends.[34] The same cannot be said for Jackson's *Dick Turpin*, a lengthier book in the next decade. It was heavy on illustrations but rather skimmed over Turpin's involvement with the Gregory gang and their crimes, and was sympathetic to its subject matter, referring to 'the lower classes took him to their hearts' and finally 'And so Dick Turpin the popular hero was finally laid to rest'. No evidence was cited for these assertions.[35]

Another short article about Turpin was largely factual but contained unsubstantiated material. The author stated 'Turpin was looked upon as being a gentleman' when he lived in Hackney 'even so he was no Robin Hood'. Yet familiar myths are introduced: Turpin rides Black Bess and when he and King see a man on the highway at Stamford Hill who has only 18d, they give him 2s 6d.[36]

This century there have been more books. Professor Sharpe wrote an excellent book about English highwaymen, including Turpin, but, unlike previous books, it focusses on a discussion of contemporary crime and the fight against it, and the myth of highwaymen, its creation and spread, as opposed to the reality. He begins by stating 'We think of Dick Turpin as a courageous and romantic figure, a man of considerable daring, who, like Robin Hood, defied corrupt officialdom and robbed the rich to help the poor'.[37] Then he asks who the real Turpin was, and why highwaymen are romantic figures, giving his answer immediately: 'In reality, Dick Turpin was a brutal criminal, who terrorised rich and poor alike'. Much of the book examines how the cult of Turpin developed, as well as giving details about detection and crime and punishment in the eighteenth century.[38]

The chapters begin by relating Turpin's execution and the events immediately leading up to it. It is a factual account. Sharpe then states Turpin's recognisability to the modern public:

'Turpin is one of that select band of figures from England's past (others might include Henry VIII, Queen Victoria, Sir Winston Churchill and, interestingly, Robin Hood) who are instantly recognisable to everyone. Even the most subliterate fourteen-year-old will have heard of Turpin… [yet] few people could give any precise details about him'.[39]

The comment feels like a rejigging of the phrase once beloved by some middlebrow mid-twentieth-century writers of history 'Every schoolboy knows', but this is unverifiable and hardly true; this author on mentioning Turpin to a friend in her mid-thirties was surprised to learn she had never heard of him; his schoolboy son found that not all his classmates at his grammar school would know the name. The general observation holds up, however.

Sharpe then states that none of this popularity and glamour would have been apparent to contemporaries; Turpin had enjoyed brief and limited infamy in life and death, but then so had many other criminals and they were soon forgotten, replaced by the brief memory of other and more recent scoundrels. How was his heroic legend created and how do history and myth co-exist, asks Sharpe. 'Why then should a totally fictitious version of the past prove so pervasive?'[40]

Sharpe shifts his gaze to highwaymen in general. Nineteenth-century paintings glamorise some of their actions, in contrast with contemporary reports of their vile villainy in reality. Contemporary officialdom certainly saw highway robbery either by men on foot or riders as a dangerous force to be combatted. They often robbed quite poor travellers. Examination revealed that 'many of the highway robbers that were indicted at that time were carried out by men of low status and on foot, and that it is the menace and brutality of these robberies which is the most marked feature of such qualitative evidence about them as we have'.[41] However, the seventeenth-century Claude Duval was highly praised by some at the time and he 'established the image of highwayman which was to prove so resilient in later generations', though even he could be heartless and vicious at times.[42] Yet highwaymen were of some interest to the public, as a number of books about them were published in the eighteenth century; interestingly enough, Turpin was not covered by all of them.[43]

Sharpe moves onto crime in general, observing that some historians have seen the eighteenth century as a wholly violent age in which the amateur forces of law and order were largely ineffectual. He discusses crime and punishment in the period and especially in and around London. The historical Turpin returns to the narrative in chapter four when his association with the Gregory/Essex gang is outlined; his fellow thieves, their crimes and how the gang was successfully dealt with by the 'amateur' forces of officialdom. Turpin does not shine in this account of his crimes and his associates. Sharpe sums up, 'Despite the later mythologising, he comes across as an unpleasant man, albeit for a short period a successful and notorious criminal, whose offences ran from robbery with violence to murder... One wonders if, three centuries into the future, any of our modern criminals will be candidates for romanticism'. And contemporary records have no reference to Black Bess or the ride to York.[44]

The next plank of the book covers the novel *Rookwood*, and its author, and his success with the book, 'a very curious literary production. Its plot is almost impossible to summarise'.[45] Sharpe points out that the ride to York on Black Bess, which features in the book, was not original but that 'it was the phenomenal success of *Rookwood* that firmly established those two crucial elements of the Turpin legend'. He also observes that the last mounted highway robbery in England occurred in 1831, three years before the first publication of *Rookwood*, due to better policing, urban growth and developments in banking meaning that travellers no longer needed to carry large sums of money with them. Turpin had been established as a hero just when the danger of highwaymen to real travellers had gone (similarly the romanticisation of Bonnie Prince Charlie and the Jacobites emerged in the early nineteenth century when they were no longer a threat).[46]

Where Ainsworth had been so successful, a host of lesser pens followed in the same vein, many of them writing for the increasingly lucrative children's market as education became more widespread. Not only Turpin, but Duval, Sheppard and other rogues, fictional or not, began to be written about for cheap booklets. Poems, folk songs, plays, toys and circuses all capitalised on the highwayman and in particular the Turpin myth, and were very popular. Films, romantic fiction and pantomimes continued to ensure the popularity of the highwayman figure throughout the twentieth and into the twenty-first century. The highwayman was always the hero and Turpin was the most famous of them all. A theatre performance at York in 2001 characterised Turpin as 'glamorous, chivalrous, a big hit with the ladies'. Sharpe notes 'This, of course, has absolutely no connection with the "real" Turpin of documentary history. Does this matter? Should people be told about it?'[47]

The final and shortest chapter concerns Turpin and the meaning of history. As Sharpe writes, 'There are a lot of Dick Turpins': the man who was hanged in 1739, and the one known to the public.[48] There is 'the clear distinction between the type of attempts to reconstruct historical reality at which historians struggle, and the historical myth that so often achieves widespread public currency and triumphs over the historians and their labours'.[49] Popular history of the type shown on the screen can be morally unambiguous, whereas attempts at reality can be more complex and so more difficult to deal with. One reason why it is important to make the effort to 'get history right' is that otherwise the past can be used by those in the present as propaganda for cultural, social and political reasons, in order to serve their future needs, and this is not the sole preserve of the totalitarian state.[50]

Rather less weighty than Sharpe's book was a book by popular children's author Terry Deary entitled *Gorgeous Georgians,* in which he briefly states the legend of Turpin and then debunks it. This treatment was extended in a later book, *Dick Turpin: Legends and Lies*, which assessed Turpin using the fictional device of having five people discuss him while waiting for him to be hanged. The narrator is a fictional twelve-year-old boy. He hears contradictory views of Turpin from the four adults (all real people) gathered near to him: John Robinson, the farmer, tells him that Turpin is a gentleman, but Mrs Shelley, the old woman, says he is a thief and she wants to see him hang in revenge. The two others do not yet speak. Each short chapter focusses on the story of each of the adults. The farmer claims Turpin was a hero, 'He was only trying to make some money to live' and relates how Turpin tried to rob King but the two became friends. The boy then compares Turpin to Robin Hood, 'a real hero'. To this Mrs Shelley retorts 'He was the most cruel man to ride the roads of Essex'.[51]

Mrs Shelley then explains how her home was broken into by Turpin and his gang and they were about to torture her prior to obtaining her money. She explained that thereafter she was too terrified to go to sleep each night. The third adult, James Smith, here a teacher, tells how Turpin shot King by accident before fleeing. The old man tries to ameliorate Turpin's actions and suggests he will die bravely, which the teacher denies will be the case.[52]

Robinson and Smith then explain their roles in the capture of Turpin. Both believe they should have the reward of £200. Robinson tells how he had the magistrates arrest Turpin when posing as Palmer in 1738 after he shot the cockerel. Smith then explains that he identified Palmer as Turpin by recognising his writing on his letter from York and then identifying him in York Castle. The old man is angry 'Traitor... giving away an old friend from school. What sort of gutter rat would do that?' Mrs Shelley tells him that Smith was doing his duty.[53]

It is revealed that the old man is Turpin's father who has come to see his son die. On the gallows Turpin makes a speech to defend himself, 'I never meant to harm anyone... I only tried to make a living. I wasn't born rich. I had to make my own way in life. I did the best I could'. The old Turpin and Mrs Shelley are reconciled as they walk away together.[54]

The author then has an epilogue about the lies and legend of Turpin. We are told that you can visit his grave in York and see the cell he was in at York Castle Museum (though which one it was is uncertain). We're told he shot his partner and that though he escaped in London he shot a cockerel later:

> 'But people need heroes. Over the years people began to add to Turpin's story. They invented a wonderful horse for him called Black Bess. Lies.
>
> 'They added a story that Turpin rode from London to York in a day to escape the law. Brave Bess dropped dead at the end. Lies.
>
> 'Films and books have made Dick Turpin look like a gallant gentleman. Lies.
>
> 'He was a cruel bully. Truth.
>
> 'He died well... but he lived badly. Truth'.[55]

Deary is attempting to debunk the myth of the heroic highwayman, as every author writing non-fiction has done since 1739. Unfortunately the book reveals limited research and knowledge on the author's part, as one might expect from the author of *Horrible Histories*. To mention a few: Smith was not a schoolmaster in 1739 but an excise officer. To castigate Smith as a traitor, as the author does, seems to suggest that the author disapproves of evidence leading to the arrest of criminals being handed over to the authorities, and thus implicitly at least, to side with the criminals. Or it may be the author's dislike of teachers, as later revealed in the book (he approves of stealing from them).

The author gives Turpin a last speech that he never made, which is all to Turpin's credit and reinforces the social injustice myth that the films and dramas perpetuate. There is no evidence that Mrs Shelley, Smith, John Turpin and Robinson were ever present at the execution and none that even if they were, that they talked to each other; in a crowded place this is unlikely. Three of four of them lived in Essex, so a journey and extended stay in York seems inherently unlikely (though Smith visited York to identify Turpin and to give evidence at the trial).

The stories about Turpin given by the characters are passed off as fact. Yet no contemporary source suggests that King and Turpin tried to rob one another when they first met. Contemporary sources are also ambiguous over whether Turpin shot King or whether Bayes did, and whether Turpin actually tortured Mrs Shelley or whether he or another gang member merely threatened to do so. Yet here it is passed off as fact that Turpin was the torturer and the shooter – as with the tabloid press, the author of *Horrible Histories* prefers the ghastlier version.

The enormously popular *Horrible Histories* series has gone from book to stage and TV and has even led to a Dick Turpin song. The singer is meant to be Turpin and he appears as a rather effeminate young man, well dressed and with unblemished skin, most unlike the appearance of the real character. The song is filmed at Osterley Park in Middlesex, which unintentionally aligns it with the glamorous myth. The song is about how, contrary to myth, Turpin is far from being a hero, and that he was discovered by a 'postman' (Smith). It does a reasonable job of debunking the many myths put about by Noyes, Ainsworth and others. Turpin begins by singing 'everybody thinks they know the story of Dick Turpin's highway glory' but admits 'I was no prince charming, nothing dandy about me' and 'the truth was... I was a ruthless killer with a ruthless killer's heart... a vicious highwayman'. Finally after fleeing to Yorkshire he adds 'I was stitched up by a postie. That's not glamorous that's lame... It's no fun hanging with a highwayman when he's hanging from a rope'. It is an entertaining and fairly accurate piece of work, though referring to James Smith as 'a postie' is a little inaccurate and stating that Turpin shot not one man but two repeats the supposition that it was Turpin not Bayes who shot King. Likewise he was arrested for shooting a cockerel not for stealing hens.

Another modern book aimed at children about ten famous historical villains includes Turpin among them, but attributes King's death to him and claims he tortured many people. In the latter case there is only one undisputed record; two if Mrs Shelley is added. The author tries to debunk the myth and gives Nevison the credit for the ride to York.[56]

Books about highwaymen for adults naturally include Turpin but many are factually slipshod. Although they do not doubt his villainy, one referring to him as 'a cruel, sadistic and ruthless highwayman' and another that he was transformed from ugly thug to gentleman hero, the primary source material they draw on is limited. They tend to put all their trust in Bayes's *Genuine History*, but as already stated, this is a dubious source. One of these authors asserts Turpin was born in East Ham, was apprenticed to a Whitechapel butcher, married a woman by the name of Palmer, stole from a Mr Plaistow, that the Gregory gang was five strong and that Smith was a postmaster. Another confuses his baptism date with his birth date, and as with the first repeats the apprenticeship story and states definitely that he roasted Mrs Shelley over a fire. And so on.[57] Other recent surveys of English highwaymen include chapters about Turpin and these are mostly accurate, attempting to cast aside the legendary image for the brutal truth. David Brandon refers to Turpin as 'the very embodiment of the dashing highwayman', before going on to decry the mythology.[58]

Some analyse Turpin. While recognising that he was 'a most unpromising candidate for the role of legendary hero', one author deems him to have been an emblem of escape and freedom. She adds that because of his close relationship with Black Bess, this was seen to be of great cultural and moral value and so helped provide him with popularity.[59] A cultural historian states that 'more than any other figure, Dick Turpin exemplifies the modern notion of the highwayman'. He adds that he had already achieved celebrity status in his own lifetime and that this was heightened by the attention the contemporary media bestowed on him, 'the eighteenth century Turpin is to a great extent the product of print journalism'. He represented the rural, athletic and masculine pursuits; a man's man. Robin Hood, Rob

Roy and Turpin 'are all successfully quarantined within a romantic nostalgic past, safely removed from the realities of the present and its grubby everyday criminals'.[60]

Unfortunately some serious historians have also unconsciously swallowed the Turpin myth uncritically. In one of his first published articles, about the trials and executions of Jacobite prisoners in York in 1746, by this author, there is a phrase about these men not being sympathetically viewed as was the case with 'a popular hero like Dick Turpin, hanged in 1739'. This is bad enough but worse is Marxist historian Peter Linebaugh, in a study of executions in London, who tells the reader that Turpin was brought to London to be tried at the Old Bailey, was the son of a farmer, was apprenticed to a butcher in Whitechapel, married Hesther Palmer, stole cattle to sell at Waltham Abbey, joined a smuggling gang and recites an exchange between Turpin and the judge; most of which fiction is taken from Bayes's *History*. Linebaugh even regurgitates the midnight ride to York and the death of Black Bess as fact and posits Turpin as a 'social bandit' beloved by Marxists who only robbed the privileged, as did the Turpin of the films and TV fables.[61] Gatrell, another who should have known better, notes the ride to York as a fact, despite its physical impossibility. He also refers to Turpin as a 'highwayman', yet that was only one of his many crimes and not even the one for which he was hanged.[62] Which just goes to show that historians and those reading their works need to be aware of making comments based on what they think they know or have read in dubious sources.

There are a number of relevant videos on the internet that have been posted in recent years. They include Vic Reeves's *Rogues Gallery* (2011) about Turpin, showing Reeves interviewing the 'real' Turpin. They are all quite short but are mostly historically accurate, though attributing the origin of the Turpin myths to Ainsworth, and in one case to Richard Bayes. The authors are in no doubt that the real Turpin was a notorious criminal and vicious thug.

There have been short television documentaries on the Discovery channel, including one in 1999, which also try to portray an accurate figure of Turpin. One features an interview with esteemed Turpin scholar Derek Barlow. Another has an actor dressed up as Turpin whom the presenter interviews. Both debunk the ride to York and show Turpin as a mean and vicious figure, but these documentaries do contain errors of fact and one includes myths of places associated with Turpin.

Other pieces online about Turpin have similar problems in that after rightly attacking the legend they then proceed, due to limited research, to state half-truths and myths as fact and so historical errors already embedded in the narrative are repeated and garner alleged factual respectability. They often credit Ainsworth with sole responsibility for changing Turpin from thug to hero and then err as to some or all of the following: Turpin's birthplace, confusing date of baptism with date of birth, misnaming his wife, giving him out to be a smuggler, as well as errors over dates, the Gregory gang and Turpin's later career. Ainsworth is given all the 'credit' for the Turpin myth.

Local histories also refer to Turpin, often to decry legends. Michael Robbins rebuts Turpin's links with Tottenham and Edmonton in Middlesex, attributing this to Ainsworth.[63] Likewise Martin Briggs refers to Edgwarebury Farm as being 'vaguely associated with Dick Turpin' and claims that there is a 'Turpin's Oak' in Oak Lane, Finchley. He adds that 'modern historians' discount the ride to York and 'dismiss him as a common rascal'.[64] Stevenson has Turpin being rumoured to haunt Camlet Moat and Finchley.[65] The *Victoria County Histories* for Middlesex make several references to Turpin; one stating that there is no evidence for him having operated on Hounslow Heath and another claiming there is no evidence for his connection with Turpin's Oak. Apparently coachmen used to shoot this as they passed it by.[66] Another recounts a rumour that Turpin's grandfather lived in Clay Hill, Enfield and the man himself lurked on the Chase.[67] Yet another states that at a farmstead in Edgware, Turpin stole silverware, threw boiling water over the householder and raped the daughter of the house.[68]

Apart from the local histories there are many general books about highwaymen and outlaws, mostly written in the twentieth century, and these usually include a chapter on Turpin. On the whole, historians have tried to paint an accurate picture of Turpin as robber, killer and horse thief. They do their best to rebut the legends about Black Bess and the ride to York, as well as the glamour, romance, chivalry and kindness of Turpin. How far they have been successful remains to be seen, given the support that screen adaptations give to the myth.

An insightful comment comes from a nineteenth-century writer:

'There never was, perhaps, a man in the particular profession to which this notorious fellow devoted himself, whose name was more familiar in the mouths of the common people than that of Turpin. But since it invariably happens that a certain proportion of curiosity respecting the life of actors of a man is sure to beget a corresponding desire to satisfy it, we find that some have unjustifiably resorted to fiction when they should have adhered scrupulously to fact. Hence it has happened that certain exploits have been attributed to Turpin which do not belong to him; with others the unparalleled ride from York to London in an uncommonly short period, performed, it is averred, on one horse. We have never been able to find any authentic account of this fact, nor have we, as yet, discovered any conceivable necessity that should compel him to so rapid a journey'.[69]

Conclusion

Dick Turpin is essentially two men. There is the one that is fondly known about by most people, a handsome, romantic, brave, kind-hearted gentleman of the road, who had a horse called Black Bess and rode from London to York in a day. He gives to the poor and fights villains. This is the Turpin of legend, and the man who has emerged from the eighteenth century to become an icon for the nineteenth and twentieth century and beyond. In reality this image is an amalgam of the stories of others, principally Dudley and Nevison, with a dash of Ainsworth's imagination. Unlike many historical figures, whose reputations have waxed and waned, the legendary Turpin's has remained on a high for the last two centuries.

This is despite the efforts of historians in these last two centuries. The real Turpin could not be more different. He was a pockmarked failed butcher who joined a gang of deer-stealers in Essex and with them attacked lonely homesteads around London. There householders and their servants were terrorised, threatened, tied up and forced to reveal the location of their valuables. On occasions, violence was used, including torture and rape. Once the gang was taken, Turpin escaped and in doing so became well known for his highway robberies in 1735–37. However, after shooting one or perhaps two men dead, he fled again, and in Yorkshire, having changed his name, was arrested for horse-stealing, correctly identified, tried and hanged at York. He had been a minor celebrity in the press and there was a contemporary biography written about him. Contrary to myth he did not restrict his highway robberies to holding up coaches but often robbed travellers on horseback or on foot.

Turpin's criminal career, in some ways, conforms to the pattern of such men. He began in 1734 as a butcher who was an associate to the Gregory gang and later that year and in the next he became an active member. Following the gang's collapse he became an independent criminal, able to adapt his *modus operandi* to his changing circumstances, and recruited other gang members. In this his fame in the press may well have been useful to him. In 1737 he was able to uproot himself geographically and change his criminal ways yet again. Compared to many criminals he was quite successful and versatile, which helped him escape capture for longer than others, though the end came eventually and was mostly of his own making.

However, none of the attributes of the legendary Turpin, save that he was a highwayman, albeit briefly, apply to the real man. To an extent it is because of that one attribute that there was an opportunity for him to be favourably remembered, this one true fact on which a whole fictional edifice was built. The image of the highwayman is, for better or worse, imbued with an undeserving glamour. In part this is because it is a crime that has ceased to exist and has been no threat to anyone for two centuries. Of course, there were many highwaymen: Duval, Dudley, Nevison and Sixteen String Jack have already been mentioned, and that is to name but four. Yet Turpin has eclipsed them all.

Certainly he had the fortune that Harrison Ainsworth chose him to appear in his novel. He saw a ball that was already there, the myth of the ride to York and a mare called Bess, and an aura of benevolence, and took it from the pitch and ran with it, and as he did so that ball gathered increasing momentum and weight until it became a full-blown historical myth, firmly embedded in the national psyche. The memory of Turpin survives because of a number of pieces of luck; his luck in escaping the round-up of the Gregory gang in 1735, and his good fortune in unknowingly turning to a crime that would soon become redundant, then lucky in escaping in 1737 and then having been picked out of numerous similar criminals by a popular novelist.

Turpin's name and myth survived, but this must never blind the public to the fact that he was a man of violence who associated with men who were similar, if not worse. His crimes apart, he was able to abandon his wife and son, and to land his father in prison, without too many qualms. However, there is much about him that we will never know. There is virtually nothing known about his early years, his personality, his exact motivations and his inner self. What we do know about are his criminal actions and in some cases the lack of them. However, it is important not to exaggerate his crimes as some have; he is 'only' known to have definitely tortured one person, possibly two; and he definitely killed one man, possibly two. Without wanting to downplay these crimes, it is also essential not to overdo them.

In *As You Like it*, Shakespeare has Jaques make his famous Seven Ages of Man speech (Act II, Scene 7) in which he states 'And one man in his time plays many parts'. This is true of everyone, but historical figures are often given labels for shorthand convenience. Thus Turpin is usually labelled 'highwayman' or less often, but less inaccurately, 'criminal'. Turpin was many things to many people: a butcher, a housebreaker, a highwayman, a horse thief, a killer; but also a son, a sibling, a friend, a husband and a father. However, virtually nothing is known about these aspects of his personal and family life and it is his criminal persona, which is far better documented, which is known about. Decades after his death he was mostly reduced/transformed into being a highwayman, a hero, a horseman and a lover. Both lists are inadequate but we can go no further beyond the limit of the known evidence. They do indicate, however, that Turpin was more than just one archetype.

One advantage that the posthumous Turpin enjoyed is that there was relatively little written about him after his death, only two short biographies in 1739 and one of these is almost a pirate copy of the other. Compare this to Jonathan Wild: over a dozen accounts of his life appeared shortly after his death. Thus we know more about Wild than Turpin, but this is to Turpin's posthumous benefit, because it means that there was a far greater field for the imagination of future authors who are free to write about him in any way they like, unhindered by historical fact. Had Turpin been tried and hanged in London, with the rest of the Gregory gang of housebreakers, there would have been no notoriety as he would have been just another criminal gang member and not a wanted individual. If, after evading capture until 1737, Turpin had been tried in London, it is likely that there would have been more written about him, as with Wild, and that a likeness of him would have been drawn by a contemporary, as with Sheppard. However, York was a provincial city with a population of about 10,000 compared to London with over half a million residents, and so his immediate infamy was not as great as it could have been.

The myth of Turpin compared to the known reality poses another, wider question. Most historical figures, if they are known at all by the general public, are known but little, perhaps just by a label and a sentence or two at best, perhaps as figureheads for a cause. Think of Mary Seacole or Winston Churchill. It has already been noted how misleading a little knowledge can be. As this is the case, how well do we know other historical figures, who are often referred to in the media and popular culture, though about whom experts often differ, and how far does that little knowledge shape our sense of the past and inspire our present and future?

Notes

Introduction

1. V.A.C. Gatrell, *The Hanging tree, Execution and the English People, 1770–1868* (1994).

Chapter 1

1. Geoffrey Holmes and Daniel Szechi, *The Age of Oligarchy: Pre Industrial England, 1722–1783*, (1993), pp.346-349.
2. W.A. Speck, *Stability and Strife: England, 1714–1760*, (1977), p.353.
3. Ibid, p.353.
4. Ibid.
5. Pat Rogers, ed., *Daniel Defoe: Tour around the Whole Island of Great Britain*, (1971), p.431.
6. Ibid, p.433.
7. Speck, *Stability and Strife*, pp.86, 89-90.
8. Henry Fielding, *Enquiry into the increase of Robbers* (1751), p.146.
9. James Sharpe, *Dick Turpin and the Myth of the English Highwayman* (2005), pp.89-91, 98.
10. *Gentleman's Magazine*, 3, (1733).
11. Jonathan Oates, *Foul Deeds and Suspicious Deaths in Lewisham and Deptford*, (2007), pp. 30-36.

12. Holmes and Szechi, *The Age of Oligarchy*, pp.352, 368, 384.
13. Speck, *Stability and Strife*, pp.59-60; J.M. Beattie, *Policing and Punishment in London, 1660–1750*, (2001), pp.41-42.

Chapter 2

1. Reed Browning, *The Duke of Newcastle* (1975), p.1.
2. Essex Record Office, D/P 314, 1/1; Thomas Kyll, *The Trial of the Notorious Highwayman, Richard Turpin* (1739), p.14.
3. Ancestry.co.uk, parish registers; *Essex Standard*, 14 February 1885.
4. *Essex County Directory*, 1848, pp.656-657; *VCH Essex*, I, (1907), p.347; Thomas Wright, *History of Essex*, II, (1836), pp.81-86.
5. ERO, D/P 314/8/1; LIB/POL/1/3.
6. Richard Bayes, *The Genuine History of the life of Richard Turpin* (1739), p.1
7. ERO, D/P 314/8/1; LIB/POL/1/3.
8. Kyll, *Trial*, pp.12-13.
9. Pevsner, *Buildings of England: Essex* (2007), p.485.
10. Kyll, *Trial*, pp.13-14.
11. ERO, D/P 314/8/1; LIB/POL1/3.
12. Ibid, D/P 314/8/1.
13. Bayes, *Genuine History*, pp.1-2.
14. Kyll, *Trial*, p.22.
15. Anon, *Lives of the Highwaymen* (1742), p.274.
16. Kyll, *Trial*, p.13.
17. Bayes, *Genuine History*, p.2.
18. Kyll, *Trial*, p.11.
19. Bayes, *Genuine History*, p.2.
20. Kyll, *Trial*, p.13.
21. Ibid.
22. Ibid, pp.14-15.
23. S.D. Smith, ed., *An Exact and Industrious Tradesman: The Letter Book of Joseph Symson of Kendal, 1711-1720*, (2003).

24. Bayes, *Genuine History*, p.2.
25. Ibid.
26. Ibid, pp.2-3.
27. Kyll, *Trial*, p.13.
28. Ibid, p.14.
29. The National Archives, T53/37, p.288.
30. Ibid, T27/25, p.396.
31. James Thorne, *Environs of London* (1876), pp.191-192.
32. TNA, SP36/29, f.99r.
33. Ibid, 23, f12v.
34. Ibid, 39, f.338r.

Chapter 3

1. TNA, T53/40, p.158.
2. *General Evening Post*, 10-13 May 1735.
3. TNA, T1/277, p.239.
4. Ruth Paley, ed., 'Justice in Eighteenth Century Hackney: Henry Norris and the Hackney Petty Sessions Note Book', *London Record Society*, 28 (1991), p.19.
5. TNA, T53/37, p.289.
6. London Metropolitan Archives, MJ/SR/2606; TNA, ASSI94/570.
7. Old Bailey online.
8. Paley, 'Justice', pp.2, 12, 21, 26.
9. LMA, MJ/SR/2652.
10. TNA, ASSI94/564.
11. TNA, T53/37, p.289, OBOL.
12. *General Evening Post*, 8-11 March 1735.
13. *Derby Mercury* 20 February 1735; *London Gazette*, 22-25 February 1735; Old Bailey online; *Political State*, 54, (1737), p.461.
14. Speck, *Stability and Strife*, p.90.
15. TNA, SP35/39, f.338r.
16. *Bayes, Genuine History*, p.3.

17. ERO, LIB/POL/6/2.
18. *London Evening Post*, 18 February 1735.
19. *Gentleman's Magazine*, 5, (1735), p.106.
20. *Bayes, Genuine History*, pp.4-5.
21. *Political State of Great Britain*, 50, (1735), p.25.
22. Ibid.
23. Paley, 'Justice', p.130, LMA, MJ/SR/2626, Calendar of Middlesex Sessions, 1732-1735, pp.121, 128, 141.
24. *General Evening Post*, 1-4 February 1735.
25. TNA, SP44/83, p.222; T53/38, pp.406-407; T53/39, p.272; T60/16, p.99.
26. *Stamford Mercury*, 25 December 1735; TNA, ASSI94/580, 639.
27. TNA, SP36/33, f.170r; T53/39, p.324.
28. *Gentleman's Magazine*, 4, (1734), p.702.
29. TNA, T53/38, p.374.
30. Ibid, ASSI94/583.
31. Ibid, SP36/33, f.171v.
32. *Bayes, Genuine History*, p.5.
33. TNA, SP36/33, f.155r.
34. Ibid, f.167r.
35. Ibid.
36. Bayes, *Genuine History*, pp.13-14.
37. *Political State*, 49, (1735), p.241.
38. TNA, SP36/34, f.164v-165r.
39. Kyll, *Trial*, p.6.
40. *Ipswich Journal*, 11 January 1735.
41. *Bayes, Genuine History*, pp.6-7.
42. *Ipswich Journal*, 18 January 1735.
43. *Gentleman's Magazine*, 5, (1735), p.50.
44. *Caledonian Mercury*, 27 January 1735.
45. *Derby Mercury*, 6 February 1735.
46. *Bayes, Genuine History,* pp.3-4.
47. Ibid, p.4.
48. *Derby Mercury*, 13 February 1735.

49. Ibid.
50. *Read's Weekly Journal*, 8 February 1735.
51. Old Bailey online.
52. Ibid.
53. Ibid.
54. Ibid.
55. TNA, SP36/34, f.52v.
56. Old Bailey online.
57. Ibid.
58. Ibid.
59. Ibid; LMA, MJ/SR/2631/16.
60. Old Bailey online.
61. TNA, SP36/34, f.38r.
62. Old Bailey online. Madam Van Muyden, ed., *Cesar De Saussure, A Foreign View of England* (1902), p.138.
63. Old Bailey online.
64. Ibid.
65. Ibid.
66. Ibid.
67. Ibid; LMA, MJ/SR/2631, 12.
68. TNA, SP44/128, p.345.
69. John Beresford, ed; *James Woodforde: Diary of a Country Parson, 1758-1802* (1987), p.236.
70. *Political State,* 49, (1735), p.242.
71. Ibid, p.243.
72. De Saussure, *A Foreign View*, p.116.
73. *Newcastle Courant*, 15 February 1735.
74. Old Bailey online.
75. LMA, MJ/SR/2631, 53.
76. *Stamford Mercury*, 27 February 1735.
77. Kyll, *Trial*, p.14.
78. *Stamford Mercury*, 27 February 1735.
79. *Caledonian Mercury*, 18 February 1735.

80. *Read's Weekly Journal*, 22 February 1735.

81. *London Gazette* 22-25 February 1735.

82. TNA, SP36/41, f.47r.

83. *Derby Mercury*, 27 February 1735.

84. *Ipswich Journal*, 27 March 1735

85. *Political State*, 49, (1735), pp.242-243.

86. Old Bailey online.

87. Ibid.

88. *General Evening Post*, 25-28 February 1735.

89. *Newcastle Courant*, 15 March 1735.

90. TNA, WO4/33, p.102.

91. *General Evening Post*, 8-11 March 1735.

92. *Gentleman's Magazine*, 5 (1735), p.102.

93. *General Evening Post*, 8-11 March 1735.

94. Christopher Morris, ed., *The Journeys of Celia Fiennes* (1949), p.310.

95. *General Evening Post*, 8-11 March 1735.

96. TNA, T90/147, p.59.

97. *Gentleman's Magazine*, 5, (1735), p.161; *Ipswich Journal*, 8 March 1735.

98. TNA, T53/38, p.160.

99. Ibid, p.195.

100. Ibid, SP44/128, p.392.

101. William Shaw, ed, *Treasury Books and Papers, 1735-1738* (1900), pp.71, 132, 90, 137.

102. Old Bailey online; TNA, T53/38, p.255.

103. *Read's Weekly Journal*, 22 March 1735.

Chapter 4

1. Paul Langford, *A Polite and Commercial people, England, 1727-1783* (1992), p.157.

2. W.S. Lewis, ed., *Correspondence of Horace Walpole*, Vol., 12, (1944), p.79.

3. Donald Gibson, ed., *A Parson in the Vale of the White Horse: George Woodward's Letters from East hundred, 1753-1761* (1984), p.64.

4. Frederick A. Pottle, ed., *Boswell's London Journal, 1762-1763* (1950), p.271.

5. Beresford, *James Woodforde*, pp. 166, 169.

6. Henri Talon, ed., *John Byrom: Selections from his Journals and Papers* (1950), p.101.

7. Ibid, p.128-129.

8. *Old Whig*, 10 April 1735.

9. *General Evening Post*, 10-13 May 1735.

10. *Political State* 49, (1735), pp.462-463; *Read's Weekly Journal*, 12 April 1735.

11. *General Evening Post*, 10-13 May 1735.

12. *Political State* 49, (1735), pp.462-463; *General Evening Post*, 10-13 May 1735.

13. Ibid, p.567.

14. *Newcastle Courant*, 10 May 1735.

15. *General Evening Post,* 10-13 May 1735.

16. *Old Whig*, 8 May 1735.

17. *Political State* 49, (1735), p.567.

18. *General Evening Post*, 20-22 May 1735.

19. Old Bailey online.

20. *Derby Mercury*, 5 June 1735.

21. *General Evening Post*, 22-24 May 1735.

22. *Gentleman's Magazine*, 5, (1735), p.161.

23. *Political State*, 50, (1735), p.8.

24. TNA, T90/147, p.59.

25. Shaw, *Treasury Books and Papers, 1735-1738*, pp.80, 137, 126.

26. *Derby Mercury*, 24 April 1735.

27. Talon, *John Byrom*, p.289.

28. *General Evening Post*, 3-5 June 1735.

29. *Grub Street Journal*, 15 May 1735.

30. *General Evening Post*, 10-12 July 1735.

31. Ibid, 24 July 1735

32. *Ipswich Journal*, 16 August 1735.

33. *Derby Mercury*, 14 August 1735; *Political State*, 49, (1735), pp.461-462; TNA, T53/39, p.271.

34. *Derby Mercury*, 14 August 1735.

35. *Political State*, 49, (1735), p.462; TNA, T53/39, p.271.

36. *Ipswich Journal*, 16 May 1735; *Derby Mercury* 14 August 1735; TNA, T53/39, p.271.

37. *Derby Mercury* 21, 14 August 1735.

38. Shaw, *Treasury Papers and Books, 1735-1738*, pp.88, 92, 598.

39. *Stamford Mercury*, 25 December 1735; TNA, T53/38, p.406-407; Paley, 'Justice', p.32.

40. *Newcastle Courant*, 27 March 1736; TNA, T53/38, p.407.

41. Shaw, *Treasury Books and Papers, 1735-1738*, pp,195, 278.

42. *Ipswich Journal*, 1 March 1735.

43. Ibid, 20 December 1735.

44. *Stamford Mercury*, 26 December 1735.

45. *Political State*, 54, (1737), p.145. TNA, T53/39, pp.374-376.

46. Ibid, p.462.

47. TNA, T90/147, p.111.

48. Ibid, 4 August; *Newcastle Courant*, 23 July 1737; *Derby Mercury*, 28 July 1737; TNA, SP44/83, p.222; T53/39, p.249.

49. Shaw, *Treasury Books and Papers, 1735-1738*, pp.383, 612.

50. TNA, SP36/39, f.145r.

51. *Newcastle Courant*, 18 February 1738.

52. *Ipswich Journal*, 18 September 1736.

53. Ibid; *Kentish Weekly Packet,* 17 March 1736.

54. Bayes, *Genuine History*, p.14.

55. Ibid, pp.14-15.

56. Ibid, p.15.

57. Ibid.

58. Ibid, pp.15-16.

59. *Country Journal*, 25 September 1736.

60. *Calendar of Middlesex Quarter Sessions, 1739-1741*, (nd) p.138.

61. *Ipswich Journal*, 15 October 1736.

62. Ibid, 11 October 1736.

63. *Caledonian Mercury*, 16 November 1736.

64. Ibid, 18 November 1736.

65. *Political State*, 53, (1737), p.255.

66. Kyll, *Trial*, pp.24-25.

67. Jean Bernard Le Blanc, *Lettres d'un Francois*, III, (1745), pp. 205-207.

68. Ibid, pp.205-206.

69. *Stamford Mercury*, 28 April 1737.

70. *Newcastle Courant*, 30 April 1737.

71. *Derby Mercury*, 21 April 1737

72. Ibid, 5 May 1737.

73. Bayes, *Genuine History*, p.17; *London Evening Post*, 10-12 February 1737.

74. TNA, ASSI94/608.

75. *Reid's Journal*, 2 April 1737.

76. *London Evening Post*, 23-26 April 1737.

77. Ibid, 30 April – 2 May 1737.

78. *Newcastle Courant*, 14 May 1737, *Stamford Mercury*, 12 May 1737, Bayes, *Genuine History*, p.17; *Reid's Journal*, 7 May 1737; LMA, MJ/SR/2680, 2676.

79. Bayes, *Genuine History*, pp.17-18.

80. Ibid.

81. *Newcastle Courant*, 14 May 1737.

82. *Derby Mercury*, 5 May 1737.

83. *Stamford Mercury*, 12 May 1737.

84. Bayes, *Genuine History*, p.18.

85. Kyll, *Trial*, p.24.

86. *Newcastle Courant*, 14 May 1737.

87. *Stamford Mercury*, 12 May 1737.

88. Bayes, *Genuine History*, pp.18-19.

89. Ibid, p.19.

90. Ibid.

91. *Stamford Mercury*, 26 May 1737.

92. TNA, PROB11/683.

93. LMA, MJ/SR/2680, 2677.

94. *London Evening Post*, 6-9 August 1737.

95. *Derby Mercury*, 12 May 1737.

96. *Newcastle Courant*, 14 May 1737.

97. Bayes, *Genuine History*, p.16.

98. *Derby Mercury*, 12 May 1737.

99. Kyll, *Trial*, p.23

100. *Newcastle Courant*, 14 May 1737.

101. *Derby Mercury*, 19 May 1737.

102. *Grub Street Journal,* 5 May 1737.

103. Ibid, 19 May 1737.

104. *Country Journal,* 2 April 1737.

105. *Stamford Mercury*, 12 May 1737; *Reid's Journal*, 14 May 1737.

106. *Country Journal*, 14 May 1737.

107. *Newcastle Courant*, 21 May 1737; *Stamford Mercury*, 19 May 1737.

108. *Kentish Weekly Packet,* 11 May 1737.

109. *Stamford Mercury*, 25 May 1737.

110. *Newcastle Courant*, 28 May 1737.

111. *Stamford Mercury* 19 May 1737.

112. *London Evening Post*, 10-12 May 1737.

113. *Old Whig*, 12 May 1737.

114. *London Gazette*, 2 June 1737.

115. *Read's Weekly Journal*, 14 May 1737.

116. *London Gazette*, 25 June 1737.

117. Van Muyden, *Foreign View*, p.101.

118. *Political State*, 51 (1737), pp.552-553.
119. Fielding, *Enquiry*, p.145.
120. *Political State*, 52, (1737), p.28.
121. *Derby Mercury*, 23 June 1737.
122. *Newcastle Courant*, 18 June 1737.
123. Ibid.
124. *Kentish Weekly Packet*, 11 June 1737.
125. *Gentleman's Magazine*, 7, (1737), p.314.
126. *London Evening Post*, 18-21 June 1737; 2-5 July 1737.
127. *Newcastle Courant*, 6 August 1737.
128. *Derby Mercury*, 18 August 1737.
129. *Fog's Weekly Journal,* 15 October 1737.
130. *Derby Mercury*, 16 June 1737.
131. *Kentish Weekly Packet*, 9 July, 17 August 12 November, 1737.
132. *Derby Mercury*, 27 October 1737.
133. *Stamford Mercury*, 15 September 1737.
134. Ibid, 18 August 1737.
135. Ancestry.co.uk
136. *The Gentleman's Magazine*, 7, (1737), p.499.
137. Ibid.
138. Ibid, p.438.
139. Ibid, p.499.
140. *Daily Post*, 27 December 1737.
141. *Country Journal*, 7 May 1737.
142. *London Evening Post*, 2-4 February 1738.
143. *New's News; great and wonderful news from London in an uproar or a Hue and Cry after the great Turpin, with his escape into Ireland*, pp.4-5.
144. Ibid, pp.6-7.
145. A. Saville, ed, 'Secret Comment: the Dairies of Gertrude Saville, 1721-1757', *Thoroton Society*, (1997), p.235.
146. *New News*, p.3.
147. *Newcastle Courant* 3 June 1738

148. *Stamford Mercury* 25 May 1738.

149. *Reid's Weekly Journal,* 25 November 1737.

150. *Newcastle Courant*, 29 April 1738.

151. Ibid, 1 July 1738.

152. *Derby Mercury*, 15 June 1738.

153. Sarah Markham, ed., *John Loveday of Caversham, 1711-1789*, (1984), p.266.

154. *Kentish Weekly Packet*, 4 March 1738.

155. *Political State*, 56, (1738), p.297.

Chapter 5

1. Kyll, *Trial*, p.iii; *Political State*, LVII, (1739) pp.191-2.

2. *Political State*, LVII, (1739), p.192.

3. TNA, ASSI94/639, 643.

4. Kyll, *Trial*, pp.iii-iv.

5. Ibid, pp.iv-v.

6. East Riding Record Office, QSF122/D8

7. Ibid, 7.

8. Kyll, *Trial*, p.v.

9. Ibid, pp.v-vi

10. Ibid, p.vi.

11. ERRO, CT, pp.31-32.

12. Kyll, *Trial*, p.vi.

13. Daniel Defoe, *Tour around the Whole Island of Great Britain*, II (1766), p.166.

14. Information York Castle Museum

15. B.R. Hartley, 'Thomas Griffiths of York', *York Historian*, 11, (1994).

16. *Newcastle Courant*, 30 September 1738.

17. *Daily Gazetteer*, 7 March 1739.

18. Bayes, *Genuine History*, p.30.

19. Beresford, *Diary*, p.113.

20. *Political State*, LVII, (1739), pp.192-193.
21. Post Office archives communication.
22. TNA, SP36/47, f.87v.
23. *Derby Mercury*, 8 March 1739; *Political State*, LVII (1739), p.193.
24. *Daily Gazetteer*, 27 February 1739.
25. C.E. Whiting, ed., 'Two Yorkshire Diaries', *Yorkshire Archaeological Society Record Series*, CXVII, (1951), pp.44-45.
26. TNA, SP36/47, f86r.
27. Ibid, f.100r.
28. Ibid, SP44/131, p.102.
29. Ibid, p.107.
30. *Derby Mercury*, 1 March 1739
31. *London and Country Journal*, 6 March 1739.
32. *Derby Mercury*, 1 March 1738.
33. *Ipswich Journal*, 17 March 1739.
34. Ibid, 10 March 1739.
35. *London and Country Journal*, 13 March 1739.
36. Ibid.
37. *Newcastle Courant*, 24 February 1739.
38. TNA, T53/40, f.158.
39. Ibid, ASSI44/54
40. Kyll, *Trial*, p.1; *York Poll Book* (1741).
41. *York Courant*, 20, 27 March 10 April 1739.
42. Kyll, *Trial*, p.4.
43. Ibid, p.5.
44. Ibid, p.6.
45. Ibid, p.7.
46. Ibid, p.8.
47. Ibid, p.9.
48. Ibid, p.10
49. Ibid, p.11.
50. Ibid, p.12.
51. Ibid, p.13.

52. Ibid, p.14.

53. Ibid, p.15.

54. Ibid, p.16.

55. Ibid, p.17.

56. Ibid, p.18.

57. Ibid, p.19.

58. Ibid, p.20.

59. Ibid, p.21.

60. *Newcastle Courant*, 31 March 1739.

61. *Derby Mercury*, 5 April 1739.

62. Ibid, 29 March 1739.

63. Bayes, *Genuine History*, p.28.

64. Ibid, p.29.

65. Ibid, pp.29-30.

66. Gerald Curtis, *The Story of the Sampfords* (1981), p.268.

67. Bayes, *Genuine History*, pp.30-32.

68. Hugh Murray, 'Sedan Chairs in York', *York Historian*, 17, (2000), p.30.

69. Henry Fielding, *Jonathan Wild*, p.12.

70. *York Courant*, 10 April 1739.

71. Kyll, *Trial*, pp.32.

72. W.E. Matthews, ed., *Diary of Dudley Ryder, 1715-1716*, (1939), p.336.

73. Beresford, *Diary*, p.14.

74. North Yorkshire Record Office, ZAZ 80.

75. *York Herald*, 27 October 1888.

76. Charles Harper, *Half Hours with the Highwaymen* (1908), p.240.

77. TNA, T90/147, p.317.

78. Henry Fielding, *An Enquiry into the late Increase of Robbers*, (1751), pp.189-190.

79. Kyll/Bayes

80. Whiting, 'Two Yorkshire Diaries', p.45.

81. *York Herald*, 20 October 1888.

82. Francis Drake, *Eboracum* (1736), p.263.

83. *Leeds Mercury*, 13 April 1739

84. Kyll, *Trial*, p.21.

85. Ibid, p.25

86. Ibid, pp.22-23

87. York Castle Museum information.

88. *London Evening Post*, 6-8 November 1746; *York Herald*, 20 October 1888. Information Dr Melia, Borthwick Institute of Historical Research.

89. Kyll, *Trial*, pp.21-22.

90. York City Archives, F16, f.194r.

91. Ibid, f.198r, 201v, 204r; *Newcastle Courant*, 2 June 1739.

92. *York Evening Post*, 17 September 1979.

93. YCA, JAR/1/2/10.

94. *Scots Magazine*, 6 April 1739.

95. Ibid, 4 May 1739

96. *Stamford Mercury* 5 July 1739.

97. William Shaw, ed, *Treasury Papers and Books, 1739-1741*, (1901), pp.43, 223, 229; TNA, T53/40, pp.156-159.

98. *Stamford Mercury*, 5 July 1739.

99. Ibid.

100. *Scots Magazine*, 22 November 1740.

101. *Derby Mercury*, 18 December 1740.

102. Stewart Marsh Ellis, *William Harrison Ainsworth and Friends,* I (1911), p.242.

103. *Oxford Journal*, 6 October 1781.

104. *Hampshire Chronicle*, 22 October 1796.

Chapter 6

1. Barlow, *Dick Turpin*, pp.444-445; Sharpe, *Myth*, p.158.

2. Anon, *The Life and Trial of Richard Turpin, A Notorious Highwayman* (1800), p.29.

3. Ibid, pp.30-31.

4. Daniel Defoe, *A Tour through the Whole Island of Great Britain* (1724-1726), pp.110-111; Alexander Smith, *A Compleat History of the Lives and Robberies of the most Notorious Highwaymen II* (1719), pp.4-5; volume I, p.45.

5. Anon, *Collection of Diverting Songs* (1817).

6. *Morning Post*, 13 November 1819.

7. Ibid, May 1822.

8. *Gore's Advertiser*, 6 February 1823.

9. *Public Ledger*, 8 May 1822.

10. *Morning Advertiser* 23 July 1827.

11. Ibid, 5 November 1830.

12. W. Harrison Ainsworth, *Rookwood: A Romance* (1836), p.xv.

13. Ibid, pp.xv-xvi.

14. Ibid, p.xvi.

15. Ibid, p.63.

16. Ibid, pp.55, 63, 65.

17. Ibid, pp.66, 69.

18. Ibid, pp.107-108.

19. Ibid, pp.179, 198.

20. Ibid, pp.201, 212, 236, 239.

21. Ibid, pp.256, 270-272.

22. Ibid, pp.273- 305, 312.

23. Stewart Marsh Ellis, *William Harrison Ainsworth and Friends* (1911), p.243.

24. Ainsworth, *Rookwood*, pp.315, 334.

25. Ibid, pp.343-344.

26. Charles Dickens, *The Pickwick Papers*, (Penguin 1999 edition), pp.580, 797.

27. Anon, The *Prince of Highwaymen: being the life and adventures of Turpin*, (nd), pp.6, 8.

28. M. Barnett, *Dick Turpin and Tom King: A Tale of Newgate: a one Act farce* (nd).

29. *York Herald*, 26 May 1843.

30. *Essex Standard*, 25 January 1879.

31. *York Herald* 5 March 1894.

32. Ibid, 9 August 1875.

33. *Essex Standard*, 12 October 1877.

34. Ibid, 22 August 1896.

35. Ibid, 17 March 1871.

36. Ibid, 11 December 1863.

37. *York Herald*, 4 November 1865

38. Ibid, 16 March 1888.

39. Ibid, 30 May 1883.

40. *Essex Times*, 29 March 1873.

41. *York Herald*, 22 December 1866

42. Ibid, 21 November 1881.

43. Ibid, 22 January 1887.

44. *Middlesex Independent*, 8 June 1892

45. *York Herald*, 13 June 1891

46. Ibid, 28 October 1848.

47. Ibid, 18 June 1864.

48. Ibid, 25 February 1854.

49. Ibid, 27 February 1893.

50. *Essex Standard*, 14 March 1896.

51. Ibid, 7 December 1889.

52. *Middlesex and Surrey Express*, 23 June 1900.

53. *York Herald*, 2 April 1875.

54. Ibid, 8 July 1876.

55. *Middlesex Independent*, 22 January 1898.

56. *Middlesex Gazette*, 13 March 1897.

57. *York Herald*, 1 October 1880.

58. *Middlesex Chronicle*, 27 May 1876.

59. *York Herald*, 18 November 1884

60. Ibid, 28 September 1892.

61. Ibid, 30 September 1891.

62. Thomas Hardy, *Far from the Madding Crowd* (1874), Chapter 50.

63. *York Herald*, 16 July 1900.

64. *Essex Times* 17 June 1887

65. Ibid, 7 July 1869.

66. *York Herald*, 1 February 1875.

67. Ibid, 25 July 1874.

68. Ibid, 19 August 1891.

69. *Middlesex and Surrey Express*, 11 November 1899.

70. *Middlesex Gazette*, 26 September 1896.

71. *Middlesex Chronicle* 13 October 1877.

72. *York Herald*, 9 January 1880.

73. *Middlesex Gazette* 25 April 1896

74. *Middlesex Independent*, 11 August 1900.

75. A Noyes, *The Ballad of Dick Turpin*.

76. Hackney Archives, MS3960/1, pp.47-52.

77. Ibid, MS3960/4.

78. *York Herald*, 24 August 1895.

79. *Yorkshire Post and Leeds Intelligencer*, 11 April 1939.

80. Ibid, 23 May 1952.

81. Ibid, 28 May 1951.

82. Ibid, 10 July 1952.

83. *Dundee Courier*, 16 April 1996.

84. *Dublin Evening Telegraph*, 2 March 2001.

85. *Yorkshire Post and Leeds Intelligencer*, 14 February 1924.

86. Ibid, 26 February 1914

87. Ibid, 18 September 1930.

88. Ibid, 14 June 1950.

89. Alastair Hagger, 'Dick Turpin: The pre-postmodern outlaw' *New Vistas*, 6, 2, (2020), pp.35-40.

90. *Middlesex County Times*, 25 June 1921.

91. Harper, *Half Hours*, p.240.

92. *Daily Mirror*, 21 April 1904.

93. *Illustrated Police News*, 29 June 1912.

94. *Luton Times and Advertiser*, 5 July 1912.

95. *Whitby Gazette*, 20 November 1911.

96. *Birmingham Daily Gazette*, 30 July 1919.

97. *Shields Daily News*, 16 May 1933.

98. *Lincolnshire Echo*, 26 August 1897.

99. *The Sketch*, 31 May 1899.

100. *Essex Newsman* 14 November 1950.

101. *Haverhill Echo*, 29 March 1984.

102. ERO, C/DP/6/2/10, p.9.

103. *The Acton Gazette*, 21 August 1987.

104. *Essex Newsman*, 18 May 1929.

105. Ibid, 27 January 1906.

106. *Essex Times*, 11 August 1950.

107. *Staffordshire Sentinel*, 13 May 1994.

108. *Essex Guardian*, 19 August 1905.

109. *Essex News*, 1 July 1933.

110. Tim Leonard and Susan Stewart, eds., *Hanwell Remembered*, II (1980), p.9.

111. *Lincolnshire Chronicle*, 10 December 1875.

112. *Essex Newsman* 7 January 1928; information from Mr John Gauss and Mrs Ruth Smith.

113. Ibid, 5 September 1931.

114. Ibid, 10 January 1950.

115. *Shields Daily News*, 23 August 1952.

116. *Essex News*, 27 November 1937.

117. Ibid, 14 May 1910.

118. *Cycling*, 6 June 1912.

119. *York Herald*, 27 October 1888

120. Richard Hills, *Dick Turpin rides again – full length pantomime* (2001), pp.1, 4, 6, 33, 41.

121. *The Stage*, 3 July 1986.

122. *Rough Guide to Yorkshire* (2015), p.153.

123. *Insight Guides to Great Britain: York* (c.2010), p.49.

124. *Lynn Advertiser*, 23 June 1987.

125. ERO, C/DP/6/2/10, pp.5-9.

126. Information from Saffron Walden Museum; *Sketch*, 31 May 1899; *Chelmsford Chronicle*, 4 September 1936; *Haverhill Echo*, 29 March 1984; *Tatler*, 2 September 1903.

127. Roger Clarke, *Natural History of Ghosts*, (2012), p.173.

128. Richard Jones, *Walking Haunted London* (2009), p.56.

129. Ibid, p.43.

130. Ibid, p.52.

131. Hinckleypastpresent.org/dickturpin

132. Jones, *Walking*, p.56.

133. Clarke *Natural History*, p.174.

134. Betty Puttick, *Ghosts of Essex*, (1997), pp.85-86.

135. *Essex News*, 6 March 1945.

136. Ibid, 20 March 1945.

137. Spookyisles.com/chequers-inn/.

138. Cambridge-news.co.uk/news-local-news/haunted-pub-inn-dick-turpin-18502852

139. Ghostwalkbrighton.co.uk/the-spirit-of dick-turpin/

140. Cool.interetsingstuff.com/mystery-of-london-heathrow-airport-ghost

141. http://www.standard.

142. http:://www.buckinghamshirelive.com

143. Occult-world.com/turpin-dick/

144. Clarke, *Natural History*, p.130.

145. *VCH Essex*, 6 (1973), p.290.

146. Hagger, 'The pre-postmodern outlaw', p.40.

Chapter 7

1. Sharpe, *Dick Turpin*, pp.198-202; *Lincolnshire Echo*, 17 July 1912.

2. Julius E. Day, *Immortal Turpin*, (1948), p.140.

3. *Sheffield Daily Telegraph*, 8 December 1925.

4. *The Bioscope*, 12 March 1925.
5. *Sketch* 15 November 1933
6. *The Era*, 15 November 1933.
7. *Lincolnshire Echo*, 6 October 1934.
8. *Yorkshire Evening Post*, 14 July 1951.
9. *Milngavie and Bearsden Herald*, 17 November 1951.
10. *Sandwell Evening Mail*, 10 November 1990.
11. *Thanet Times*, 12 November 1974.
12. *Middlesex County Times*, 15 June 1979.
13. *York Herald*, 29 December 2015.
14. *The Sun*, 13 April 2022.

Chapter 8

1. Kyll, *Trial*, p.1.
2. *Newcastle Courant*, 14 April 1739; *York Courant* 17 April 1739.
3. *York Courant*, 1, 22, 29 May, 5 June 1739.
4. *Ipswich Journal*, 2 February 1740.
5. *Reading Mercury,* 30 April – 14 May 1739.
6. *A Select and Impartial Account of the Lives, Behaviour and Dying words of the most remarkable convicts from the year 1700*, III, (1760), p.151.
7. *The Life of Richard Turpin, a notorious Highwayman and The Life of Sawney Beane, the Man eater* (1800), p.19.
8. *Newgate Calendar*, I (1824), pp.385-394.
9. Anon, *The Life and Adventures of Dick Turpin*, (1825), p.1.
10. Ibid, pp.2-4.
11. Ibid, pp.5-8.
12. Anon *The Life of Richard Turpin, the Notorious Highwayman* (no date), pp.1, 22.
13. Anon, *The Life of Richard Turpin, a most notorious highwayman* (1872), p.18.

14. ERO, LIB/PAM1/7/51.
15. *Dictionary of National Biography*, (1899), pp.1302-1303.
16. *ODNB*, (2004), Vol. pp.700-701.
17. *Essex Guardian*, 27 September 1902.
18. *Essex Times*, 25 March 1911.
19. *Dundee Evening Telegraph*, 2 March 1950.
20. *York Herald*, 5 August 1899.
21. Ibid, 9 September 1899
22. Thomas Secombe, *Richard Turpin* (c.1903), pp.27, 32.
23. Harper, *Half Hours*, p.173.
24. Ibid, I, p.ix.
25. Ibid, p.181.
26. Ibid, pp.205-208.
27. Ibid, p.230.
28. Ibid, p.234.
29. ERO, T/Z 164/2.
30. Ibid, T/Z 164/1, pp.8, 11, 19.
31. Ibid, T/Z 164/5.
32. Arty Ash and Julius Day, *Immortal Turpin* (1948), pp.9-10.
33. Barlow, *Dick Turpin and the Gregory Gang*.
34. Anon, *Dick Turpin in York* (1976).
35. Peter Jackson, *Dick Turpin* (1988), pp.82, 86.
36. Clifford Gully, 'Dick Turpin in Hackney', *East London Record*, 13 (1990), pp.30, 32.
37. James Sharpe, *Dick Turpin and the Myth of the English Highwayman* (2005), inner cover.
38. Ibid.
39. Ibid, p.7.
40. Ibid, pp.8-9.
41. Ibid, pp.43-44.
42. Ibid, p.58.
43. Ibid, p.73.
44. Ibid, pp.137-138.

45. Ibid, p.148.
46. Ibid, p.159.
47. Ibid, pp.171-207.
48. Ibid, p.208.
49. Ibid, p.210.
50. Ibid, pp.216-217.
51. Terry Deary, *Gorgeous Georgians* (2007), pp.54-55; *Dick Turpin: Legends and Lies*, (2007), pp.7-15.
52. Ibid, pp.16-22.
53. Ibid, pp.26-36.
54. Ibid, pp.41-45.
55. Ibid, pp.55-56.
56. Jim Pipe, *Top Ten Worst Vicious Villains* (2012), pp.12-13.
57. Stephen Basdeo, *The Lives and Exploits of the Most notorious Highwaymen, Rogues and Murderers* (2018), pp.89-100; Michael Billett, *Highwaymen and Outlaws* (1997), pp.95-96.
58. Gillian Spraggs, *Outlaws and Highwaymen* (2001), pp.250, 257.
59. David Brandon, *Stand and Deliver: A History of Highway Robbery* (2001), pp.115-124; Fiona McDonald, *Gentlemen Rogues and Wicked Ladies* (2009).
60. Erin Mackie, *Rakes, Highwaymen and Pirates* (2009), pp.96-105.
61. Oates, 'York and the Jacobite Prisoners, 1745-1751', *York Historian*, 17, (2000); Peter Linebaugh, *The London Hanged* (2003), pp.203-205, 214.
62. Gatrell, *The Hanging Tree*, pp.133, 626.
63. Michael Robbins, *Middlesex*, (1953), p.125.
64. Martin Briggs, *Middlesex Old and New* (1934), pp.140, 116.
65. Michael Stevenson, *Middlesex* (1972), pp. 34, 49.
66. *Victoria County History* for Middlesex, Vol. III (1962), p. and vol. VI (1980), p.40.
67. Ibid, V, (1976), p.208.
68. Ibid, IV, (1971), p. 157.
69. Anon, *Lives of the Most Notorious and Daring Highwaymen* (1867), p.208.

Bibliography

Manuscripts

National Archives
Assizes
ASSI 44/54
ASSI 94/564, 570, 580, 583, 593, 608, 639, 643

Probate
PROB 11/683

State Papers Domestic
SP36/22-23, 33, 36, 39, 47

State Papers Letter Books
SP44/83
SP44/128, 130, 131

Treasury:
T1/277
T27/25
T52/39
T53/37-40, 58-59
T60/16
T90/147

War Office
WO4/33, 35

East Riding Record Office
QSF122/D7-8

Essex Record Office
C/DP/6/2/10
D/P314/8/1
LIB/PAM1/7/51.
T/Z 164/1-5

Hackney Archives
MS 3960/1,4

London Metropolitan Archives
MJ/SR/2606
MJ/SR/2626
MJ/SR/2631
MJ/SR/2652
MJ/SR/2676
MJ/SR/2677
MJ/SR/2680

York City Archives
F16
JAR/1/2/10

Printed

Anon, *New's News; great and wonderful news from London in an uproar or a Hue and Cry after the great Turpin, with his escape into Ireland (1737).*

Richard Bayes, *The Genuine History of Richard Turpin* (1739)

John Beresford, ed., *James Woodforde: Diary of a Country parson, 1758-1802* (1987).

Calendar of Printed Minutes, Middlesex Quarter Sessions, 1732-1735

Ibid, 1739-1741.

Francis Drake, *Eboracum* (1736).

Stewart Marsh Ellis, *William Harrison Ainsworth and Friends* (1911).

Essex Directory (1848).

Essex Poll Books (1715, 1734).

Henry Fielding, *The History of Jonathan Wild* (1743).

Henry Fielding, *An Enquiry into the Late Increase of Robbers* (1751).

Donald Gibson, ed., *A Parson in the Vale of the White Horse: George Woodward's Letters from East Hendred, 1753-1761* (1982).

Thomas Kyll, *The Trial of Richard Turpin the notorious highwayman at York* (1739).

Jean Bernard Le Blanc, *Lettres d'un Francois*, III, (1745).

W.S. Lewis, ed., *The Correspondence of Horace Walpole*, 12 (1944).

Sarah Markham, ed., *John Loveday of Caversham, 1711-1789*, (1984).

W.E. Matthews, ed., *Diary of Dudley Ryder, 1715-1716*, (1939).

Christopher Morris, ed., *The Journeys of Celia Fiennes* (1949).

Madam Van Muyden, ed., *Cesar de Saussure: A Foreign View of England* (1902).

Ruth Paley, ed., 'Justice in Eighteenth Century Hackney: The Justicing Notebook of Henry Norris and the Hackney Petty Sessions Book', *London Record Society* 28, (1991).

Frederick Pottle, ed., *James Boswell's London Diary, 1762-1763* (1950).

Pat Rogers, ed., *Daniel Defoe's Tour of the Whole Island of Great Britain* (1971).

Alan Saville, ed., 'Secret Comment: Diaries Gertrude Saville, 1721-1757', *Thoroton Society* (1998).

William Shaw, ed., *Calendar of Treasury Books and Papers, 1735-1738* (1900).

Ibid, *1739-1741* (1901).

Alexander Smith, *A Compleat History of the Lives and Robberies of the most Notorious Highwaymen* (1719).

Henri Talon, ed., *John Byrom: Selections from his Journals and Papers* (1950).

C.E. Whiting, ed., 'Two Yorkshire Diaries', *Yorkshire Archaeological Society Record Series*, CXVII, (1951).

Thomas Wright, *History of Essex* II (1836).

Newspapers and Magazines

Acton Gazette, 1987.

Caledonian Mercury, 1735-1736, 1739.

Country Journal, 1736-1737.

Daily Gazetteer, 1738

Daily Post, 1737.

Derby Mercury, 1734-1735, 1737-1739

Dublin Evening Telegraph, 2001

Dundee Courier, 1996

Ealing Gazette, 1979

Essex Guardian, 1905

Essex News, 1910, 1933, 1937, 1945

Essex Newsman, 1906, 1928-1929, 1931, 1950

Essex Standard, 1851, 1871, 1873, 1879, 1879, 1887, 1889, 1896

Essex Telegraph,

Essex Times, 1950

General Evening Post, 1735

Gentleman's Magazine, 1733-1737.

Gore's Advertiser, 1823

Grub Street Journal, 1735, 1737

Haverhill Echo, 1984

Ipswich Journal, 1735-1737, 1739-1740

Kentish Weekly Packet, 1737, 1739

Leeds Mercury, 1739

Lincolnshire Chronicle, 1875

Lincolnshire Echo, 1897

London Evening Post, 1737

London Gazette, 1735, 1737

London and Country Journal, 1739

Lynn Advertiser, 1987

Middlesex Chronicle, 1876-1877

Middlesex County Times, 1921

Middlesex Gazette, 1896-1897

Middlesex Independent, 1892, 1898

Middlesex and Surrey Express, 1900

Morning Advertiser, 1827, 1830

Morning Post, 1819, 1822

Newcastle Courant, 1735, 1737-1739

Old Whig, 1735, 1737.

Political State of Great Britain, 1735-1739

Public Ledger, 1822

Reading Mercury, 1739.

Reid's Weekly Journal, 1735, 1737.

Scots Magazine, 1739-1740.

Shields Daily News, 1952

Staffordshire Sentinel, 1994

The Stage, 1986

Stamford Mercury, 1735, 1737-1738.

Thanet Times, 1974

York Courant, 1739.

York Evening Press, 1979

York Herald, 1843, 1858, 1854, 1864-1866, 1871, 1874-1876, 1880, 1883-1884, 1887-1888, 1891-1895, 1900, 2015.

Yorkshire Post and Leeds Intelligencer, 1924, 1930, 1939, 1950- 1952

Secondary Sources

Anon, *The Life of Richard Turpin, the notorious highwayman* (nd).

Anon, *The Life of Richard Turpin, a most notorious highwayman,* (1872).

Anon, *The Prince of Highwaymen: being the life and adventures of Dick Turpin* (c.1885).

Anon, *Dick Turpin in Yorkshire* (1978)

Anon, *Rough Guide to Yorkshire* (2015).

Anon, *Insight Guides: Yorkshire* (2010)

William Harrison Ainsworth, *Rookwood* (1836).

M. Barnett, *Richard Turpin and Tom King; a tale of Newgate* (nd).

Stephen Basdeo, *The Lives and Exploits of the most noted Highwaymen, Rogues and Murderers* (2018).

John Beattie, *Policing and Punishment in London, 1660-1750: Urban Crime and the limits of terror* (2001).

Michael Billett, *Highwaymen and Outlaws* (1997).

David Brandon, *Stand and deliver: A History of Highway Robbery* (2001).

Martin Briggs, *Middlesex Old and New* (1934).

Derek Barlow, *Dick Turpin and the Gregory Gang* (1973).

Reed Browning, *The Duke of Newcastle* (1975).

Roger Clarke, *Natural History of Ghosts*, (2012).

Gerald Curtis, *The Story of the Sampfords* (1981).

Julius E. Day, *Immortal Turpin: The authentic Story of England's most notorious Highwayman* (1948).

Terry Deary, *Dick Turpin: Legends and Lies* (2007).

Ibid, *Horrible Histories: Gorgeous Georgians* (2007).

V.A.C. Gatrell, *The Hanging Tree: Execution and the English People, 1770-1868* (1994).

Clifford Gully, 'Dick Turpin in Hackney', *East London Record*, 13 (1990).

Alistair Hagger, 'Dick Turpin: The pre-postmodern Outlaw', *New Vistas*, 6, 2, (2020).

Charles Harper, *Half Hours with the Highwaymen* (1908).

B.R. Hartley, 'Thomas Griffiths, Governor of York Prison', *York Historian*, 11 (1994).

Richard Hill, *Dick Turpin Rides Again – full length pantomime*, (2001).

Geoffrey Holmes and Daniel Szechi, *The Age of Oligarchy: Pre Industrial England, 1722-1783*, (1993).

Peter Jackson, *Dick Turpin* (1988).

Richard Jones, *Walking Haunted London* (2009).

William Knipe, *Criminal Chronology of York Castle* (1867).

Paul Langford, *A Polite and Commercial People, England, 1727-1783*, (1992).

Peter Linebaugh, *The London Hanged* (2003).

Tim Leonard and Susan Stewart, eds., *Hanwell Remembered*, II (1980).

Fiona McDonald, *Gentlemen Rogues and Wicked Ladies* (2009).

Erin Mackie, *Rakes, Highwaymen and Pirates* (2009).

Hugh Murray, 'Sedan Chairs in York', *York Historian*, 17 (2000).

Alfred Noyes, *The Ballad of Dick Turpin* (unknown date).

Jonathan Oates, 'York and the Rebel prisoners, 1745-1751', *York Historian*, 17 (2000).

Nikolas Pevsner, *Buildings of England: Essex* (2009).

Michael Robbins, *Middlesex* (1953).

Thomas Secombe, *Richard Turpin* (1903).

James Sharpe, *Dick Turpin: The Myth of the English Highwayman* (2005).

Robert Shoemaker, *The London mob: Violence and disorder in eighteenth century England*, (2004).

W.A. Speck, *Stability and Strife*: *England, 1714-1760*, (1977).

Gillian Spraggs, *Outlaws and Highwaymen* (2001).

Bruce Stevenson, *Middlesex* (1972).

Victoria County History: Essex, Vol. II, IV, VI (1907-1973).

Victoria County History: Middlesex, Vols. III-VI (1961-1980).

Online

Ancestry.co.uk (baptisms, wills)

Horrible Histories: Dick Turpin Song

Carry on Dick

The Legend of Young Dick Turpin

Dick Turpin

Dick Turpin's Ride

Index